AN INTRODUCTION TO ECONOMETRIC THEORY

An Introduction to Econometric Theory

Measure-Theoretic Probability and Statistics with Applications to Economics

A. RONALD GALLANT

PRINCETON UNIVERSITY PRESS

PRINCETON, NEW JERSEY

Published by Princeton University Press, 41 William Street,
Princeton, New Jersey 08540
In the United Kingdom: Princeton University Press,
Chichester, West Sussex

Library of Congress Cataloging-in-Publication Data

Gallant, A. Ronald, 1942–
An introduction to econometric theory : measure-theoretic
probability and statistics with applications to economics /
A. Ronald Gallant.
p. cm.
Includes bibliographical references and index.
ISBN 0-691-01645-3 (alk. paper)
1. Econometrics. I. Title.
HB139.G35 1997
330′.01′5195—dc21 97-7561

This book has been composed in Bitstream Dutch

Princeton University Press books are printed on
acid-free paper and meet the guidelines for permanence
and durability of the Committee on Production
Guidelines for Book Longevity of the
Council on Library Resources

Printed in the United States of America
by Princeton Academic Press

10 9 8 7 6 5 4 3 2 1

To the Latané family

Contents

Preface

The topics presented here are a selection from probability and statistics intended to prepare first-year graduate students for their courses in econometrics, microeconomics, and macroeconomics. They are also intended to provide students with a basis for deciding early in their studies if theoretical econometrics is a field in which they would like to write their dissertation. With these goals guiding selection, several topics that are not in a standard first-year graduate course in probability and statistics are included, such as the asymptotics of generalized method of moments. Some topics that are standard, such as optimal small sample inference, are excluded. One year of calculus is a prerequisite. An additional year of advanced calculus, or any other course providing experience with mathematical proofs, would be helpful.

The material is intended to be taught in a one-semester or two-quarter course. There is little here beyond what is needed for that purpose. The rule guiding selection is that what is presented should be directly useful to students in their later courses. Those who are attracted to theoretical econometrics would be expected to study probability and statistics in more depth by taking further graduate courses in mathematics and statistics. Those who are not attracted should find this an adequate preparation in the theory of probability and statistics for both their applied courses in econometrics and their courses in microeconomics and macroeconomics.

The intent is to develop a fundamental understanding of probability and mathematical statistics and a sound intuition. Much effort is devoted to motivating ideas and to presenting them as the solution to practical problems. For instance, correlation, regression, and conditional expectation are developed as a means to obtain the best approximation of one random variable by some function of another. Linear, polynomial, and unrestricted functions are considered. One is led naturally to the notion of conditioning on a σ-algebra as a means to finding the unrestricted solution, and gains an understanding of the relationships among linear, polynomial, and unrestricted solutions. Proofs of results are presented when the proof itself aids understanding or when the proof technique has practical value.

George Holmes, Garland Durham, and the students in the Fall 1996 class of Economics 271 read the manuscript carefully and are responsible for the elimination of many errors. I apologize for the errors that remain and would appreciate an e-mail message to ron_gallant@unc.edu reporting those you find.

AN INTRODUCTION
TO ECONOMETRIC THEORY

1

Probability

1.1 Examples

This chapter introduces the basic ideas of probability theory. Four examples are used throughout to motivate the theoretical constructs. The first two, craps and keno, are games of chance, the third is a coin tossing experiment, and the fourth is the triangle map, which generates deterministic chaos. The theory that we shall develop is applicable to each of these examples.

1.1.1 *Craps*

Craps is a dice game that has one feature that makes it especially interesting as an example in our study of probability: The number of rolls of the dice required to decide the outcome of a bet is indeterminate. Conceptually the dice might have to be rolled forever and the bet never decided. Dealing with this contingency forces us to develop a theory of probability that turns out to be rich enough to support the study of econometrics in general and the study of time series phenomena, such as weekly interest rates, in particular. Moreover, there is nothing abstract about craps. The game is real; it is tangible; you can play it yourself in Las Vegas, Reno, Atlantic City, and elsewhere; and people have been playing it in something like its present form since at least the time of the Crusades.

The game is played at a table laid out as shown in Figure 1.1. The casino crew consists of a boxman, a stickman, and two dealers who occupy positions as shown in the figure. Dealers manage betting at their end of the table. The stickman manages the dice and the bets at the center of the table, which are hardway and one roll bets. The boxman makes change and supervises the game. The players crowd around the table at either side of the stickman. Play is noisy with players and crew announcing, deciding, and paying bets, encouraging the dice, talking to one another, etc. It is great fun.

The flow of the game is determined by the *pass line* bet. Custom and social pressure require the shooter, who is the player throwing the dice,

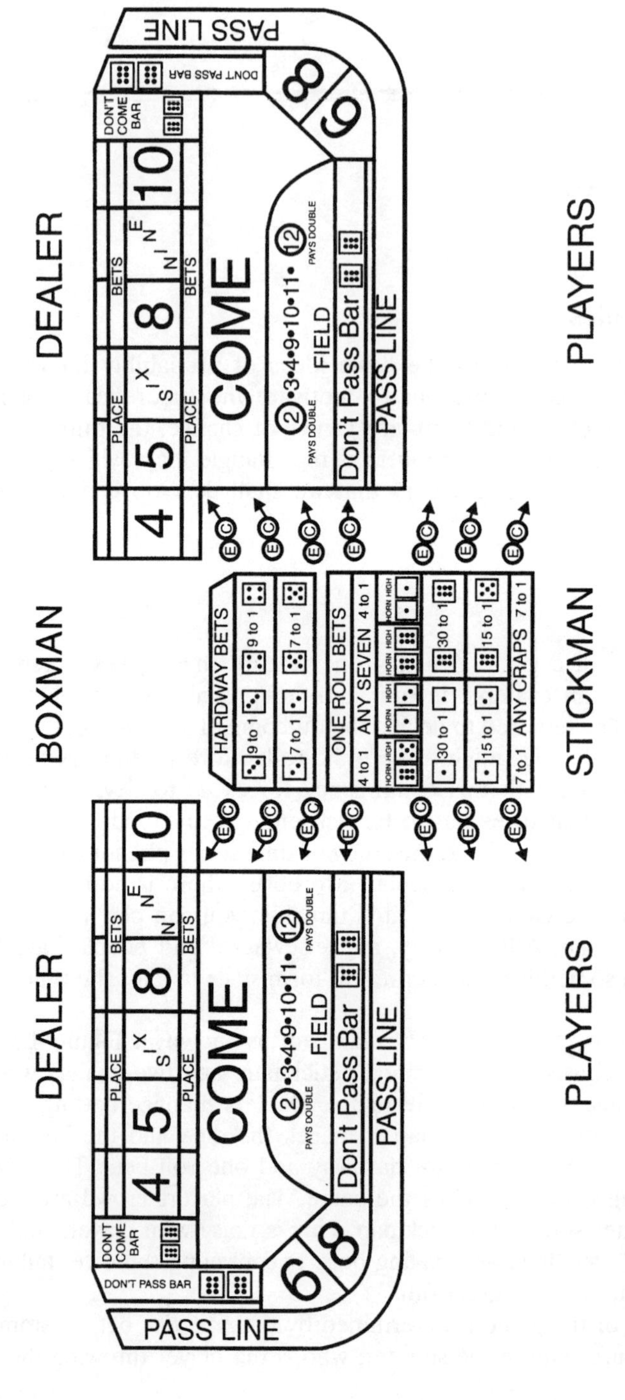

Figure 1.1 The layout of a crap table and the positions of players and crew.

to place a bet on the pass line before the first roll, which is called a *come out* roll, although the rules do permit a bet on the don't pass bar instead. A come out roll occurs immediately after the previous pass line bet has been decided. If the previous pass line bet lost on the roll of a seven, then the losing shooter also loses the dice and they are offered to players to the shooter's left, in turn, until a player accepts them to become the new shooter. The payoff on the pass line is stated as either "1 to 1" or "2 for 1." Each means that a winning player who bet $1 gets that $1 back plus $1.

Figure 1.2 shows the 36 possible positions in which the dice may land when thrown. The stickman will disallow rolls that bounce off the table, land on a pile of chips, or in the dice bin, and will scold a shooter who does not throw hard enough to hit the opposite end of the table or players who get their hands in the way of the dice.

If the sum of the dice on the come out roll is *craps*, which is a 2, 3, or 12, then the roll is called a miss and the pass line loses. If the come out roll is a 7 or 11, it wins. Otherwise, a 4, 5, 6, 8, 9, or 10 has been thrown. Whichever it is becomes the *point*. The shooter then continues to roll the dice until either the point recurs, in which case the pass line wins, or a 7 occurs, in which case the pass line loses and the dice pass leftward. It is this indeterminate number of rolls after the point is established that makes the game of craps interesting to us as an example.

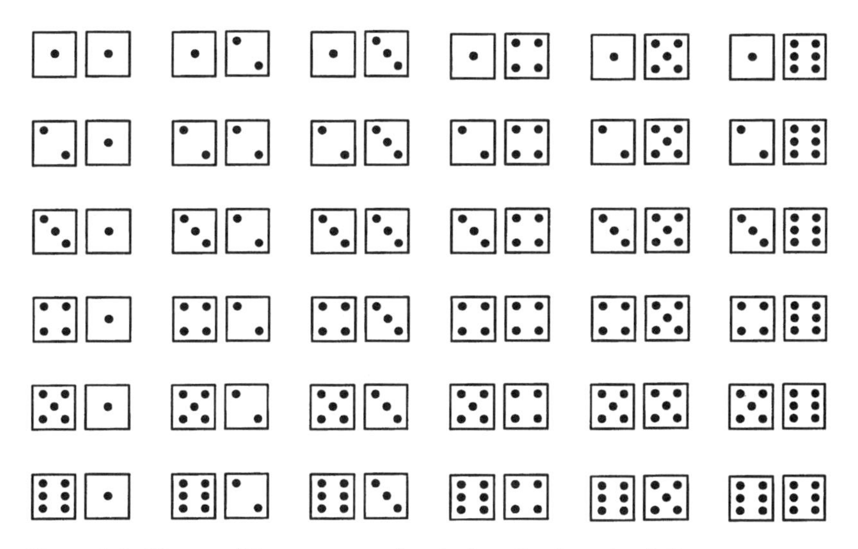

Figure 1.2. The possible outcomes of a single roll of a pair of dice.

If the come out roll is 4, 5, 6, 8, 9, or 10, then players who have bet the pass line are offered *free odds*. They can make a fair bet—called odds, taking the odds, or a right bet—that wins if the point recurs before a 7 is rolled. Minimally, one can bet $1 for every $1 bet on the pass line, but some casinos (e.g., Golden Horseshoe, Downtown Las Vegas) have allowed as much as seven times the pass line bet. This is a form of price competition among casinos. Free odds pay 6 to 5 if the point is 6 or 8, 3 to 2 if the point is 5 or 9, and 2 to 1 if the point is 4 or 10.

The *don't pass* bar bet is the opposite of the pass line bet, in the sense that the don't pass bet wins when the pass line bet loses and conversely, except that the don't pass bet neither wins nor loses if a 12 is thrown on the come out roll. Of course, the free odds bet is also reversed; it wins if a 7 is thrown before the point is made. Don't pass free odds pay 5 to 6 if the point is 6 or 8, 2 to 3 if the point is 5 or 9, and 1 to 2 if the point is 4 or 10.

The *come* and *don't come* bets are the same as the pass and don't pass bets except that a player may place that bet before any roll except the come out roll.

If you play craps, and want to keep the house advantage to a percentage that is nearly irrelevant, then play the pass, don't pass, come, don't come, and always take maximum odds. Stay away from all other bets. Admittedly, this strategy takes much of the entertainment value out of the game.

A *place* bet to win is the same as a pass line bet without the initial skirmish of the come out roll. The bettor chooses a point, a 4, 5, 6, 8, 9, or 10, and the bet wins if the point is rolled before a 7. The bet is usually off on any come out roll. Similarly, a place bet to lose is the same as a don't pass bar bet without the initial skirmish. Payoffs vary somewhat from casino to casino on place bets. Typical payoffs are shown in Table 1.1. Casinos that are more generous with free odds are often more generous with place bet payoffs as well.

A *hardway* bet on the 8 wins if a hard 8 is rolled before either an easy 8 or a 7. A hard 8 occurs when (4, 4) is thrown; an easy 8 occurs when either (2, 6) or (3, 5) is thrown. The other hardway bets are 4, 6, and 10. Typical payoffs are shown in Table 1.1.

Other bets, whose definitions are plainly marked in Figure 1.1, are the field and the single roll bets at the center of the table. The single roll bets at the center are 2 (snake eyes), 3, 12 (box cars), any craps, 11 (the yo), and any 7. Typical payoffs are shown in Table 1.1.

TABLE 1.1
True Odds, Payoff Odds, and Casino Advantage at Craps.

Bet	True Odds	Payoff Odds	% Casino Advantage
Multiple Roll Bets			
Pass or Come	251 to 244	1 to 1	1.414
with free odds			0.848
with double odds			0.606
Don't Pass or Don't Come	976 to 949	1 to 1	1.402
with free odds			0.832
with double odds			0.591
Place 4 or 10 to win	2 to 1	9 to 5	6.666
5 or 9	3 to 2	7 to 5	4.000
6 or 8	6 to 5	7 to 6	1.515
Place 4 or 10 to lose	1 to 2	5 to 11	3.030
5 or 9	2 to 3	5 to 8	2.500
6 or 8	5 to 6	4 to 5	1.818
Hardway 4 or 10	8 to 1	7 to 1	11.111
6 or 8	10 to 1	9 to 1	9.090
Big 6 or Big 8	6 to 5	1 to 1	9.090
Buy 4 or 10	2 to 1	True odds less 5% of bet	4.761
5 or 9	3 to 2	True odds less 5% of bet	4.761
6 or 8	6 to 5	True odds less 5% of bet	4.761
Lay 4 or 10	1 to 2	True odds less 5% of payoff	2.439
5 or 9	2 to 3	True odds less 5% of payoff	3.225
6 or 8	5 to 6	True odds less 5% of payoff	4.000
Single Roll Bets			
Field	5 to 4	1 to 1, 2 to 1 on 2 and 12	5.556
Any 7	5 to 1	4 to 1	16.666
2 or 12	35 to 1	30 to 1	13.890
3 or 11	17 to 1	15 to 1	11.111
Any craps	8 to 1	7 to 1	11.111

Source: Patterson and Jaye 1982 and Dunes Hotel 1984.

These are all the bets we shall need as examples. For the remainder, see a casino brochure or Patterson and Jaye 1982.

1.1.2 *Keno*

Keno has the appeal of a state lottery: for a small wager you can win a lot of money. Unlike a state lottery, one does not have to wait days to learn the outcome of the bet. A new game is played every half hour or so, twenty-four hours a day. Moreover, the game comes to you, you do not have to go to it. Keno runners are all over the casino, in the restaurant, bars; they are ubiquitous. Or, there is a keno parlor set aside for the game where you can place wagers directly and watch the numbers be drawn. The game is played by marking a ticket such as is shown in the top panel of Figure 1.3. One can mark any number of spots from 1 to 15. The ticket in the figure has eight spots marked.

Write the amount of the wager at the top of the ticket and hand it in with the wager to a writer at the keno parlor or to a keno runner. You receive back an authorized game ticket marked as shown in the second panel of Figure 1.3. The authorized game ticket is a full receipt that shows the amount wagered, the number of the game, the number of spots marked, and the marked spots.

Twenty numbered balls are drawn from 80. The mechanism that draws the balls is usually made of clear plastic and sounds, acts, and functions much as a hot air corn popper; one sees similar machines in bingo parlors. These numbers are displayed on electronic boards throughout the casino. The boards look much like a huge ticket with the draws lit up. The *catch* is the number of *draws* that match those marked on the game ticket.

If you are in the keno parlor you can pick up a draw card such as is shown in the bottom of Figure 1.3. This card has the game number on it with the draws indicated by punched holes. The catch can be determined quickly by laying the draw card over the game card. The draw card is a convenience to keno runners and to players who play multiple tickets per game.

Payoffs vary somewhat from casino to casino. A typical set of payoffs is shown in Table 1.2.

1.1.3 *Coin Tossing*

Consider $x \in [0, 1]$ written as a decimal (or base 10) number. For example,

$$.625 = 6\frac{1}{10} + 2\frac{1}{100} + 5\frac{1}{1000}.$$

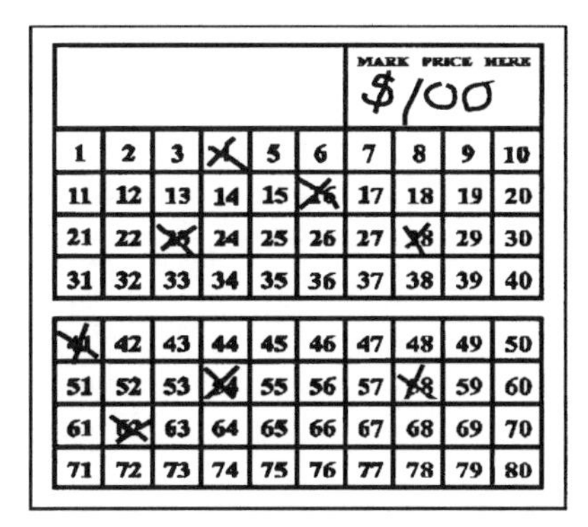

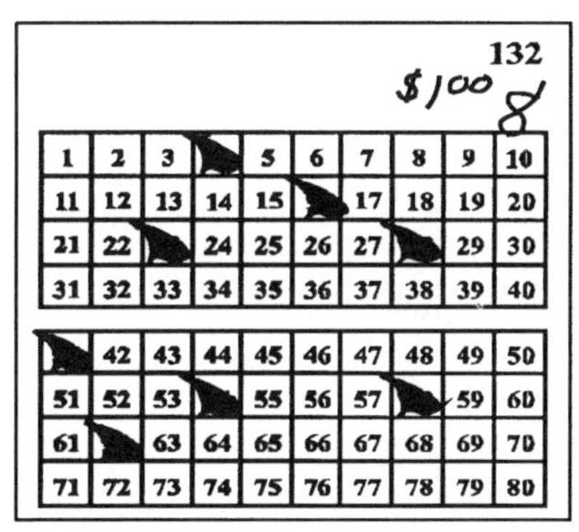

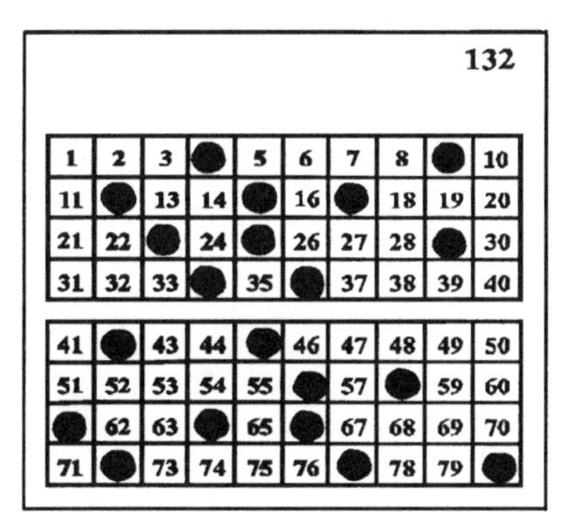

Figure 1.3. Keno player's ticket, authorized game ticket, and draw card. The top panel is a blank keno ticket as marked by a player. The middle panel is the authorized game ticket issued by the casino for a wager as specified by the player's ticket. The game ticket shows the spots marked, the amount wagered, and the game number, which is 132 in this instance. The bottom panel gives the twenty numbers that were drawn on game number 132. The catch is the number of draws that match those marked on the game ticket, which is three in this instance.

TABLE 1.2
Keno Payoffs.

Wager	*$1.00*	*$5.00*	*$10.00*
Catch	*Win*	*Win*	*Win*
Mark 1 Spot			
1	3.00	15.00	30.00
Mark 2 Spots			
2	12.00	60.00	120.00
Mark 3 Spots			
2	1.00	5.00	10.00
3	40.00	200.00	400.00
Mark 4 Spots			
2	1.00	5.00	10.00
3	3.00	15.00	30.00
4	112.00	560.00	1,120.00
Mark 5 Spots			
3	1.00	5.00	10.00
4	22.00	110.00	220.00
5	500.00	2,500.00	5,000.00
Mark 6 Spots			
3	1.00	5.00	10.00
4	3.00	15.00	30.00
5	85.00	425.00	850.00
6	1,500.00	7,500.00	15,000.00
Mark 7 Spots			
4	2.00	10.00	20.00
5	23.00	115.00	230.00
6	350.00	1,750.00	3,500.00
7	5,000.00	25,000.00	50,000.00
Mark 8 Spots			
5	9.00	45.00	90.00
6	85.00	425.00	850.00
7	1,500.00	7,500.00	15,000.00
8	18,000.00	50,000.00	50,000.00
Mark 9 Spots			
5	4.00	20.00	40.00
6	40.00	200.00	400.00
7	300.00	1,500.00	3,000.00
8	4,000.00	20,000.00	40,000.00
9	18,000.00	50,000.00	50,000.00
Mark 10 Spots			
5	2.00	10.00	20.00
6	20.00	100.00	200.00
7	126.00	630.00	1,260.00
8	950.00	4,750.00	9,500.00
9	4,000.00	20,000.00	40,000.00
10	18,000.00	50,000.00	50,000.00
Mark 11 Spots			
6	9.00	45.00	90.00
7	75.00	375.00	750.00
8	380.00	1,900.00	3,800.00
9	2,000.00	10,000.00	20,000.00
10	12,000.00	50,000.00	50,000.00
11	25,000.00	50,000.00	50,000.00
Mark 12 Spots			
6	5.00	25.00	50.00
7	30.00	150.00	300.00
8	240.00	1,200.00	2,400.00
9	600.00	3,000.00	6,000.00
10	1,500.00	7,500.00	15,000.00
11	8,000.00	40,000.00	50,000.00
12	25,000.00	50,000.00	50,000.00
Mark 13 Spots			
6	1.00	5.00	10.00
7	16.00	80.00	160.00
8	80.00	400.00	800.00
9	700.00	3,500.00	7,000.00
10	2,000.00	20,000.00	40,000.00
11	8,000.00	40,000.00	50,000.00
12	20,000.00	50,000.00	50,000.00
13	25,000.00	50,000.00	50,000.00
Mark 14 Spots			
6	1.00	5.00	10.00
7	10.00	50.00	100.00
8	40.00	200.00	400.00
9	300.00	1,500.00	3,000.00
10	1,000.00	5,000.00	10,000.00
11	3,500.00	17,500.00	35,000.00
12	12,000.00	50,000.00	50,000.00
13	25,000.00	50,000.00	50,000.00
14	36,000.00	50,000.00	50,000.00
Mark 15 Spots			
7	8.00	40.00	80.00
8	25.00	125.00	250.00
9	130.00	650.00	1,300.00
10	300.00	1,500.00	3,000.00
11	2,600.00	13,000.00	26,000.00
12	8,000.00	40,000.00	50,000.00
13	25,000.00	50,000.00	50,000.00
14	32,000.00	50,000.00	50,000.00
15	50,000.00	50,000.00	50,000.00

Source: MGM Grand Hotel 1984.
Notes: No limit to betting. $50,000.00 aggregate payoff limit to all players per game.

This number also has a binary (or base 2) form

$$.625 = .101_2 = 1\frac{1}{2} + 0\frac{1}{4} + 1\frac{1}{8}.$$

Similarly to decimals, every number $x \in [0, 1]$ has a binary representation and, conversely, every sequence of 0's and 1's represents a number in $[0, 1]$.

If the sequence of 0's and 1's is repetitive, then the formula

$$\frac{1}{1-r} = 1 + r + r^2 + r^3 + \cdots \qquad 0 \leq r < 1$$

for the sum of a geometric progression (Abramowitz and Stegun 1964) may be used to determine which $x \in [0, 1]$ the sequence represents. For example,

$$.010101\cdots_2 = 0\frac{1}{2} + 1\frac{1}{4} + 0\frac{1}{8} + 1\frac{1}{16} + \cdots = \frac{1}{4}\left(1 + \frac{1}{4} + \frac{1}{4^2} + \cdots\right) = \frac{1}{3}.$$

Moreover, one can observe from this that every repetitive sequence of 0's and 1's must be a ratio of positive integers and therefore a rational number. A sequence of 0's and 1's that terminates is a rational number also. A sequence that terminates has more than one representation. For example, $.1_2 = .011\cdots_2$.

Suppose that we select the 0's and 1's by tossing a fair coin. We can determine to which $x \in [0, 1]$ the sequence corresponds to any desired accuracy by tossing the coin long enough. We can also determine whether or not $x \in [a, b]$ for $0 \leq a < b \leq 1$. There is a problem with endpoints. For example, if $b = 1/2$, then in principle one would have to toss the coin an infinite number of times to determine if x were either of the two sequences $.011\cdots_2$ or $.100\cdots_2$ that represent 1/2. As a practical matter, the chance of this occurring is $0 = \lim_{n\to\infty}(1/2)^n$. Thus, endpoints can be disregarded and the chance that $x \in (a, b)$ or $x \in (a, b]$ or $x \in [a, b)$ or $x \in [a, b]$ is the same.

Disregarding endpoints, what are the chances of getting a sequence that represents $x \in (0, 1/2]$? Observe that each $x \in (0, 1/2]$ has first digit 0 and has an exact counterpart in $(1/2, 1]$ obtained by putting that 0 to a 1. Therefore, all that matters is the first toss. The chance of a 0 is 1/2 so the chance of $x \in (0, 1/2]$ is 1/2.

By similar logic one concludes that the chance of x being in $(0, 1/4]$ or $(1/4, 1/2]$ or $(1/2, 3/4]$ or $(3/4, 1]$ is 1/4. The terminus of this reasoning is that the chance that x is in $(a, b]$ where $0 \leq a < b \leq 1$ is the length $b - a$ of the interval.

To summarize, we see that it is quite possible to describe a physical mechanism that generates numbers x in $[0, 1]$ for which it is reasonable to state that the chance that x is in some subinterval $(a, b]$ is the length $b - a$ of that subinterval.

1.1.4 *Triangular Map*

The next example is interesting because there is nothing random to it at all; it is completely deterministic. Yet probability theory can be used to describe the salient characteristics of sequences $\{x_t\}_{t=0}^{\infty}$ generated according to this deterministic recipe.

The triangular map is

$$T(x) = 1 - 2\left|\frac{1}{2} - x\right| = \begin{cases} 2x & x \in \left[0, \frac{1}{2}\right] \\ 2 - 2x & x \in \left(\frac{1}{2}, 1\right] \end{cases}.$$

Consider a sequence $\{x_t\}_{t=1}^{\infty}$ generated by starting with some point $x_0 \in [0, 1]$ and using the recursion

$$x_{t+1} = T(x_t)$$

for $t = 1, 2, \ldots$ to generate the rest of the sequence. If we let x have binary representation (see Section 1.1.3), then we see that the action of the triangular map is to discard the leading 0 or 1 and occasionally flip digits. For example,

$$\begin{aligned} T(.0101_2) &= .101_2 \\ T(.101_2) &= 10.0_2 - 1.01_2 = 1.111\ldots_2 - 1.01_2 \\ &= .10111\ldots_2 = .11_2 \\ T(.110\,110\ldots_2) &= 1.111\,111\,111\ldots_2 - 1.101\,101\,101\ldots_2 \\ &= .010\,010\,010\ldots_2\,. \end{aligned}$$

Notice if we start the recursion with an x_0 whose binary representation terminates, then from some point on the sequence $\{x_t\}_{t=0}^{\infty}$ has $x_t \equiv 0$. If we start with x_0 whose digits repeat, then the sequence $\{x_t\}_{t=0}^{\infty}$ cycles among some finite set of points. Starting the recursion with a rational number leads to uninteresting sequences.

However, if we start with an irrational number, the sequence $\{x_t\}_{t=0}^{\infty}$ is interesting. It is an example of what is known as a chaotic process. The fact that it is chaotic and various properties of the process are discussed in Chapter 1 of Schuster 1988. Of these properties, one is of special interest to us: For any a and b with $0 \leq a < b \leq 1$,

$$\lim_{n\to\infty} \frac{1}{n} \sum_{t=1}^{n} I_{(a,\,b]}(x_t) = b - a,$$

where $I_{(a,\,b]}(x_t)$ denotes the *indicator function* of the set $(a, b]$. That is, for a set A,

$$I_A(x) = \begin{cases} 1 & x \in A, \\ 0 & x \notin A. \end{cases}$$

What this means is that the proportion of the sequence $\{x_t\}_{t=0}^{\infty}$ that is in the interval $(a, b]$ is given by the interval's length $b - a$.

1.2 Sample Space

A useful first step in building a mathematical model with which to analyze data that might arise from the examples of Section 1.1 is to list all possible outcomes. The set of all possible outcomes is called the *sample space*, which, following custom, we shall denote by Ω. This listing of all possible outcomes is context dependent and is not unique. There may be many acceptable listings for a given application. What is important is that the listing be exhaustive; that is, there is a sample point to represent every outcome. We now illustrate.

Suppose one should like to analyze the single roll bets in the game of craps (described in Section 1.1.1). The set of ordered pairs of the numbers from 1 to 6,

$$\Omega_p = \left\{ \begin{matrix} (1,1), & (1,2), & (1,3), & (1,4), & (1,5), & (1,6) \\ (2,1), & (2,2), & (2,3), & (2,4), & (2,5), & (2,6) \\ (3,1), & (3,2), & (3,3), & (3,4), & (3,5), & (3,6) \\ (4,1), & (4,2), & (4,3), & (4,4), & (4,5), & (4,6) \\ (5,1), & (5,2), & (5,3), & (5,4), & (5,5), & (5,6) \\ (6,1), & (6,2), & (6,3), & (6,4), & (6,5), & (6,6) \end{matrix} \right\}$$

consisting of 36 points would be an adequate sample space. It exhausts the possibilities (see Figure 1.2). Since order is not important in deciding the outcome of any single roll bet, the sample space

$$\Omega_u = \left\{ \begin{array}{llllll} (1,1), & (1,2), & (1,3), & (1,4), & (1,5), & (1,6) \\ (2,2), & (2,3), & (2,4), & (2,5), & (2,6), & (3,3) \\ (3,4), & (3,5), & (3,6), & (4,4), & (4,5), & (4,6) \\ (5,5), & (5,6), & (6,6) & & & \end{array} \right\}$$

consisting of 21 points would also be adequate. As a practical matter, it is usually easier to work with Ω_p.

An analysis of the field bet requires only knowledge of the sum of the spots showing on the thrown dice; therefore the sample space

$$\Omega_s = \{2, 3, 4, 5, 6, 7, 8, 9, 10, 11, 12\}$$

consisting of 11 points would suffice.

Bets on the pass line require an indeterminate number of rolls to decide. In principle, it is possible that neither the shooter's point nor a seven will ever be rolled and the game could continue indefinitely. One possible choice of Ω is all possible infinite sequences of ordered pairs (n_1, n_2) of the numbers from 1 to 6. If we let $\Omega_{p,i}$ be a copy of Ω_p above, then all possible sequences of ordered pairs can be written as the Cartesian product of the $\Omega_{p,i}$

$$\Omega_p^\infty = \mathsf{X}_{i=1}^\infty \Omega_{p,i}.$$

This choice of Ω is rich enough to support the analysis of any bet on the table. For example, consider the point

$$\omega = [(1,6), (1,3), (6,1), (4,3), \ldots]$$

from Ω_p^∞. If the first throw is a come out roll, then bets on the pass line would win, lose, win in the first four rolls. Field bets would win once and lose thrice in the first four rolls. Hardway bets on the four would lose on each of the first four rolls.

If one only wanted to analyze place bets, come bets, and bets on the pass line, it would be enough to keep track of the sum of the dice on each roll. In this case the sample space could consist of all infinite sequences of the numbers from 2 to 12, namely,

$$\Omega_s^\infty = \mathsf{X}_{i=1}^\infty \Omega_{s,i},$$

where each $\Omega_{s,i}$ is a copy of Ω_s above.

For the game of keno (Section 1.1.2), the sample space comprised of all sequences of length 20 made up of the numbers from 1 to 80 where no number is repeated within the sequence is adequate. We could let order be important so that $(3, 5, 6, \ldots)$ and $(6, 3, 5, \ldots)$ count as different sequences, or we could let order be unimportant so they count as the same sequence. The order of draws is not important in determining whether or not a keno bet wins, so either is acceptable.

For the coin tossing example (Section 1.1.3), one could put $\Omega = (0, 1]$ or take Ω to be all possible sequences of 0's and 1's. Recall that endpoints do not matter so that $\Omega = (0, 1), [0, 1)$, or $[0, 1]$ are also acceptable choices.

For the triangular map example (Section 1.1.4), one could put $\Omega = [0, 1]$ or take Ω to be all the irrational numbers in $[0, 1]$.

1.3 Events

An *event* E is a subset of the sample space Ω. It may be empty, a proper subset of the sample space, or the sample space itself. Situations such as Section 1.1 describe are often called *experiments*. An event *occurs* if the experiment is performed, ω is the outcome, and $\omega \in E$. We illustrate using the game of craps, which is described in Section 1.1.1.

The event "snake eyes" is a single roll bet that pays 30 to 1. Relative to the sample space Ω_p consisting of all pairs (n_1, n_2) of the numbers 1 through 6, which is displayed in Section 1.2 and again later in this section, snake eyes is the singleton set

$$E = \{(1, 1)\}.$$

The shooter rolls. If the dice land $\omega = (1, 1)$, then snake eyes occurs. The event "any seven" is another single roll bet. It pays 4 to 1. It is

$$E = \{(1, 6), (6, 1), (2, 5), (5, 2), (3, 4), (4, 3)\}.$$

As noted in Section 1.2, multiple roll bets such as a place bet on the eight to win require a more complicated sample space. For place bets, the sample space Ω_s^∞ consisting of all infinite sequences of the numbers from 2 to 12 is adequate. With this sample space, one wins a place bet on the eight if the event

$$\begin{aligned} E &= \{\text{"an eight before a seven"}\} \\ &= \left\{\omega\colon \omega = (\omega_1, \omega_2, \ldots), \min\{i\colon \omega_i = 8\} < \min\{i\colon \omega_i = 7\}\right\} \end{aligned}$$

occurs. For instance, if the shooter rolls the sequence

$$\omega = (\omega_1, \omega_2, \omega_3, \ldots) = (5, 6, 8, \ldots),$$

then a place bet on the eight wins and E occurs. If the shooter rolls

$$\omega = (\omega_1, \omega_2, \omega_3, \omega_4, \omega_5, \ldots) = (6, 6, 9, 4, 7, \ldots),$$

then it loses and E does not occur.

Subsetting, or *containment*, is indicated by $A \subset B$, which means that every ω that is in A is also in B. The definition can be written symbolically as

$$A \subset B \quad \overset{\text{def}}{\Leftrightarrow} \quad (\omega \in A \Rightarrow \omega \in B),$$

which reads

> A is a subset of B if and only if ω in A implies that ω is in B.

As an example, consider $A = \{x : x < 5\}$ and $B = \{x : x < 8\}$:

$$\begin{aligned} x \in A &\Rightarrow x < 5 \\ x < 5 &\Rightarrow x < 8 \\ x < 8 &\Rightarrow x \in B, \end{aligned}$$

therefore

$$x \in A \Rightarrow x \in B.$$

By the definition,

$$A \subset B.$$

Two events A and B are *equal*, written $A = B$, if they contain the same elements. This can be written symbolically as

$$A = B \quad \overset{\text{def}}{\Leftrightarrow} \quad (A \subset B \text{ and } B \subset A).$$

To prove equality, one must take an arbitrary element ω from A and show that it is in B and then take an arbitrary element ω from B and show that it is in A.

The *union* of A and B, written $A \cup B$, is the set of elements that belong to either A or B, or both,

$$A \cup B = \{\omega\colon \omega \in A \text{ or } \omega \in B\}.$$

The *intersection* of A and B, written $A \cap B$, is the set of elements that belong to both A and B,

$$A \cap B = \{\omega\colon \omega \in A \text{ and } \omega \in B\}.$$

The *complement* of A, written as $\tilde{A}$ or $\sim A$, is the set of elements in Ω that are not in A,

$$\tilde{A} = \{\omega \in \Omega\colon \omega \notin A\}.$$

We illustrate complement, union, and intersection with some single roll bets from craps:

$$\Omega_p = \left\{\begin{matrix} (1,1), & (1,2), & (1,3), & (1,4), & (1,5), & (1,6) \\ (2,1), & (2,2), & (2,3), & (2,4), & (2,5), & (2,6) \\ (3,1), & (3,2), & (3,3), & (3,4), & (3,5), & (3,6) \\ (4,1), & (4,2), & (4,3), & (4,4), & (4,5), & (4,6) \\ (5,1), & (5,2), & (5,3), & (5,4), & (5,5), & (5,6) \\ (6,1), & (6,2), & (6,3), & (6,4), & (6,5), & (6,6) \end{matrix}\right\} \quad \text{“sample space”}$$

$$F = \left\{\begin{matrix} (1,1), & (1,2), & (1,3), & (2,1), & (2,2), & (3,1), \\ (3,6), & (4,5), & (4,6), & (5,4), & (5,5), & (5,6), \\ (6,3), & (6,4), & (6,5), & (6,6) & & \end{matrix}\right\} \quad \text{“field”}$$

$$\tilde{F} = \left\{\begin{matrix} (1,4), & (1,5), & (1,6), & (2,3), & (2,4), & (2,5), \\ (2,6), & (3,2), & (3,3), & (3,4), & (3,5), & (4,1), \\ (4,2), & (4,3), & (4,4), & (5,1), & (5,2), & (5,3), \\ (6,1), & (6,2) & & & & \end{matrix}\right\} \quad \text{“no field”}$$

$$H = \{(4,4)\} \quad \text{“hard eight”}$$

$$E = \{(2,6), (6,2), (3,5), (5,3)\} \quad \text{“easy eight”}$$

$$H \cup E = \{(4,4), (2,6), (6,2), (3,5), (5,3)\} \quad \text{“any eight”}$$

$$H \cap E = \{\,\} = \emptyset \quad \text{“empty set.”}$$

The union and intersection operations are *commutative*, *associative*, and *distributive*. Specifically, if A, B, and C are subsets of Ω, then union and intersection commute

$$A \cup B = B \cup A$$
$$A \cap B = B \cap A,$$

associate

$$A \cup (B \cup C) = (A \cup B) \cup C$$
$$A \cap (B \cap C) = (A \cap B) \cap C,$$

and distribute

$$A \cup (B \cap C) = (A \cup B) \cap (A \cup C)$$
$$A \cap (B \cup C) = (A \cap B) \cup (A \cap C).$$

Also useful are *DeMorgan's laws*

$$\sim(A \cup B) = \tilde{A} \cap \tilde{B}$$
$$\sim(A \cap B) = \tilde{A} \cup \tilde{B}.$$

The first is proved as follows:

$$\begin{aligned}
\omega^o \in (\widetilde{A \cup B}) &\Rightarrow \omega^o \notin (A \cup B) \\
&\Rightarrow \omega^o \notin \{\omega: \omega \in A \text{ or } \omega \in B\} \\
&\Rightarrow \omega^o \notin A \text{ and } \omega \notin B \\
&\Rightarrow \omega^o \in \tilde{A} \text{ and } \omega \in \tilde{B} \\
&\Rightarrow \omega^o \in \{\omega: \omega \in \tilde{A} \text{ and } \omega \in \tilde{B}\} \\
&\Rightarrow \omega^o \in (\tilde{A} \cap \tilde{B}).
\end{aligned}$$

Thus

$$(\widetilde{A \cup B}) \subset \tilde{A} \cap \tilde{B}.$$

A similar argument yields

$$\tilde{A} \cap \tilde{B} \subset (\widetilde{A \cup B}),$$

which proves the result.

It is possible to take the union or intersection of a countable number of sets. A point is in $\bigcup_{i=1}^{\infty} A_i$ if it is in at least one of the A_i; that is,

$$\bigcup_{i=1}^{\infty} A_i = \{\omega : \exists i \text{ in } 1 \le i < \infty \text{ such that } \omega \in A_i\}$$
$$= \{\omega : \omega \in A_i \text{ for some } i \text{ in } 1 \le i < \infty\}.$$

A point is in $\bigcap_{i=1}^{\infty} A_i$ if it is in every one of the A_i; that is,

$$\bigcap_{i=1}^{\infty} A_i = \{\omega : 1 \le i < \infty \Rightarrow \omega \in A_i\}$$
$$= \{\omega : \omega \in A_i \text{ for every } i \text{ in } 1 \le i < \infty\}.$$

To illustrate, if the game is craps, the sample space is Ω_s^{∞}, and E_i is the event "the shooter rolls 8 on roll i," then $\bigcap_{i=1}^{\infty} E_i$ contains the single point $\omega = (8, 8, \ldots)$ and $\bigcup_{i=1}^{\infty} E_i$ is the set of all sequences that have at least one 8 as an element. Other examples are

$$\bigcup_{i=1}^{\infty}\left[\frac{1}{i}, 1\right] = \left\{x : \frac{1}{i} \le x \le 1 \text{ for some } 1 \le i < \infty\right\} = (0, 1]$$

and

$$\bigcap_{i=1}^{\infty}\left[\frac{1}{i}, 1\right] = \left\{x : \frac{1}{i} \le x \le 1 \text{ for every } 1 \le i < \infty\right\} = [1].$$

DeMorgan's laws apply to countable intersections and unions:

$$\sim \bigcup_{i=1}^{\infty} A_i = \bigcap_{i=1}^{\infty} \tilde{A}_i,$$
$$\sim \bigcap_{i=1}^{\infty} A_i = \bigcup_{i=1}^{\infty} \tilde{A}_i.$$

Consider the event E consisting of those sample points

$$\omega = (\omega_1, \omega_2, \omega_3, \ldots) \in \Omega_s^{\infty}$$

for which an infinite number of the ω_i are equal to 8. Let E_i be the event "8 on roll i" as above. If $\omega \in E$, then ω is in infinitely many of the events in the sequence $E_1, E_2, E_3, \ldots$; that is, events in the sequence occur infinitely often. For this reason, the event E is called "E_i *infinitely often*" and is written $[E_i \text{ i.o.}]$. We can characterize $[E_i \text{ i.o.}]$ in terms of countable unions and intersections of the E_i as follows:

$$\omega \in [E_i \text{ i.o.}] \Leftrightarrow \text{ for every } I \geq 1 \text{ there is an } i \geq I \text{ such that } \omega \in E_i$$

$$\omega \in [E_i \text{ i.o.}] \Leftrightarrow \text{ for every } I \geq 1 \text{ we have } \omega \in \bigcup_{i=I}^{\infty} E_i$$

$$\omega \in [E_i \text{ i.o.}] \Leftrightarrow \omega \in \bigcap_{I=1}^{\infty} \bigcup_{i=I}^{\infty} E_i.$$

Therefore

$$[E_i \text{ i.o.}] = \bigcap_{I=1}^{\infty} \bigcup_{i=I}^{\infty} E_i.$$

Another event of interest is E_i occurs all but a finite number of times. By a similar logic this event is $\bigcup_{I=1}^{\infty} \bigcap_{i=I}^{\infty} E_i$. One sometimes sees the notation $\liminf E_i$ to mean $\bigcup_{I=1}^{\infty} \bigcap_{i=I}^{\infty} E_i$ and $\limsup E_i$ to mean $\bigcap_{I=1}^{\infty} \bigcup_{i=I}^{\infty} E_i$.

Two events A and B are *disjoint* (or *mutually exclusive*) if $A \cap B = \emptyset$. A sequence of events $A_1, A_2, \ldots$ is disjoint (or mutually exclusive) if the sets A_i are pairwise disjoint; that is, if $A_i \cap A_j = \emptyset$ for all $i \neq j$. A sequence of events is called *exhaustive* if $\Omega = \bigcup_{i=1}^{\infty} A_i$. In the coin tossing experiment (Section 1.1.3) with $\Omega = [0, 1]$, the sets

$$A_0 = [0], \qquad A_i = \left(\frac{1}{i+1}, \frac{1}{i}\right], \qquad i = 1, 2, \ldots$$

are mutually exclusive and exhaustive.

1.4 Probability Spaces

1.4.1 *Coin Tossing: One Dimension*

Probability theory is designed to permit a mathematical analysis of the situations described in the examples of Section 1.1 and similar situations. The coin tossing example serves best to illustrate the ideas. Recall that the salient feature of that example is that it is a physical mechanism that generates numbers ω in $(0, 1]$ for which it is reasonable to state that the chance that ω is in some subinterval $(a, b]$ is the length $b - a$ of that subinterval. A sample space for the coin tossing example is $\Omega = (0, 1]$. With this choice of sample space, an event A is a subset of $(0, 1]$. To determine if an event occurs, one tosses the coin long enough to determine if

$$\omega = t_1\frac{1}{2} + t_2\frac{1}{4} + t_3\frac{1}{8} + \cdots$$

is in A, where t_i is 1 if the coin lands heads on toss i and is 0 if it lands tails.

The probability function P assigns to an event A the chance $P(A)$ that it will occur. If the event A is a subinterval of $\Omega = (0, 1]$, then its probability is its length, viz.

$$P\{(a, b]\} = b - a.$$

If A is the union of two disjoint subintervals, then its probability is the sum of the lengths of the two subintervals,

$$P\{(a, b] \cup (c, d]\} = b - a + d - c.$$

From this together with $P(\Omega) = P\{(0, 1]\} = 1$, one can infer that

$$P\{\sim (a, b]\} = 1 - P\{(a, b]\}.$$

If A is the finite union of disjoint subintervals, that is, $A = \bigcup_{i=1}^{n}(a_i, b_i]$ and $(a_i, b_i] \cap (a_j, b_j] = \emptyset$ for $i \neq j$, then

$$P(A) = \sum_{i=1}^{n}(b_i - a_i).$$

The empty set has no length and cannot occur so it is natural to put

$$P(\emptyset) = 0.$$

If we let $\mathscr{A}$ denote the collection of sets of the form $(a, b]$ with $0 \leq a < b \leq 1$, finite unions of such sets, plus the empty set $\emptyset$, then, at present, we have P defined over $\mathscr{A}$. Note that (i) the empty set is in $\mathscr{A}$, (ii) $\tilde{A} \in \mathscr{A}$ whenever A is, and (iii) $A \cup B \in \mathscr{A}$ whenever A and B are. A collection of sets with these three properties is called an *algebra* of sets. This is as far as the notion of length will take us. Unfortunately it is not far enough. We will need P to be defined for a larger class of events than the algebra $\mathscr{A}$.

A *σ-algebra* (or *σ-field* or *Borel field*) is a collection of sets $\mathscr{B}$ that satisfy the following three properties: (i) $\emptyset \in \mathscr{B}$ (the empty set is a member of $\mathscr{B}$), (ii) if $B \in \mathscr{B}$, then $\tilde{B} \in \mathscr{B}$ ($\mathscr{B}$ is closed under complementation), and (iii) if $B_1, B_2, \ldots \in \mathscr{B}$, then $\bigcup_{i=1}^{\infty} B_i \in \mathscr{B}$ ($\mathscr{B}$ is closed under countable union).

Let $\mathscr{F}$ denote the smallest σ-algebra that contains $\mathscr{A}$ (Problem 11). Note that $\mathscr{F}$ will contain intervals of the form (a, b), $[a, b)$, and $[a, b]$ because they can be constructed from countable unions and intersections of sets of the form $(a, b] \in \mathscr{A}$. For instance, $(a, b) = \bigcup_{i=1}^{\infty}(a, b - 1/i]$. We can extend the definition of P to $\mathscr{F}$.

Before doing so, let us introduce or recall, as the case may be, the definitions of the *supremum* and *infimum* of a subset B of the real line, denoted $\sup B$ and $\inf B$, respectively. If B has an upper bound, that is, there is some real number b such that $x \leq b$ for all $x \in B$, then $\sup B$ is the smallest such b. If B does not have an upper bound, then $\sup B = \infty$. Define $\sup \emptyset = -\infty$. For example, $\sup(0, 1] = \sup(0, 1) = 1$, $\sup(-\infty, \infty) = \infty$, and $\sup\{x: x = 1 - 1/i, i = 1, 2, \ldots\} = 1$. $\operatorname{Inf} B$ is defined analogously: If B has a lower bound, then $\inf B$ is the largest lower bound. If B does not have a lower bound, then $\inf B = -\infty$. Also, $\inf \emptyset = \infty$. As examples, $\inf[0, 1) = \inf(0, 1) = 0$, $\inf(-\infty, \infty) = -\infty$, and $\inf\{x: x = 1/i, i = 1, 2, \ldots\} = 0$. Supremum and infimum are related by $\inf B = -\sup\{-x: x \in B\}$. If $A \subset B$, then $\sup A \leq \sup B$ and $\inf B \leq \inf A$.

Returning to the extension of P to $\mathscr{F}$, for $F \in \mathscr{F}$ define

$$P(F) = \inf \sum_{i=1}^{\infty} P(A_i),$$

where $\{A_i\}$ ranges over all sequences $A_1, A_2, \ldots$ from $\mathscr{A}$ such that $F \subset \bigcup_{i=1}^{\infty} A_i$. That is,

$$P(F) = \inf\left\{p: p = \sum_{i=1}^{\infty} P(A_i), F \subset \bigcup_{i=1}^{\infty} A_i, A_i \in \mathscr{A}\right\}.$$

The probability function so defined will satisfy three properties: (i) $P(F) \geq 0$ for all $F \in \mathscr{F}$ (P is *positive*), (ii) $P(\Omega) = 1$, and (iii) if $F_1, F_2, \ldots \in \mathscr{F}$ are disjoint, then $P(\bigcup_{i=1}^{\infty} F_i) = \sum_{i=1}^{\infty} P(F_i)$ (P is *count-*

ably additive). Because the function P takes as its argument the elements of $\mathcal{F}$, which are sets, P is called a *set function*. Properties (i) through (iii) are called the *axioms of probability*. Thus, a *probability function* P is a positive, countably additive, set function that is defined over a σ-algebra $\mathcal{F}$ of subsets of a sample space Ω and satisfies $P(\Omega) = 1$. A *probability space* is the triplet $(\Omega, \mathcal{F}, P)$.

For later reference, we note that if P is countably additive, then it must also be *finitely additive*; that is, if $F_1, F_2, \ldots, F_n \in \mathcal{F}$ are disjoint, then $P(F) = \sum_{i=1}^{n} P(F_i)$. This is proved by noting that sequence $F_1, F_2, \ldots, F_n, \emptyset, \emptyset, \ldots$ is disjoint and that for this sequence $\sum_{i=1}^{n} P(F_i) = \sum_{i=1}^{\infty} P(F_i)$ and $\bigcup_{i=1}^{n} F_i = \bigcup_{i=1}^{\infty} F_i$.

1.4.2 *Coin Tossing: Two Dimensions*

As the coin tossing example suggests, probability is akin to the notions of length, area, and volume and we will make use of this analogy frequently in the sequel. Because area lends itself better to graphical illustration than length or volume, we shall extend the coin tossing example to two dimensions.

Consider performing the coin tossing experiment of Section 1.1.3 twice with two different coins and letting the outcome be recorded as the two-dimensional point (x, y) where x corresponds to the tosses of the first coin and y to the tosses of the second. The relevant sample space is $\Omega^2 = (0, 1] \times (0, 1]$. The probability of a rectangle is its area $P\{(a, b] \times (c, d]\} = \text{Area}\{(a, b] \times (c, d]\} = (b - a) \times (d - c)$. The probability of the union $\bigcup_{i=1}^{n} A_i$ of disjoint rectangles of the form $A_i = (a_i, b_i] \times (c_i, d_i]$ is the sum of the areas of the rectangles: $P(\bigcup_{i=1}^{n} A_i) = \sum_{i=1}^{n} \text{Area}(A_i)$. The collection $\mathcal{A}$ consisting of $\emptyset$ and all finite unions of rectangles of the form $(a, b] \times (c, d]$ is an algebra. Let $\mathcal{F}$ be the smallest σ-algebra that contains $\mathcal{A}$. A covering $\bigcup_{i=1}^{n} A_i$ of $F \in \mathcal{F}$ by a union of disjoint rectangles $A_i \in \mathcal{A}$ is shown in Figure 1.4. The probability of F is approximated by the smallest value of $\sum_{i=1}^{n} \text{Area}(A_i)$ that can be achieved by rectangles such as those shown. Indeed, this is how the area of irregular objects is computed in practice. The approximation converges to $P(F)$ as n tends to infinity. More generally, to accommodate sets less regularly shaped than shown in Figure 1.4, the probability of $F \in \mathcal{F}$ is

$$P(F) = \inf\left\{p\colon p = \sum_{i=1}^{\infty} \text{Area}(A_i), F \subset \bigcup_{i=1}^{\infty} A_i, A_i \in \mathcal{A}\right\}.$$

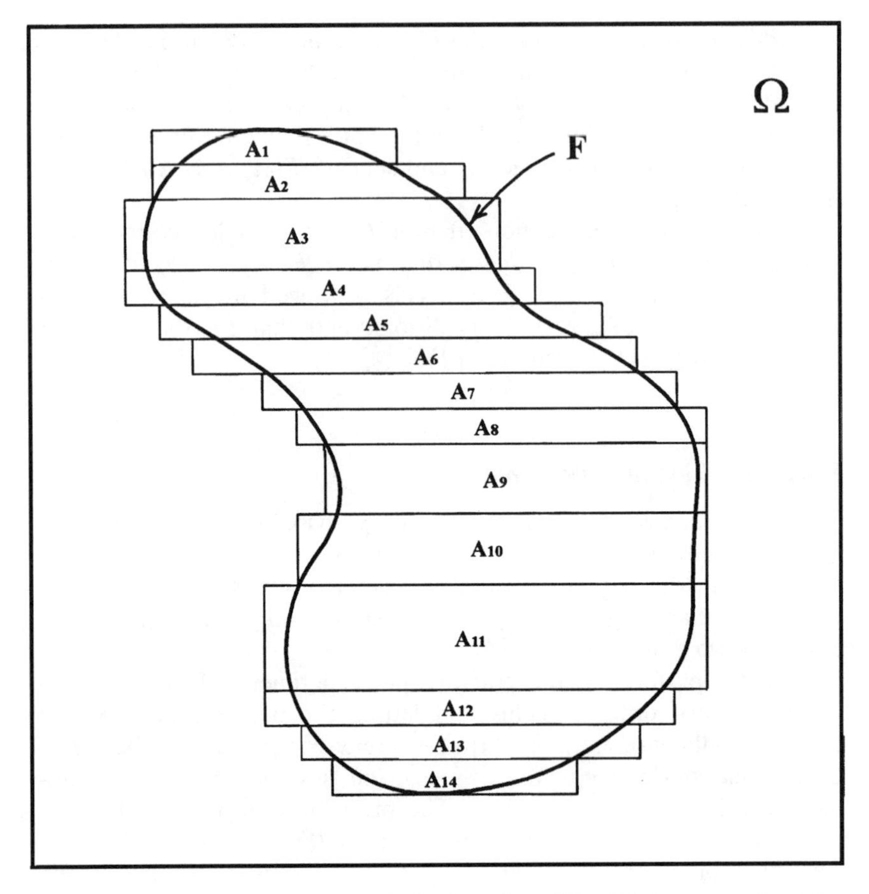

Figure 1.4. A covering of an irregularly shaped set F by disjoint rectangles. The probability of F is approximated by the smallest value of $\sum_{i=1}^{n} \text{Area}(A_i)$ that can be achieved by rectangles such as those shown. The approximation converges to $P(F)$ as n tends to infinity.

1.4.3 *Craps: Single Roll Bets*

To illustrate how these ideas can be extended beyond the coin tossing example, we shall apply them to the game of craps described in Subsection 1.1.1. For a given bet, our goal shall be to describe an appropriate sample space Ω, a σ-algebra $\mathcal{F}$, and a probability function P.

To analyze the single roll bets, we take Ω_p, defined in Section 1.2, as the sample space. The σ-algebra $\mathcal{F}_p$ over which P is defined is the collection of all possible subsets of Ω_p. $\mathcal{F}_p$ contains $\emptyset$, all singleton sets, of which there are 36, all sets containing two elements, of which there are $1260 = 36 \times 35$, and so on. Every outcome in Ω_p is equally likely—presumably state gaming commissions make sure that this is true—so the probability assigned to any singleton set is $P(\{\omega\}) = 1/36$.

We extend the definition beyond singleton sets by making P be finitely additive. Thus, the probability assigned to an event with two elements is $P(\{w_1, w_2\}) = P(\{w_1\}) + P(\{w_2\}) = 1/36 + 1/36 = 1/18$, and, in general, the probability of any event is the number of points in it divided by 36. For example, the probability that a place bet on the 4 wins on the first roll is $P[\{(1, 3), (2, 2), (3, 1)\}] = 1/12$.

1.4.4 *Craps: Multiple Roll Bets*

If we consider two tosses of the dice, we would let $\Omega_{p,1}$ and $\Omega_{p,2}$ each be copies of Ω_p, and let the sample space be the Cartesian product

$$\begin{aligned}\Omega_p^2 &= \Omega_{p,1} \times \Omega_{p,2} \\ &= \{(\omega_1, \omega_2): \omega_1 \in \Omega_{p,1}, \omega_2 \in \Omega_{p,2}\} \\ &= \{[(n_1, n_2), (n_3, n_4)]: (n_1, n_2) \in \Omega_{p,1}, (n_3, n_4) \in \Omega_{p,2}\}.\end{aligned}$$

Let $\mathcal{F}_{p,1}$ and $\mathcal{F}_{p,2}$ each be copies of $\mathcal{F}_p$. The σ-algebra $\mathcal{F}_p^2$ over which P is defined is the smallest σ-algebra that contains

$$\mathcal{F}_{p,1} \times \mathcal{F}_{p,2} = \{E_1 \times E_2: E_1 \in \mathcal{F}_{p,1}, E_2 \in \mathcal{F}_{p,2}\},$$

where

$$\begin{aligned}E_1 \times E_2 &= \{(\omega_1, \omega_2): \omega_1 \in E_1, \omega_2 \in E_2\} \\ &= \{[(n_1, n_2), (n_3, n_4)]: (n_1, n_2) \in E_1, (n_3, n_4) \in E_2\}.\end{aligned}$$

The operation of taking the smallest σ-algebra containing some class of sets $\mathcal{A}$ is often written $\sigma(\mathcal{A})$ so that

$$\mathcal{F}_p^2 = \sigma(\mathcal{F}_{p,1} \times \mathcal{F}_{p,2}).$$

As above, each of the outcomes $(\omega_1, \omega_2) \in \Omega_p^2$ is equally likely and there are $36 \times 36 = 1{,}296$ such points so that, as above, to assign a probability $P(E)$ to an event E is a matter of counting up the number of points in E and dividing by 1,296.

Let us consider the probability that a place bet on the 4 wins on the second roll. This is the event

$$E = \left\{ \begin{matrix} (1,1), & (1,2), & (1,4), & (1,5), & (2,1), & (2,3), & (2,4), \\ (2,6), & (3,2), & (3,3), & (3,5), & (3,6), & (4,1), & (4,2), \\ (4,4), & (4,5), & (4,6), & (5,1), & (5,3), & (5,4), & (5,5), \\ (5,6), & (6,2), & (6,3), & (6,4), & (6,5), & (6,6) & \end{matrix} \right\} \times \left\{ \begin{matrix} (1,3), \\ (2,2), \\ (3,1) \end{matrix} \right\}.$$

There are 27×3 points in this event so that

$$P(E) = \frac{27 \times 3}{36 \times 36} = \frac{3}{4} \times \frac{1}{12}.$$

By continuing along these lines, one can determine the probability space $(\Omega_p^n, \mathcal{F}_p^n, P)$ for n rolls. One would conclude that the probability of the event E_i = "a place bet on the 4 wins on roll i" is

$$P(E_i) = \frac{1}{12} \times \left(\frac{3}{4}\right)^{i-1}.$$

Note that these probability spaces are consistent in that if one computed the probability that a place bet wins on roll i in any of them for which $n \geq i$, one would get the same answer. That is,

$$P(E_i) = P(E_i \times \Omega_{p,\,i+1} \times \cdots \times \Omega_{p,\,n}).$$

For multiple roll bets the sample space is

$$\Omega_p^\infty = \mathsf{X}_{i=1}^\infty \Omega_{p,\,i},$$

as described in Section 1.2, where each $\Omega_{p,\,i}$ is a copy of Ω_p. The σ-algebra on which P is defined is constructed as follows. Let $\mathcal{A}$ be the collection of sets formed by taking events E^n from $\mathcal{F}_p^n$ and appending an infinite number of copies of Ω_p for $n = 1, 2, \ldots$. That is,

$$\mathcal{A} = \bigcup_{n=1}^{\infty} \{A: A = E_n \times \Omega_{p,\,n+1} \times \Omega_{p,\,n+2} \times \cdots, E_n \in \mathcal{F}_p^n,\ \Omega_{p,\,i} = \Omega_p\}.$$

Probabilities are assigned to $A \in \mathscr{A}$ according to

$$P(E_n \times \Omega_{p,\,n+1} \times \Omega_{p,\,n+2} \times \cdots) = P(E_n).$$

Put $\mathscr{F}_p^\infty = \sigma(\mathscr{A})$. The definition is extended to $F \in \mathscr{F}_p^\infty$ by putting $P(F) = \inf \sum_{i=1}^\infty P(A_i)$, where the sequence $A_1, A_2, \ldots$ ranges over all disjoint sequences of sets from $\mathscr{A}$ whose union contains F. The triple $(\Omega_p^\infty, \mathscr{F}_p^\infty, P)$ so constructed is a probability space.

Notations such as

$$E = \bigcup_{n=1}^\infty E_n \times \Omega_{p,\,n+1} \times \Omega_{p,\,n+2} \times \cdots \quad \text{and} \quad P(E_n \times \Omega_{p,\,n+1} \times \Omega_{p,\,n+2} \times \cdots)$$

are cumbersome. Henceforth, we will let the fact that copies of Ω_p must be appended to $E_n \in \mathscr{F}_p^n$ in order to get membership in $\mathscr{F}_p^\infty$ be understood and we will write

$$E = \bigcup_{n=1}^\infty E_n \quad \text{and} \quad P(E_n)$$

instead.

In applications, the only probabilities one actually needs to compute are probabilities for sets from $\mathscr{A}$, which is a matter of counting as we have seen. For example, to compute the probability of the event $E =$ "a place bet on the 4 wins," one notes that the events $E_i =$ "a place bet on the 4 wins on roll i" are disjoint and that

$$E = \bigcup_{i=1}^\infty E_i.$$

By countable additivity and the definition of P, the probability that a place bet on the 4 wins is

$$P(E) = \sum_{i=1}^\infty P(E_i) = \frac{1}{12} \sum_{i=1}^\infty \left(\frac{3}{4}\right)^{i-1} = \frac{1}{12} \times 4 = \frac{1}{3}.$$

This can be compared to the true odds of 3 for 1—3 for 1 is the same as 2 to 1—in Table 1.1. Our computation agrees!

By the same logic used to work out the place bet, $A_i =$ "a place bet on the 4 is decided on roll i" occurs with probability $P(A_i) = (1/4)(3/4)^{i-1}$ so that $P(\bigcup_{i=1}^\infty A_i) = 1$. Since $\omega \in \bigcup_{i=1}^\infty A_i \Leftrightarrow \exists i$ such that $\omega \in A_i$, the bet is decided in a finite number of rolls with probability 1. The probability of other multiple roll bets will be easier to work out after some more ideas from probability theory are in place, in particular, the notion of conditional probability.

1.4.5 *Coin Tossing: Countable Dimensions*

We extended the coin tossing example from one dimension to two. The same construction can be used to extend it to n dimensions. Having extended to n dimensions, the extension to $\Omega^\infty = \mathsf{X}_{i=1}^{\infty}(0, 1]$ is the same as for multiple roll bets in craps: $\mathscr{A}$ is the collection of all events from the finite-dimensional spaces with an infinite number of copies of $(0, 1]$ appended. Probabilities $P(A)$ are assigned to events $A \in \mathscr{A}$ using probabilities from the finite-dimensional spaces. $\mathscr{F} = \sigma(\mathscr{A})$. For $F \in \mathscr{F}$, $P(F) = \inf \sum_{i=1}^{\infty} P(A_i)$, where the sequence $A_1, A_2, \ldots$ ranges over all disjoint sequence of sets from $\mathscr{A}$ whose union contains F. The reader who would like to pursue the ideas behind these constructions in more depth should see Royden 1988, Chapter 11.

1.5 Properties of Probability Spaces

We can summarize the previous section in the following definition.

Definition 1.1. A *probability space* is the triple $(\Omega, \mathscr{F}, P)$ consisting of a sample space Ω, a σ-algebra $\mathscr{F}$ of subsets of Ω, and a function P defined on $\mathscr{F}$ that satisfies the axioms of probability:

1. $P(A) \geq 0$ for all $A \in \mathscr{F}$.
2. $P(\Omega) = 1$.
3. If $A_1, A_2, \ldots \in \mathscr{F}$ are disjoint, then $P(\bigcup_{i=1}^{\infty} A_i) = \sum_{i=1}^{\infty} P(A_i)$.

In this section we derive some useful properties of probability spaces that follow from the definition, which we can summarize as follows.

Proposition 1.1. *Let $(\Omega, \mathscr{F}, P)$ be a probability space and let A, B, and $A_1, A_2, \ldots$ be sets in $\mathscr{F}$. Then*

1. $P(\emptyset) = 0$.
2. $P(A) \leq 1$.
3. $P(A) + P(\tilde{A}) = 1$.
4. $P(A \cap B) + P(A \cap \tilde{B}) = P(A)$.
5. $P(A \cup B) = P(A) + P(B) - P(A \cap B)$.
6. *If $A \subset B$, then $P(A) \leq P(B)$.*
7. *If A_1, $A_2, \ldots$ are mutually exclusive and exhaustive, then $P(A) = \sum_{i=1}^{\infty} P(A \cap A_i)$.*
8. $P(\bigcup_{i=1}^{\infty} A_i) \leq \sum_{i=1}^{\infty} P(A_i)$ *(countable subadditivity).*

As pointed out in the previous section, probability is akin to area. More precisely, the properties of the probability function are similar

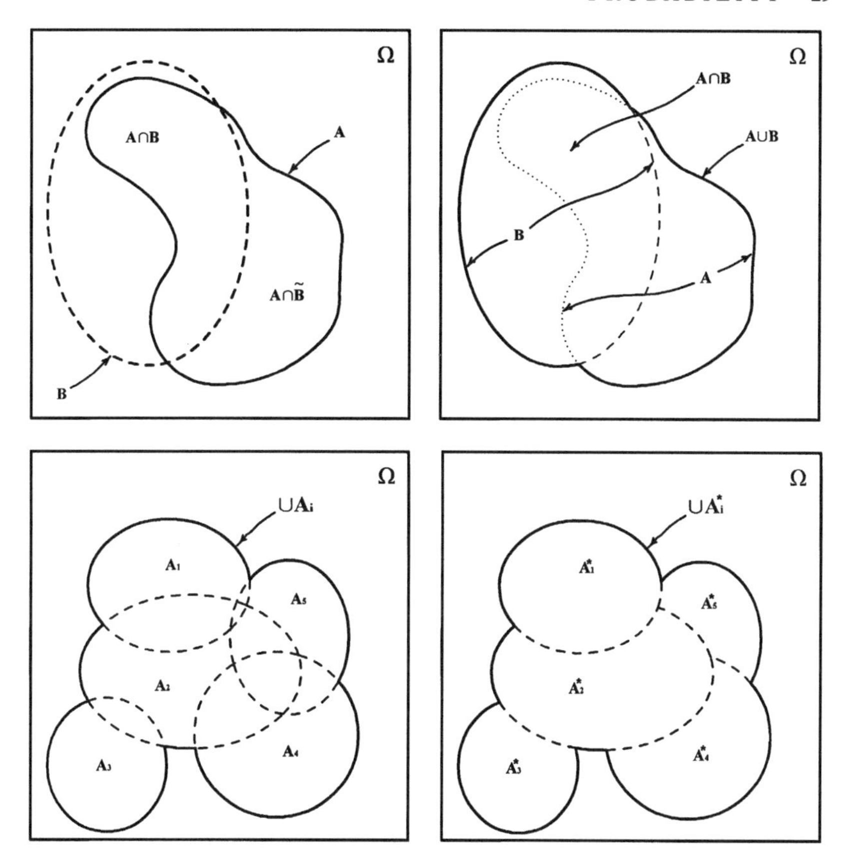

Figure 1.5. Illustration of Proposition 1.1. The sample space is $\Omega = (0,1] \times (0,1]$. The area of a set A is equal to its probability $P(A)$. The upper left panel shows $P(A \cap B) + P(A \cap \tilde{B}) = P(A)$. The upper right panel shows $P(A \cup B) = P(A) + P(B) - P(A \cap B)$. The lower two panels show that $\bigcup_{i=1}^{5} A_i = \bigcup_{i=1}^{5} A_i^*$, where $A_1^* = A_1$ and $A_i^* = A_i \cap [\sim (\bigcup_{j=1}^{i-1} A_j)]$. Therefore, $P(\bigcup_{i=1}^{5} A_i) = P(\bigcup_{i=1}^{5} A_i^*) = \sum_{i=1}^{5} P(A_i^*) \leq \sum_{i=1}^{5} P(A_i)$.

to those of area if all sets under consideration are confined to some bounded region that has total area 1, such as $\Omega = (0,1] \times (0,1]$. As may be seen from inspection of Figure 1.5, the properties listed in Proposition 1.1 are properties of area. We shall verify a few of them rigorously in the remainder of this section.

To show Property 4, note that $\Omega = B \cup \tilde{B}$. Therefore, by the distributive laws,

$$A = A \cap \Omega = A \cap (B \cup \tilde{B}) = (A \cap B) \cup (A \cap \tilde{B}).$$

Moreover, by the commutative and associative laws,

$$(A \cap B) \cap (A \cap \tilde{B}) = A \cap (B \cap \tilde{B}) = A \cap \emptyset = \emptyset,$$

which shows that $(A \cap B)$ and $(A \cap \tilde{B})$ are disjoint. By finite additivity, which is a consequence of countable additivity as verified in Section 1.4, we have

$$P(A) = P(A \cap B) + P(A \cap \tilde{B}).$$

This proves Property 4.

To show Property 5, we apply the distributive law to get

$$(A \cap \tilde{B}) \cup B = (A \cup B) \cap (\tilde{B} \cup B) = (A \cup B) \cap \Omega = A \cup B.$$

The sets $(A \cap \tilde{B})$ and B are disjoint because, by the associative law,

$$(A \cap \tilde{B}) \cap B = A \cap (\tilde{B} \cap B) = A \cap \emptyset = \emptyset.$$

Therefore, by finite additivity,

$$P(A \cup B) = P(A \cap \tilde{B}) + P(B).$$

Using $P(A) = P(A \cap B) + P(A \cap \tilde{B})$ from above,

$$P(A \cup B) = P(A) - P(A \cap B) + P(B),$$

which proves Property 5.

To show Property 7, we apply the distributive law to get

$$A = A \cap \Omega = A \cap \left(\bigcup_{i=1}^{\infty} A_i \right) = \bigcup_{i=1}^{\infty} (A \cap A_i).$$

The sets $(A \cap A_1), (A \cap A_2), \ldots$ are disjoint because the associative law implies that for $i \neq j$ we have

$$(A \cap A_i) \cap (A \cap A_j) = (A \cap A) \cap (A_i \cap A_j) = A \cap \emptyset = \emptyset.$$

Countable additivity implies

$$P(A) = \sum_{i=1}^{\infty} P(A \cap A_i),$$

which proves Property 7.

Lastly, we shall verify Property 8. As indicated in the bottom two panels of Figure 1.5, the idea is to show that $\bigcup_{i=1}^{\infty} A_i = \bigcup_{i=1}^{\infty} A_i^*$, where $A_1^*, A_2^*, \ldots$ are disjoint and $A_i^* \subset A_i$, so that $P(\bigcup_{i=1}^{\infty} A_i) = \sum_{i=1}^{\infty} P(A_i^*) \le \sum_{i=1}^{\infty} P(A_i)$ by countable additivity and Property 6.

The A_i^* are defined by

$$A_1^* = A_1, \qquad A_i^* = A_i \cap \left[\sim \left(\bigcup_{k=1}^{i-1} A_k\right)\right] = A_i \cap \left(\bigcap_{k=1}^{i-1} \tilde{A}_k\right)$$

for $i = 1, 2, \ldots$, where the last equality is due to DeMorgan's laws.

To see that $A_1^*, A_2^*, \ldots$ are disjoint, let $i < j$ and apply the commutative and associative laws repeatedly to get

$$\begin{aligned} A_i^* \cap A_j^* &= A_i \cap \left(\bigcap_{k=1}^{i-1} \tilde{A}_k\right) \cap A_j \cap \left(\bigcap_{k=1}^{j-1} \tilde{A}_k\right) \\ &= A_i \cap \left[\left(\bigcap_{k=1}^{i-1} \tilde{A}_k\right) \cap \tilde{A}_1\right] \cap A_j \cap \left(\bigcap_{k=2}^{j-1} \tilde{A}_k\right) \\ &= A_i \cap \left(\bigcap_{k=1}^{i-1} \tilde{A}_k\right) \cap A_j \cap \left(\bigcap_{k=2}^{j-1} \tilde{A}_k\right) \\ &\;\;\vdots \\ &= A_j \cap \left(\bigcap_{k=1}^{i-1} \tilde{A}_k\right) \cap \left(\tilde{A}_i \cap A_i\right) \cap \left(\bigcap_{k=i+1}^{j-1} \tilde{A}_k\right). \end{aligned}$$

But $\tilde{A}_i \cap A_i = \emptyset$ which implies $A_i^* \cap A_j^* = \emptyset$.

To see that $\bigcup_{i=1}^{\infty} A_i = \bigcup_{i=1}^{\infty} A_i^*$, let $\omega \in \bigcup_{i=1}^{\infty} A_i$. Then ω is in one or more A_i; let A_j be the first such A_i. Then $\omega \in A_j^*$ by the definition of A_j^*. We have $\bigcup_{i=1}^{\infty} A_i \subset \bigcup_{i=1}^{\infty} A_i^*$. Conversely, let $\omega \in \bigcup_{i=1}^{\infty} A_i^*$. Since $A_1^*, A_2^*, \ldots$ are disjoint, ω is in exactly one A_i^*; denote it by A_j^*. Then $\omega \in A_j$ by the definition of A_j^*. We have $\bigcup_{i=1}^{\infty} A_i \supset \bigcup_{i=1}^{\infty} A_i^*$. Because both $\bigcup_{i=1}^{\infty} A_i \subset \bigcup_{i=1}^{\infty} A_i^*$ and $\bigcup_{i=1}^{\infty} A_i \supset \bigcup_{i=1}^{\infty} A_i^*$ hold, it follows that $\bigcup_{i=1}^{\infty} A_i = \bigcup_{i=1}^{\infty} A_i^*$.

We now have $P(\bigcup_{i=1}^{\infty} A_i) = \sum_{i=1}^{\infty} P(A_i^*)$ and $A_i^* \subset A_i$ which proves Property 8 as remarked above.

1.6 Combinatorial Results

A sample space Ω for the game of keno, described in Section 1.1.2, consists of all sequences of length 20 made up of the numbers 1 to 80 with no number repeated within the sequence. As we have seen in

Section 1.4, if N denotes the total number of such sequences, then the probability function will assign probability $1/N$ to each singleton set; that is, $P(\{\omega\}) = 1/N$. In order to do this, we need to be able to compute N.

The σ-algebra $\mathcal{F}$ for keno is the set of all possible subsets of Ω. For each event F in $\mathcal{F}$ the probability function will assign the value $P(F) = C/N$, where C is the number of points in F. For example, to determine the probability of catching three on an 8-spot ticket we need to determine the number C of sequences of length 20 made up of the numbers 1 to 80 with no number repeated within the sequence that have exactly three numbers from our specified list of eight.

These are the sorts of questions that this section addresses. Specifically, we seek the answers to four questions:

1. *Ordered samples with replacement.* How many different sequences of r numbers can be formed from the numbers $1, 2, \dots, n$ if numbers can be repeated within the sequence and the order in which the numbers appear matters?
2. *Ordered samples without replacement.* How many different sequences of r numbers can be formed from the numbers $1, 2, \dots, n$ if numbers cannot be repeated within the sequence and the order in which the numbers appear matters?
3. *Unordered samples without replacement.* How many different sequences of r numbers can be formed from the numbers $1, 2, \dots, n$ if numbers cannot be repeated within the sequence and the order in which the numbers appear does not matter?
4. *Unordered samples with replacement.* How many different sequences of r numbers can be formed from the numbers $1, 2, \dots, n$ if numbers can be repeated within the sequence and the order in which the numbers appear does not matter?

We will answer each of these questions in turn.

Question 1. Consider the sequence $(n_1, n_2, n_3, n_4, \dots, n_r)$. There are n choices for n_1 and n choices for n_2, making $n \times n = n^2$ choices for the first two entries. Continuing thus, there are $n^2 \times n = n^3$ choices for the first three entries, $n^3 \times n = n^4$ for the first four, and so on up to n^r, which is the answer.

Question 2. Again consider $(n_1, n_2, \dots, n_r)$. There are n choices for n_1, there are $n - 1$ choices for n_2, making $n \times (n - 1)$ choices for the first two entries. Continuing thus, there are

$$P_r^n = n \times (n-1) \times \cdots \times (n - r + 1)$$

choices for a sequence of length r, which is the answer.

For a positive integer n, define

$$n! = n \times (n-1) \times (n-2) \times \cdots 3 \times 2 \times 1$$

and define $0! = 1$. Read *n factorial* for $n!$. In factorial notation

$$P_r^n = \frac{n!}{(n-r)!}.$$

By the logic of Question 2, $n!$ is the number of permutations $(n_1, n_2, \ldots, n_n)$ of the numbers 1 through n.

Question 3. There are at least three ways of looking at this problem:

Answer 1. Suppose we denote the answer by $\binom{n}{r}$. If we took this answer, and multiplied it by the number of permutations of r objects, then we would have the answer to Question 2. Thus $r!\binom{n}{r} = P_r^n$ or

$$\binom{n}{r} = \frac{n!}{r!(n-r)!}.$$

Read *n choose r* for $\binom{n}{r}$.

Answer 2. We know that the answer is P_r^n when order is important. What we need to do is divide out the redundant permutations of $(n_1, n_2, \ldots, n_r)$ because they are no longer regarded as important. Thus, the answer is

$$\binom{n}{r} = \frac{P_r^n}{r!} = \frac{n!}{r!(n-r!)}.$$

Answer 3. Consider the permutations of n objects where we have added some grouping,

$$n! = [n \times (n-1) \times \cdots \times (n-r+1)] \times [(n-r) \times \cdots \times 3 \times 2 \times 1].$$

As the grouping suggests, this is the number of ways of dividing n objects into two groups, the first of size r and the second of size $n-r$, where the order of the objects within each group matters. What we want to do is disregard the permutations within each group. Therefore we must divide them out to get

$$\binom{n}{r} = \frac{[n \times (n-1) \times \cdots \times (n-r+1)]}{r!} \times \frac{[(n-r) \times \cdots \times 3 \times 2 \times 1]}{(n-r)!}.$$

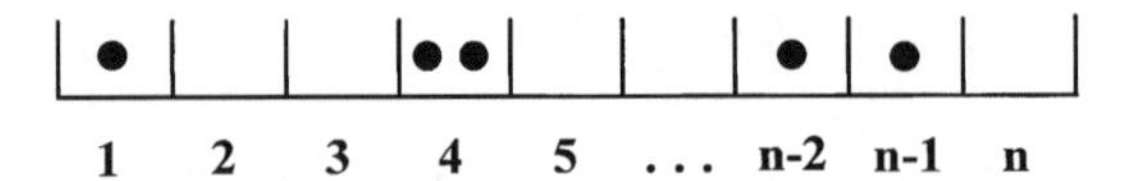

Figure 1.6. Unordered samples with replacement. The number of different sequences of r numbers that can be formed from the numbers $1, 2, \ldots, n$ when numbers can be repeated within the sequence and the order in which the numbers appear does not matter is given by the number of ways that r balls can be placed in n bins. From Casella and Berger 1990.

Other interpretations of $\binom{n}{r}$ are

$\binom{n}{r}$ is the number of permutations of n objects of which r are alike and of one kind and $n-r$ are alike and of another kind; and

$\binom{n}{r}$ is the number of ways n distinct objects can be put in two boxes, r in the first box and $n-r$ in the second box.

Some extensions are

$n!/(n_1! \times n_2! \times \cdots \times n_k!)$, where $n_1 + n_2 + \cdots + n_k = n$, is the number of permutations of n objects of which n_1 are alike and of one kind, n_2 are alike and of another, and so on; and

$n!/(n_1! \times n_2! \times \cdots \times n_k!)$, where $n_1 + n_2 + \cdots + n_k = n$, is the number of ways n distinct objects can be put in k boxes, n_1 in the first box, n_2 in the second box, and so on up to the kth box.

Question 4. As seen from Figure 1.6, the number of ways a sequence $(n_1, n_2, \ldots, n_r)$ can be formed from the numbers $1, 2, \ldots, n$ when numbers can be repeated is the number of ways that r balls can be placed in n bins. This number can be obtained by dropping the two outer bin partitions and considering the number of permutations of $n-1+r$ objects of which $n-1$ are alike and of one kind and r are alike and of another. This number is $\binom{n-1+r}{r}$, which is the answer.

The game of keno is covered by Question 3. Consider the probability C/N of catching three on an 8-spot ticket. There are 80 numbers of which 20 are chosen; order is not important. Thus, $N = \binom{80}{20}$. Of the 80 numbers, eight are marked on the player's ticket. The number of ways of choosing three from eight is $\binom{8}{3}$. The number of ways of choosing 17 misses from the 72 unmarked numbers is $\binom{72}{17}$. Therefore, $C/N = \binom{8}{3}\binom{72}{17}/\binom{80}{20}$. This analysis will work for any number of catches i and spots S, where $0 \leq i \leq S$ and $1 \leq S \leq 20$, so we have

$$P(\text{catch } i \text{ of } S \text{ spots}) = \frac{\binom{S}{i}\binom{80-S}{20-i}}{\binom{80}{20}}.$$

These probabilities for $S = 8$ are shown in Table 1.3.

TABLE 1.3
Probabilities for an 8-Spot Keno Ticket.

i	$P(F_i)$
0	0.0882662377
1	0.2664641139
2	0.3281456217
3	0.2147862251
4	0.0815037015
5	0.0183025856
6	0.0023667137
7	0.0001604552
8	0.0000043457

Note: F_i is the event "catch i spots on an 8-spot ticket."

If our logic is correct, then it must be true that

$$\sum_{i=0}^{S} \frac{\binom{S}{i}\binom{80-S}{20-i}}{\binom{80}{20}} = 1$$

because the events

$$F_i = \{\text{catch } i \text{ of } S \text{ spots}\}, \qquad i = 1, 2, \ldots, S,$$

are mutually exclusive and exhaustive. More generally, the following is true:

$$\sum_{i=\max(0,\, n+D-N)}^{\min(n,\, D)} \binom{D}{i}\binom{N-D}{n-i} = \binom{N}{n}$$

for any $n, N, D \geq 0$ such that $n \leq N$ and $D \leq N$. We shall need this fact several times in Chapter 2.

1.7 Conditional Probability

Consider Figure 1.7, which displays the sample space Ω for a roll of a pair of dice and the events A and B. Given that B has occurred, the relevant sample space becomes

$$\Omega_0 = B = \left\{ \begin{array}{cccccc} (1,4), & (1,5), & (2,4), & (2,5), & (3,4), & (3,5) \\ (4,4), & (4,5), & (5,4), & (5,5), & (6,4), & (6,5) \end{array} \right\}.$$

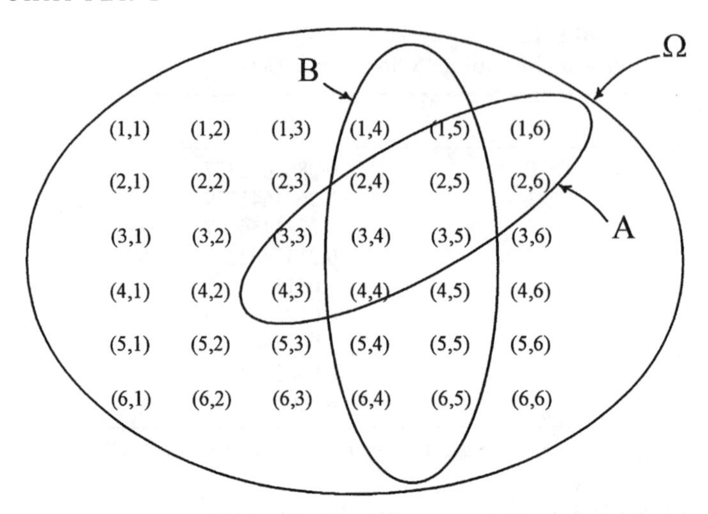

Figure 1.7. Conditional probability. The unconditional probability of A is 10/36=0.28. The conditional probability of A is 6/12=0.50.

The other points in Ω are now irrelevant. Furthermore, the only points in A that are now relevant are

$$A \cap \Omega_0 = A \cap B = \left\{ \begin{array}{ccc} (1,5), & (2,4), & (2,5) \\ (3,4), & (3,5), & (4,4) \end{array} \right\}.$$

Because there is no information available that suggests otherwise, it seems appropriate to assume that the points in Ω_0 bear the same relative probability to one another as they did in Ω. That is, it seems appropriate that the new probability function P_0 defined on $(\Omega_0, \mathscr{F}_0)$ satisfies

$$\frac{P_0(\{\omega_i\})}{P_0(\{\omega_j\})} = \frac{P(\{\omega_i\})}{P(\{\omega_j\})},$$

where ω_i, $\omega_j \in \Omega_0$ and P is the probability function defined on $(\Omega, \mathscr{F})$. As in Section 1.4, $\mathscr{F}_0$ consists of all possible subsets of Ω_0 and $\mathscr{F}$ all possible subsets of Ω. Because $P_0(\Omega_0) = 1$, we can recover the constant of proportionality from

$$\frac{1}{P_0(\{\omega_j\})} = \sum_{\omega_i \in \Omega_0} \frac{P_0(\{\omega_i\})}{P_0(\{\omega_j\})} = \sum_{\omega_i \in B} \frac{P(\{\omega_i\})}{P(\{\omega_j\})} = \frac{P(B)}{P(\{\omega_j\})},$$

giving

$$P_0(\{\omega_j\}) = \frac{P(\{\omega_j\})}{P(B)}$$

for $\omega_j \in \Omega_0$. From this it follows that for $A_0 \in \mathcal{F}_0$,

$$P_0(A_0) = \sum_{\omega_j \in A_0} \frac{P(\{\omega_j\})}{P(B)} = \frac{P(A \cap B)}{P(B)}.$$

This seems the obvious way to proceed, and motivates the following definition.

Definition 1.2. If A and B are events in $\mathcal{F}$, then the *conditional probability of A given B*, denoted $P(A|B)$, is

$$P(A|B) = \frac{P(A \cap B)}{P(B)}.$$

If $P(B) = 0$, then define $P(A|B) = 0$ for every $A \in \mathcal{F}$.

It is nearly obvious at sight that $(\Omega \cap B, \mathcal{F} \cap B, P(\cdot|B))$ is a probability space, where $\mathcal{F} \cap B = \{F \cap B: F \in \mathcal{F}\}$ (Problem 12). The connection with the example above is $\Omega \cap B = \Omega_0$, $\mathcal{F} \cap B = \mathcal{F}_0$, and $P(\cdot|B) = P_0(\cdot)$.

Conditional probability makes it easy to work out the probabilities of some of the multiple roll bets in craps. Consider a place bet on the 4. Conditional on the game terminating, the last roll must be a 7 or a 4. Thus, the relevant sample space is

$$\Omega_0 = \left\{ \begin{matrix} (1,3), & (1,6), & (2,2) \\ (2,5), & (3,1), & (3,4) \\ (4,3), & (5,2), & (6,1) \end{matrix} \right\}.$$

The bet wins if the event $A_0 = \{(1,3), (2,2), (3,1)\}$ occurs. Thus, the conditional probability that a place bet on the 4 wins is $P_0(A_0) = 3/9 = 1/3$.

If we are convinced that the game terminates with unconditional probability 1, then the conditional probability is the unconditional probability, which may be verified as follows. If $P(B) = 1$, then $P(\tilde{B}) = 1 - P(B) = 0$ so that $P(A \cap B) = P(A) - P(A \cap \tilde{B}) = P(A)$, because $A \cap \tilde{B} \subset \tilde{B}$ implies $0 \le P(A \cap \tilde{B}) \le P(\tilde{B}) = 0$. Then $P(A|B) = P(A \cap B)/P(B) = P(A)/1$.

The conditional argument above is a little slippery because, for instance, it represents all infinite sequences $\omega \in \Omega_p^\infty$ that have $(1,3)$ before $(1,6)$, $(2,5)$, $(3,4)$, $(4,3)$, $(5,2)$, or $(6,1)$ by the single point $(1,3)$ (Ω_p^∞ is defined in Section 1.2). Perhaps it could be made rigorous. It is certainly intuitively obvious and does give the correct answer with a lot less bother than we were put to in Section 1.4. Referring to Figure 1.8,

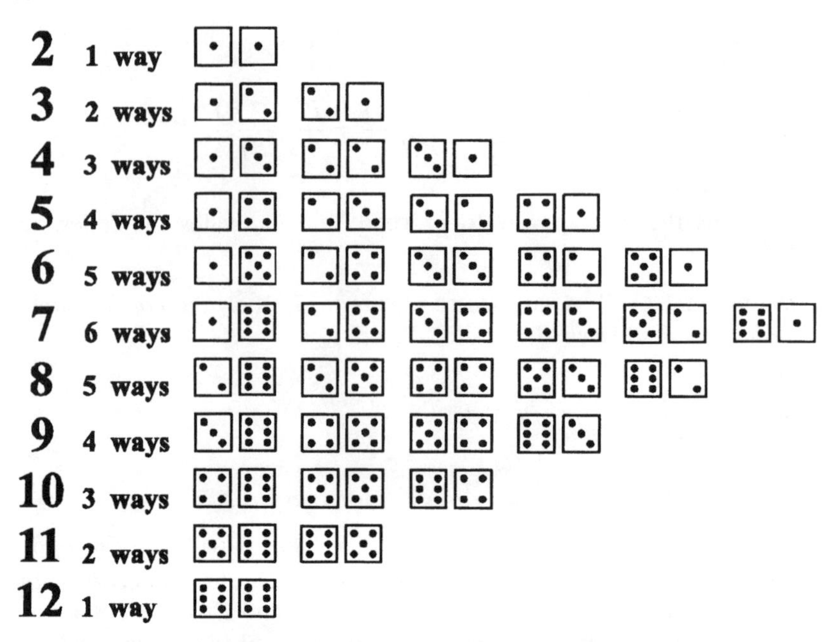

Figure 1.8. The possible outcomes of a single roll of a pair of dice.

we can use the conditional argument to deduce quickly that a place bet on the 10 wins with probability 3/(3+6)=1/3; the 5 and 9 win with probability 4/(4+6)=2/5; and the 6 and 8 win with probability 5/11. These computations agree with the true odds from Table 1.1 of 3 for 1, 5 for 2, and 11 for 5, respectively.

Some useful relationships that follow from

$$P(A \cap B) = P(A|B)P(B)$$

are the following:

$$\begin{aligned} P(A \cap B \cap C) &= P(A|B \cap C)P(B \cap C) \\ &= P(A|B \cap C)P(B|C)P(C). \end{aligned}$$

If $B_1, B_2, \ldots$ are mutually exclusive and exhaustive, then

$$\begin{aligned} P(A) &= \sum_{t=1}^{\infty} P(A \cap B_i) \\ &= \sum_{t=1}^{\infty} P(A|B_i)P(B_i). \end{aligned}$$

Obviously the relationship holds for a finite sequence of events $B_1, \ldots, B_n$ as well.

We can use it to work out the probability of a win on the pass line in craps. The conditioning events are $B_i =$ "i on the come out roll," for $i = 2, 3, \ldots, 12$. The conditional probability that the pass line wins given a 4 on the first roll is the same as the unconditional probability that a place bet on the 4 wins. Similarly for points 5, 6, 8, 9, and 10. Thus

$$\begin{aligned}
P(\text{pass line wins}) = {} & 0 \times [P(B_2) + P(B_3) + P(B_{12})] \\
& + 1 \times [P(B_7) + P(B_{11})] \\
& + \frac{1}{3}P(B_4) + \frac{2}{5}P(B_5) + \frac{5}{11}P(B_6) \\
& + \frac{1}{3}P(B_{10}) + \frac{2}{5}P(B_9) + \frac{5}{11}P(B_8) \\
= {} & \frac{6}{36} + \frac{2}{36} \\
& + \frac{1}{3} \times \frac{3}{36} + \frac{2}{5} \times \frac{4}{36} + \frac{5}{11} \times \frac{5}{36} \\
& + \frac{1}{3} \times \frac{3}{36} + \frac{2}{5} \times \frac{4}{36} + \frac{5}{11} \times \frac{5}{36} \\
= {} & 488/(2 \times 3 \times 3 \times 5 \times 11) = 244/495 \approx 0.492929.
\end{aligned}$$

1.7.1 *A Digression*

The theory of probability, which is a mathematical model, has a variety of applications. When applied to a game of chance such as craps, most people, if asked, would say that the statement "$P\{(3,3),(4,4)\} = 2/36$" means that in many tosses of a pair of dice the fraction that will land hard six $(3,3)$ or hard eight $(4,4)$ is approximately 2/36. They would expect the approximation to improve as the number of tosses increases.

Restated in terms of our probability model $(\Omega_p^\infty, \mathcal{F}_p^\infty, P)$ for multiple roll bets, described in Subsection 1.4.4, what this means is that for each outcome

$$\omega = (\omega_1, \omega_2, \ldots, \omega_n, \ldots) \in \Omega_p^\infty$$

we expect that

$$\lim_{n\to\infty} \frac{1}{n} \sum_{i=1}^{n} I_H(\omega_i) = \frac{2}{36},$$

where $H = \{(3,3),(4,4)\}$ and $I_H(\omega_i)$ denotes the indicator function, which is the function that has the value 1 if ω_i is in the set H and has the value 0 if it is not. Similarly, if $A = \{(2,6),(3,5),(4,4),(5,3),(6,2)\}$, which is the event "any eight," we expect that

$$\lim_{n\to\infty} \frac{1}{n}\sum_{i=1}^{n} I_A(\omega_i) = \frac{5}{36}$$

$$\lim_{n\to\infty} \frac{1}{n}\sum_{i=1}^{n} I_{H\cap A}(\omega_i) = \frac{1}{36}.$$

If we have set up both our single roll model $(\Omega_p, \mathcal{F}_p, P)$ and multiple roll model $(\Omega_p^\infty, \mathcal{F}_p^\infty, P)$ correctly, this is how we expect them to relate to each other.

Jumping ahead, Theorem 4.1 implies that every outcome ω in Ω_p^∞ exhibits the desired behavior except for outcomes in events E_H, E_A, $E_{A\cap H} \subset \Omega_p^\infty$ that occur with probability zero. This result, coupled with the fact that there are only a finite number of events in the single roll σ-algebra $\mathcal{F}_p$ and therefore only a finite number of events that can cause trouble, would allow us, if desired, to modify the multiple roll probability space by deleting from Ω_p^∞ all outcomes in the union of these troublesome sets so that every outcome in the sample space has the requisite behavior (Problem 31).

The interpretation of our probability model just described is a bit odd because the meaning attached to the probability of an event in the single roll probability space $(\Omega_p, \mathcal{F}_p, P)$ is derived from behavior that the single roll space induces in the multiple roll space $(\Omega_p^\infty, \mathcal{F}_p^\infty, P)$. Nonetheless, this is the most common interpretation of probability when applied to games of chance and our model is consistent with this interpretation.

What most people would say that the statement "$P(H|A) = 1/5$" means in the single roll model is that in many tosses of a pair of dice the fraction that will land hard eight $(4,4)$ of those that land eight $\{(2,6),(3,5),(4,4),(5,3),(6,2)\}$ is approximately 1/5. They would expect the approximation to improve as the number of tosses increases.

In terms of our multiple roll model $(\Omega_p^\infty, \mathcal{F}_p^\infty, P)$, this means that for each outcome

$$\omega = (\omega_1, \omega_2, \ldots, \omega_n, \ldots) \in \Omega_p^\infty$$

we expect that

$$\lim_{n\to\infty} \frac{\sum_{i=1}^{n} I_{H\cap A}(\omega_i)}{\sum_{i=1}^{n} I_A(\omega_i)} = \frac{1}{5}.$$

However,

$$\lim_{n\to\infty} \frac{\sum_{i=1}^{n} I_{H\cap A}(\omega_i)}{\sum_{i=1}^{n} I_A(\omega_i)} = \frac{\lim_{n\to\infty}(1/n)\sum_{i=1}^{n} I_{H\cap A}(\omega_i)}{\lim_{n\to\infty}(1/n)\sum_{i=1}^{n} I_A(\omega_i)} = \frac{1/36}{5/36} = \frac{1}{5}.$$

Therefore, the multiple roll probability model $(\Omega_p^\infty, \mathcal{F}_p^\infty, P)$ does exhibit the desired behavior and the formula $P(H|A) = P(H \cap A)/P(A)$ does give the desired answer for the single roll model $(\Omega_p, \mathcal{F}_p, P)$.

This digression provides another justification for the formula for conditional probability introduced in Definition 1.2. The formula produces answers that are consistent with most people's interpretation of probability when applied to games of chance.

1.8 Independence

Suppose that $P(A) > 0$ and $P(B) > 0$. If $P(A|B) = P(A)$, then we learn nothing about A from observing B. Figure 1.9 is an illustration: We learn nothing about the first toss by observing that the second is a four or a five. Not only that, if $P(A|B) = P(A)$, then $P(A \cap B) = P(A)P(B)$, which implies $P(B|A) = P(B)$. Therefore, $P(A|B) = P(A)$ not only implies that we learn nothing about A from observing B but also that we learn nothing about B from knowing A. Actually, this argument has shown that if $P(A) > 0$ and $P(B) > 0$, then

$$P(A|B) = P(A) \quad \Leftrightarrow \quad P(B|A) = P(B) \quad \Leftrightarrow \quad P(A \cap B) = P(A)P(B).$$

In this situation, the events A and B are called *independent*. We shall adopt the last of the three equivalent statements above as the definition because it also covers the case when $P(A) = 0$ or $P(B) = 0$.

Definition 1.3. Two events A and B are *independent* if $P(A \cap B) = P(A)P(B)$.

If the events A and B are independent, then the events A and $\tilde{B}$ are independent and the events $\tilde{A}$ and $\tilde{B}$ are independent (Problem 18).

The requirements for more than two events are more stringent than mere pairwise independence.

Definition 1.4. A sequence $A_1, A_2, \ldots$ of events from $\mathcal{F}$ are *mutually independent* if, for any subsequence $A_{i_1}, \ldots, A_{i_k}$, we have

$$P\left(\bigcap_{j=1}^{k} A_{i_j}\right) = \prod_{j=1}^{k} P(A_{i_j}).$$

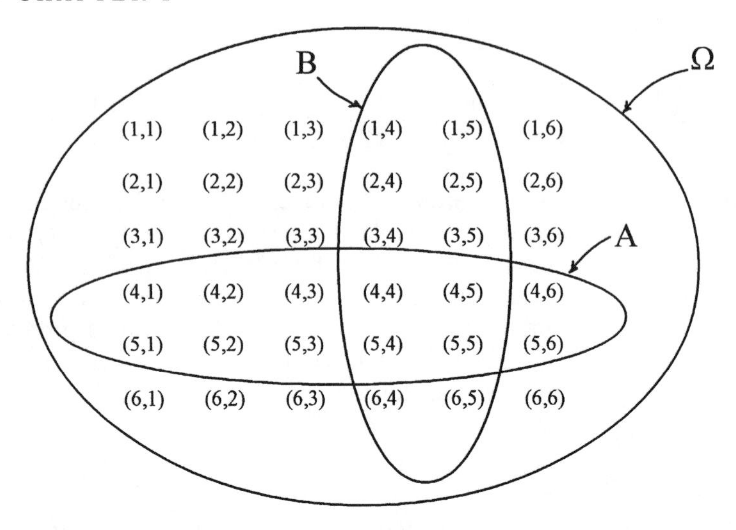

Figure 1.9. Independence. The unconditional probability of A is $12/36 = 0.33$. The conditional probability of A is $4/12 = 0.33$.

1.9 Problems

1. For each of the following experiments, describe the sample space. (i) Toss a coin five times. (ii) Count fish in a pond. (iii) Measure time to failure of a memory chip. (iv) Observe the number of defectives in a shipment. (v) Observe the proportions of defectives in a shipment.
2. Prove DeMorgan's laws for countable unions and intersections.
3. Prove that union and intersection are commutative, associative, and distributive.
4. Let F_i where $i = 1, 2, \ldots$ be an infinite sequence of events from the sample space Ω. Let F be the set of points that are in all but a finite number of the events F_i. Prove that $F = \bigcup_{k=1}^{\infty} \bigcap_{i=k}^{\infty} F_i$. Make sure that the proof is done carefully: First, take a point ω from F and show that it is in $\bigcup_{k=1}^{\infty} \bigcap_{i=k}^{\infty} F_i$. Second, take a ω point from $\bigcup_{k=1}^{\infty} \bigcap_{i=k}^{\infty} F_i$ and show that it is in F.
5. Find the supremum and infimum of the following sets: $\emptyset$, $(-10, 10)$, $(-\infty, \infty)$, $\bigcap_{i=1}^{\infty}\{1/i\}$, $\bigcup_{i=1}^{\infty}\{1/i\}$, $\bigcap_{i=1}^{\infty}[1/i, 1]$, $\bigcup_{i=1}^{\infty}[1/i, 1]$, $\{x\colon x = 1/i, i = 1, 2, \ldots\}$, $\{x\colon x = -1/i, i = 1, 2, \ldots\}$, $\{x\colon x = i, i = 1, 2, \ldots\}$, and $\{x\colon x = -i, i = 1, 2, \ldots\}$.
6. Show that $\mathcal{F} = \{\emptyset, \Omega\}$ is a σ-algebra.
7. Show the collection of all subsets of Ω is a σ-algebra.
8. Show that if $F_1, F_2, \ldots, F_N$ are mutually exclusive and exhaustive, then the collection of all finite unions plus the empty set is an algebra.

9. Show that if $F_1, F_2, \dots$ are mutually exclusive and exhaustive, then the collection of all countable unions plus the empty set is a σ-algebra.
10. Show that the intersection of two σ-algebras is a σ-algebra.
11. Let $\mathscr{A}$ be some collection of subsets of Ω. Problem 7 implies that there exists at least one σ-algebra that contains $\mathscr{A}$ (Why?). Let $\mathscr{F}$ be the intersection of all σ-algebras that contain $\mathscr{A}$. Show that $\mathscr{F}$ is a σ-algebra. Show that $\mathscr{F}$ is not empty. Why is $\mathscr{F}$ the smallest σ-algebra that contains $\mathscr{A}$?
12. Show that if $\mathscr{F}$ is a σ-algebra, then $\mathscr{F} \cap B = \{F \cap B : F \in \mathscr{F}\}$ is a σ-algebra.
13. Show that $P(\emptyset) = 0$, $P(A) \leq 1$, $P(A) + P(\tilde{A}) = 1$, and that if $A \subset B$, then $P(A) \leq P(B)$.
14. If $P(A) = 1/3$ and $P(\tilde{B}) = 1/4$, can A and B be disjoint?
15. Find formulas for the probabilities of the following events: (i) either A or B or both, (ii) either A or B but not both.
16. A pair of dice are thrown and the sum is noted. The throws are repeated until either a sum of 6 or a sum of 7 occurs. What is the sample space for this experiment? What is the probability that the sequence of throws terminates in a 7? Be sure to include an explanation of the logic that you used to reach your answer.
17. In a shipment of 1,000 transistors, 100 are defective. If 50 transistors are inspected, what is the probability that five of them will be defective. Be sure to include an explanation of the logic that you used to reach your answer.
18. Show that if two events A and B are independent, then so are A and $\tilde{B}$ and $\tilde{A}$ and $\tilde{B}$.
19. Assume that $P(A) > 0$ and $P(B) > 0$. Prove that if $P(B) = 1$, then $P(A|B) = P(A)$ for any A. Prove that if $A \subset B$, then $P(B|A) = 1$.
20. Assume that $P(A) > 0$ and $P(B) > 0$. Prove that if A and B are mutually exclusive, then they cannot be independent. Prove that if A and B are independent, then they cannot be mutually exclusive.
21. Prove that if $P(\cdot)$ is a legitimate probability function and B is a set with $P(B) > 0$, then $P(\cdot|B)$ also satisfies the axioms of probability.
22. Compute the probability of a win for each of the one roll bets in craps.
23. Compute the probability of a win for each of the place bets in craps. Work the problem two ways: (i) Compute the probability of the union of the events "win on roll i." (ii) Compute the probability of a win conditional on termination.
24. How many different sets of initials can be formed if every person has one surname and (i) exactly two given names; (ii) either one or two given names; (iii) either one, two, or three given names?

25. If n balls are placed at random into n cells, what is the probability that exactly one cell remains empty?
26. If a multivariate function has continuous partial derivatives, the order in which the derivatives are calculated does not matter (Green's theorem). For example, $(\partial^3/\partial x^2\,\partial y)f(x, y) = (\partial^3/\partial y\,\partial x^2)f(x, y)$. (i) How many third partial derivatives does a function of two variables have? (ii) Show that a function of n variables has $\binom{n+r-1}{r}$ rth partial derivatives.
27. Suppose that an urn contains n balls all of which are white except one which is red. The urn is thoroughly mixed and all the balls are drawn from the urn without replacement by a blindfolded individual. Show that the probability that the red ball will be drawn on the kth draw is $1/n$.
28. Two people each toss a coin n times that lands heads with probability 1/3. What is the probability that they will each have the same number of heads? What is the probability if the coin lands heads with probability 1/4?
29. For the game of craps, compute the probability that a shooter coming out will roll the first 7 on the kth roll.
30. For the two-dimensional coin tossing experiment described in Subsection 1.4.2, let $A = (0, 1/2] \times (0, 1]$, $B = (0, 1] \times (0, 1/2]$, and $C = \{(x, y): x < y\}$. Show that $P(C) = 1/2$ and that $P(A \cap C) = 1/8$. Are A and B independent? Are A and C independent? Compute $P(A)$ and $P(A|C)$.
31. Let $(\Omega, \mathcal{F}, P)$ be a probability space. Show that if $P(E) = 0$, then $P(F \cap \tilde{E}) = P(F)$ for every F in $\mathcal{F}$. Why are the two probability spaces $(\Omega, \mathcal{F}, P)$ and $(\Omega \cap \tilde{E}, \mathcal{F} \cap \tilde{E}, P)$ equivalent? See Problem 12 for the definition of $\mathcal{F} \cap \tilde{E}$.

2

Random Variables and Expectation

2.1 Random Variables

A random variable is a function defined on a sample space. Its purpose is to facilitate the solution of a problem by transferring considerations to a new probability space with a simpler structure.

Consider an analysis of the 8-spot ticket in keno, described in Section 1.1.2. The sample space Ω consists of all unordered sequences of length 20 that can be made up from 80 numbers and has $N = \binom{80}{20}$ elements. This is a huge number. However, for the purpose of analyzing play on an 8-spot ticket, the probability function P_X displayed in Table 2.1 is adequate. It is defined on the sample space $\mathscr{X} = \{0, 1, \ldots, 8\}$ whose elements denote the number of spots caught. One gets to this simpler structure by means of a random variable.

The random variable for the 8-spot ticket maps each $\omega \in \Omega$ to the number of spots caught. For instance, if ω is that shown in the draw card in the bottom panel of Figure 1.3 and the player's ticket is that shown in the top panel, then $X(\omega) = 3$. On the new sample space $\mathscr{X}$, probabilities are assigned according to $P_X(\{x\}) = P\{\omega: X(\omega) = x\}$. The event $\{\omega: X(\omega) = i\}$ is the event $F_i =$ "catch i spots on an 8-spot ticket" whose probability we computed in Section 1.6; see Table 1.3. The generalization of these ideas is as follows. We begin with a probability space $(\Omega, \mathscr{F}, P)$ and we wish to transfer considerations to a new probability space $(\mathscr{X}, \mathscr{A}, P_X)$. $\mathscr{A}$ is a σ-algebra of subsets of $\mathscr{X}$. The most common choice for $\mathscr{X}$ is the real line; that is, $\mathscr{X} = \Re = (-\infty, \infty)$. The most common choice of $\mathscr{A}$ is the smallest σ-algebra that contains all the open intervals (a, b). This σ-algebra is known as the collection of *Borel sets.* It is also the smallest σ-algebra that contains the algebra of all finite unions of intervals of the form $(a, b]$ that we considered in Section 1.4. The probability function on the new space is defined by

$$P_X(A) = P\big[\{\omega \in \Omega: X(\omega) \in A\}\big].$$

Of course, for this to work, the set $\{\omega \in \Omega: X(\omega) \in A\}$ must be in $\mathscr{F}$. We discuss this issue next.

TABLE 2.1
Probability of Catching x Spots on an 8-Spot Keno Ticket.

x	$P_X(\{x\})$
0	0.0882662377
1	0.2664641139
2	0.3281456217
3	0.2147862251
4	0.0815037015
5	0.0183025856
6	0.0023667137
7	0.0001604552
8	0.0000043457

Note: Table 2.1 is derived from Table 1.3.

If X is a function mapping Ω into $\mathscr{X}$ and A is a subset of $\mathscr{X}$, then the *inverse image* of A is denoted by $X^{-1}(A)$ and is defined by

$$X^{-1}(A) = \{\omega \in \Omega: X(\omega) \in A\}.$$

If F is a subset of Ω, the *image* of F is denoted by $X(F)$ and is defined by

$$X(F) = \{x \in \mathscr{X}: x = X(\omega) \text{ for some } \omega \in F\}.$$

See Figure 2.1 for an illustration. This is not the best notation because $X(\cdot)$ can mean either a function $x = X(\omega)$ that maps points to points or a set-valued set function $A = X(F)$ that maps sets to sets, as determined by context. Similarly for $X^{-1}(\cdot)$. Nevertheless, the notation is standard.

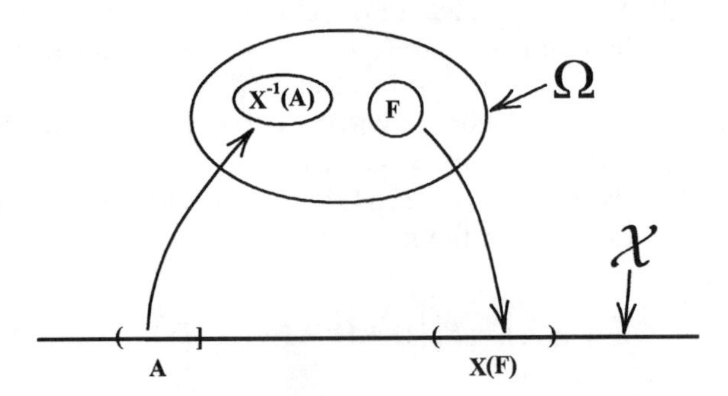

Figure 2.1. Image and inverse image. The set $X(F) \in \mathscr{X}$ is the image of $F \subset \Omega$. The set $X^{-1}(A)$ is the inverse image of the set $A \subset \mathscr{X}$.

If A and B are subsets of $\mathscr{X}$, and $A_1, A_2, \ldots$ is a sequence of subsets from $\mathscr{X}$, then the inverse image satisfies these properties:

1. If $A \subset B$, then $X^{-1}(A) \subset X^{-1}(B)$.
2. $X^{-1}(A \cup B) = X^{-1}(A) \cup X^{-1}(B)$.
3. $X^{-1}(A \cap B) = X^{-1}(A) \cap X^{-1}(B)$.
4. $X^{-1}\left(\bigcup_{i=1}^{\infty} A_i\right) = \bigcup_{i=1}^{\infty} X^{-1}(A_i)$.
5. $X^{-1}\left(\bigcap_{i=1}^{\infty} A_i\right) = \bigcap_{i=1}^{\infty} X^{-1}(A_i)$.
6. If $h(\omega) = g[X(\omega)]$, then $h^{-1}(B) = X^{-1}[g^{-1}(B)]$.
7. $X^{-1}(\sim A) = \sim X^{-1}(A)$.

A consequence of these facts is that

$$\mathscr{F}_0 = \{F \subset \Omega : F = X^{-1}(A),\, A \in \mathscr{A}\}$$

is a σ-algebra. This σ-algebra is often denoted by $X^{-1}(\mathscr{A})$.

What we need for the validity of the formula

$$P_X(A) = P[X^{-1}(A)] = P\big[\{\omega \in \Omega : X(\omega) \in A\}\big], \qquad A \in \mathscr{A}$$

is that $\mathscr{F}_0 \subset \mathscr{F}$. A function with this property is called *measurable*. When it is important to indicate to which σ-algebra inverse images belong, one says X is $\mathscr{F}$-measurable. When it is important to indicate both σ-algebras, one says X is measurable $\mathscr{F}/\mathscr{A}$.

In many applications, we consider functions that map the real line, $\mathfrak{R} = (-\infty, \infty)$, into the real line. $\mathscr{B}$, the collection of Borel sets, is the σ-algebra most often used in connection with the real line. A pair, such as $(\mathfrak{R}, \mathscr{B})$, consisting of a set and a σ-algebra of subsets of it is called a *measurable space*. Thus, one asks what functions mapping $(\mathfrak{R}, \mathscr{B})$ into $(\mathfrak{R}, \mathscr{B})$ are measurable $\mathscr{B}/\mathscr{B}$. The continuous functions are measurable $\mathscr{B}/\mathscr{B}$. Therefore, the transcendental functions, such as $\exp(x)$, $\log(x)$, and $\sin(x)$, are measurable and the polynomials are measurable. A step function that takes different values on sets from $\mathscr{B}$ is measurable $\mathscr{B}/\mathscr{B}$.

If one starts with functions $X(\omega)$ and $Y(\omega)$ that are measurable mappings from one measurable space $(\Omega, \mathscr{F})$ into another $(\mathscr{X}, \mathscr{A})$, then new functions $Z(\omega)$ constructed by ordinary algebraic operations such as $Z(\omega) = aX(\omega)$, $Z(\omega) = X(\omega) + Y(\omega)$, $Z(\omega) = X(\omega)Y(\omega)$, and $Z(\omega) = X(\omega)/Y(\omega)$ are measurable. If one has a sequence $X_1(\omega), X_2(\omega), \ldots$ of measurable functions and constructs $Z(\omega)$ through limiting operations such as $Z(\omega) = \lim_{i\to\infty} X_i(\omega)$ or $Z(\omega) = \sup_{1\le i<\infty}\{X_i(\omega)\}$, then $Z(\omega)$ is measurable.

A proof of these claims is not particularly difficult, but it would be time consuming and take us away from our main interests. If one is interested, see Royden 1988, Section 3.5. All that is important for our purposes is to know that standard functions are measurable and that any standard sequence of countable operations on such functions will not destroy measurability.

We summarize this section with two definitions and a theorem.

Definition 2.1. The pair $(\Omega, \mathcal{F})$ consisting of a set Ω and a σ-algebra $\mathcal{F}$ of subsets of Ω is called a *measurable space*. A function X mapping a measurable space $(\Omega, \mathcal{F})$ into a measurable space $(\mathcal{X}, \mathcal{A})$ is a *measurable function* if $X^{-1}(A) \in \mathcal{F}$ for every $A \in \mathcal{A}$.

Definition 2.2. A *random variable* X is a measurable function mapping the measurable space $(\Omega, \mathcal{F})$ into a measurable space $(\mathcal{X}, \mathcal{A})$.

Theorem 2.1. *If X is a random variable mapping the probability space $(\Omega, \mathcal{F}, P)$ into a measurable space $(\mathcal{X}, \mathcal{A})$, and*

$$P_X(A) = P[X^{-1}(A)] = P[\{\omega \in \Omega : X(\omega) \in A\}], \qquad A \in \mathcal{A},$$

then $(\mathcal{X}, \mathcal{A}, P_X)$ is a probability space.

Theorem 2.1 is, of course, true enough. Our claim that it has practical relevance rests on the examples.

2.2 Continuous Random Variables

The sample space $\Omega = (0, 1]$ for the coin tossing experiment of Section 1.1.3 is a continuum. It is not immediately obvious how to extend the ideas of Section 2.1 in a way that is useful in computations in this case. How this can be done is the subject of this section. We will develop the ideas by means of the coin tossing experiment because an example seems to get the ideas across better than generalities.

2.2.1 *Univariate Continuous Random Variables*

As noted in Section 1.1.3, with respect to the coin tossing experiment, endpoints do not matter. Here it will be more convenient to put $\Omega = (0, 1)$ instead of $(0, 1]$. In the coin tossing experiment, the probability assigned to an interval is its length: $P\{(a, b)\} = P\{[a, b)\} = P\{(a, b]\} = P\{[a, b]\} = b - a$.

Let $\mathcal{X} = (-\infty, \infty)$, let $\mathcal{A}$ be the Borel sets, and consider the random variable

$$X(\omega) = \log\left(\frac{\omega}{1 - \omega}\right).$$

We shall now try to derive a representation of the probability function

$$P_X(A) = P[X^{-1}(A)] = P[\{\omega \in \Omega : X(\omega) \in A\}], \qquad A \in \mathscr{A},$$

given by Theorem 2.1 that is useful for computations.

For $(c, d) \in \mathscr{X}$, the inverse image is

$$X^{-1}\{(c,d)\} = \left\{\omega: \frac{e^c}{1+e^c} < \omega < \frac{e^d}{1+e^d}\right\}.$$

Thus

$$P_X\{(c,d)\} = \frac{e^d}{1+e^d} - \frac{e^c}{1+e^c}.$$

We can achieve a more convenient form for P_X if we notice that

$$P_X\{(c,d)\} = \int_{e^c/(1+e^c)}^{e^d/(1+e^d)} d\omega$$

and apply the change of variable

$$x = \log\left(\frac{\omega}{1-\omega}\right), \qquad \omega = \frac{e^x}{1+e^x}, \qquad d\omega = \frac{e^x}{(1+e^x)^2}\,dx$$

to get

$$P_X\{(c,d)\} = \int_c^d \frac{e^x}{(1+e^x)^2}\,dx.$$

The function

$$f_X(x) = \frac{e^x}{(1+e^x)^2}$$

is called the *density function* of the random variable X. This particular density is known as the logistic density. A random variable X whose probability function can be given the representation $P_X\{(c,d)\} = \int_c^d f_X(x)\,dx$ is called a *continuous random variable*.

Once we have the formula $P_X\{(c,d)\} = \int_c^d f_X(x)\,dx$ for computing the probability of an interval, we can compute the probability of a finite union of disjoint intervals $A = \bigcup_{i=1}^n (c_i, d_i)$ using $P_X(A) = \sum_{t=1}^n P_X\{(c_i, d_i)\}$, or a countable union of disjoint intervals $A = \bigcup_{i=1}^\infty (c_i, d_i)$ using $P_X(A) = \sum_{t=1}^\infty P_X\{(c_i, d_i)\}$. The properties of the Riemann integral allow us to represent these facts collectively by writing

$$P_X(A) = \int_A f_X(x)\,dx. \qquad (2.1)$$

Rarely is anything beyond this needed in applications.

2.2.2 *Indicator Functions*

We shall now repeat this derivation for a general continuous random variable X rather than the specific choice $X(\omega) = \log[\omega/(1 - \omega)]$ primarily so that we can acquire facility with indicator functions, which see heavy use in the sequel. Recall the definition of the *indicator function* of a set A,

$$I_A(x) = \begin{cases} 1 & x \in A, \\ 0 & x \notin A. \end{cases}$$

Using indicators, an application of the probability function P to the interval (a, b) can be written

$$P\{(a, b)\} = \int_0^1 I_{(a,\, b)}(\omega)\, d\omega.$$

Similarly, for a disjoint union of intervals $F = \bigcup_{i=1}^{n}(a_i, b_i)$,

$$P(F) = \int_0^1 I_F(\omega)\, d\omega = \sum_{i=1}^{n} \int_0^1 I_{(a_i,\, b_i)}(\omega)\, d\omega;$$

see Figure 2.2. The limits of integration can be inferred from Ω and are therefore often omitted, writing

$$P(F) = \int I_F(\omega)\, d\omega.$$

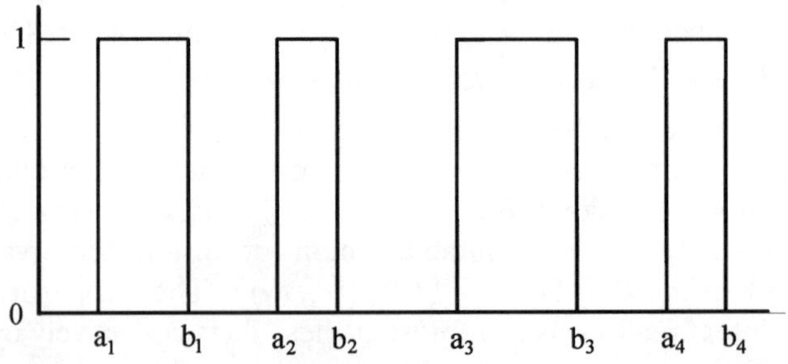

Figure 2.2. The indicator function of a union of disjoint intervals. Shown is indicator function $I_F(\omega)$ of $F = \bigcup_{i=1}^{4}(a_i, b_i)$. The combined length of the intervals $\sum_{t=1}^{n}(b_i - a_i)$ is given by the integral $\int I_F(\omega)\, d\omega$.

If attention is to be directed to the limits of integration, it is often indicated by writing

$$P(F) = \int_{\Omega} I_F(\omega)\, d\omega.$$

The formula $P(F) = \int I_F(\omega)\, d\omega$ is also valid for any $F \in \mathcal{F}$ for which the integral exists, not just when F is a finite union of intervals. In fact, the definition of the integral can be extended to what is known as the Lebesque integral (Royden 1988, Chapter 4) so that integral exists and the formula is valid for every $F \in \mathcal{F}$. As a practical matter, we do not need this extra generality. For computations, the ordinary Riemann integral, which handles intervals, finite unions of disjoint intervals, and countable unions of disjoint intervals, is adequate.

Another facet of indicator functions that is useful is

$$I_{X^{-1}(F)}(\omega) = I_F[X(\omega)].$$

To see that this is so, note that

$$\begin{aligned} I_{X^{-1}(F)}(\omega) = 1 &\Leftrightarrow \omega \in X^{-1}(F) \\ &\Leftrightarrow X(\omega) \in F \\ &\Leftrightarrow I_F[X(\omega)] = 1. \end{aligned}$$

Using this fact, the formula given by Theorem 2.1,

$$P_X(A) = P[X^{-1}(A)] = P[\{\omega \in \Omega : X(\omega) \in A\}],$$

can be reexpressed for the coin tossing experiment as

$$P_X(A) = \int_0^1 I_A[X(\omega)]\, d\omega = \int_{\Omega} I_A[X(\omega)]\, d\omega.$$

The advantage of this representation is that it can be easily manipulated using the rules of integral calculus.

Consider a random variable X. We shall leave $\mathcal{X}$ and $\mathcal{A}$ unspecified for the moment because, as we shall see, our analysis permits a choice. If $x = X(\omega)$ is an increasing function with differentiable inverse $\omega = X^{-1}(x)$, then the change of variable formula

$$x = X(\omega), \qquad \omega = X^{-1}(x), \qquad d\omega = \left[\frac{d}{dx} X^{-1}(x)\right] dx$$

gives

$$P_X(A) = \int_{X(0)}^{X(1)} I_A(x)\left[\frac{d}{dx}X^{-1}(x)\right]dx = \int_{X(\Omega)} I_A(x)\left[\frac{d}{dx}X^{-1}(x)\right]dx.$$

If $x = X(\omega)$ is a decreasing function with differentiable inverse $\omega = X^{-1}(x)$, then the change of variable formula gives

$$P_X(A) = \int_{X(1)}^{X(0)} I_A(x)\left[\frac{d}{dx}X^{-1}(x)\right]dx = -\int_{X(\Omega)} I_A(x)\left[\frac{d}{dx}X^{-1}(x)\right]dx.$$

These two formulas can be combined by writing

$$P_X(A) = \int_{X(\Omega)} I_A(x)\left|\frac{d}{dx}X^{-1}(x)\right|dx, \tag{2.2}$$

which is valid for both increasing and decreasing random variables. We will consider more general cases later.

Using indicator functions, we can rewrite Equation (2.1), which is the equation that defines a density function, as

$$P_X(A) = \int_{\mathscr{X}} I_A(x) f_X(x)\,dx. \tag{2.3}$$

Our task now is to manipulate Equation (2.2) to obtain a form similar to Equation (2.3) and thereby define the density function of the random variable X.

We have a choice. We can put $\mathscr{X} = (-\infty, \infty)$, write

$$P_X(A) = \int_{\mathscr{X}} I_A(x) I_{X(\Omega)}(x)\left|\frac{d}{dx}X^{-1}(x)\right|dx,$$

and take

$$f_X(x) = I_{X(\Omega)}(x)\left|\frac{d}{dx}X^{-1}(x)\right|$$

to be the density. Or, we can put $\mathscr{X} = X(\Omega)$, the image of Ω, write

$$P_X(A) = \int_{\mathscr{X}} I_A(x)\left|\frac{d}{dx}X^{-1}(x)\right|dx,$$

and take

$$f_X(x) = \left|\frac{d}{dx}X^{-1}(x)\right|$$

to be the density. For the random variable $X(\omega) = \omega^2$, which is increasing on $(0, 1)$, the choice would make a difference; for the random variable $X(\omega) = \log[\omega/(1-\omega)]$, it would not. In the former case, $\mathscr{A}$ is the collection of Borel sets $\mathscr{B}$; in the latter, $\mathscr{A} = \mathscr{X} \cap \mathscr{B} = \{\mathscr{X} \cap B : B \in \mathscr{B}\}$, which is the smallest σ-algebra that contains all the intervals in $\mathscr{X}$. Sometimes one choice seems more convenient, sometimes the other. Both are common.

2.2.3 *Bivariate Continuous Random Variables*

We can also apply these ideas to the double coin tossing example of Section 1.4, using $\Omega = (0, 1) \times (0, 1)$, or $\Omega = (0, 1] \times (0, 1]$, or whatever is convenient; endpoints do not matter. Denoting a point in Ω by $\omega = (\omega_1, \omega_2)$, we can define two random variables

$$x = X(\omega_1, \omega_2)$$
$$y = Y(\omega_1, \omega_2),$$

and, upon application of Theorem 2.1, we will have

$$P_{(X,Y)}(A) = \int_0^1 \int_0^1 I_A\big[X(\omega_1, \omega_2), Y(\omega_1, \omega_2)\big]\, d\omega_1\, d\omega_2,$$

where A is a rectangle, or union of disjoint rectangles, and $\mathscr{X} = \Re^2 = (-\infty, \infty) \times (-\infty, \infty)$. Notice, as the notation $P_{(X,Y)}$ suggests, that, from the point of view of Theorem 2.1, the two random variables X, Y are regarded as the one random variable (X, Y) that takes its values in $\Re^2$. See Figure 2.3 for an example.

A change of variables gives

$$P_{(X,Y)}(A) = \int_{-\infty}^{\infty} \int_{-\infty}^{\infty} I_A(x, y) f_{X,Y}(x, y)\, dx\, dy.$$

The function $f_{X,Y}(x, y)$ is called a *joint density*. We will attend to the details of the change of variable formula for several variables in a later chapter. For the moment it is enough to know that it can be done and leads to the result above. Also, having made our point regarding Theorem 2.1, we will write $P_{X,Y}(A)$ hereafter.

The joint density satisfies the consistency relationships

$$f_X(x) = \int_{-\infty}^{\infty} f_{X,Y}(x, y)\, dy$$
$$f_Y(y) = \int_{-\infty}^{\infty} f_{X,Y}(x, y)\, dx,$$

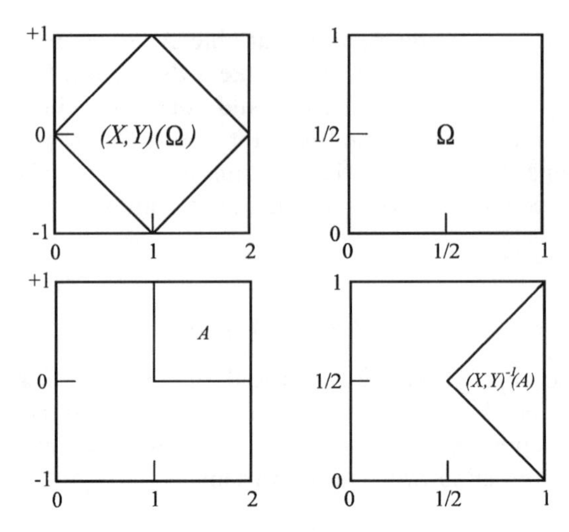

Figure 2.3. A bivariate random variable defined on the double coin toss probability space. The upper right panel shows the sample space $\Omega = (0, 1) \times (0, 1)$ on which is defined the random variable $(X, Y)(\omega_1, \omega_2) = (\omega_1 + \omega_2,\ \omega_1 - \omega_2)$; its range $R = (X, Y)(\Omega)$ is shown in the upper left panel. The lower left panel shows $A = (1, 2) \times (0, 1)$; its inverse image $F = (X, Y)^{-1}(A)$ is shown in the lower right panel. Note that part of A lies outside R. The probability assigned to A is $P_{(X,Y)}(A) = P(F) = 1/4$. The density of (X, Y) is $f_{X,Y}(x, y) = (1/2)I_R(x, y)$, which is defined over $\mathscr{X} = (-\infty, \infty) \times (-\infty, \infty)$.

where $f_X(x)$ and $f_Y(y)$ are the densities of the random variables X and Y considered separately. When $f_X(x)$ and $f_Y(y)$ are derived from the joint density $f_{X,Y}(x, y)$ in this fashion they are called *marginal densities*.

2.3 Discrete Random Variables

2.3.1 *Univariate Discrete Random Variables*

Discrete random variables are those whose image $X(\Omega)$ is a finite or countable set of points. Thus, either

$$X(\Omega) = \{x_1, x_2, \ldots, x_N\}$$

or

$$X(\Omega) = \{x_1, x_2, \ldots\}.$$

If we let

$$F_i = X^{-1}(\{x_i\}) = \{\omega \in \Omega : X(\omega) = x_i\},$$

then a discrete random variable either has the representation

$$X(\omega) = \sum_{i=1}^{N} x_i I_{F_i}(\omega)$$

or the representation

$$X(\omega) = \sum_{i=1}^{\infty} x_i I_{F_i}(\omega).$$

We can achieve an economy of notation by writing

$$X(\omega) = \sum_{x_i \in X(\Omega)} x_i I_{F_i}(\omega)$$

for both. Because a function cannot map one ω to different x_i, the F_i must be disjoint.

For a discrete random variable, usually one puts $\mathscr{X} = X(\Omega)$ and takes $\mathscr{A}$ to be all subsets of $\mathscr{X}$. However, for the sake of a general discussion, that is, so that discrete and continuous random variables can be discussed simultaneously, one sometimes puts $\mathscr{X} = \Re = (-\infty, \infty)$ and takes $\mathscr{A}$ to be the collection of Borel sets. The Borel sets contain all possible subsets of $X(\Omega)$ because they contain the intervals $[x_i, x_i]$ and all possible countable unions of them. Because discrete probability spaces have a simple structure, and because probability can be assigned to any set, worrying with $\mathscr{A}$ is actually unnecessary. Measurability considerations, while necessary in the continuous case, are just excess baggage in the discrete case.

The density function f_X of a discrete random variable is defined by

$$f_X(x_i) = P(F_i) = P\big[\{\omega \in \Omega: X(\omega) = x_i\}\big]$$

for $x_i \in X(\Omega)$. The probability that an event A occurs is gotten by summation:

$$P_X(A) = \sum_{x_i \in A} f_X(x_i).$$

An example of a discrete random variable with a finite image $X(\Omega)$ is the random variable that gives the payoff to a \$1 wager on an 8-spot keno ticket. The image, from Table 1.2, is $X(\Omega) = \{\$0, \$9, \$85, \$1500, \$18000\}$. The density function, derived from Table 1.3, is shown in Table 2.2.

TABLE 2.2
The Density of the Payoff to a $1 Wager on an 8-Spot Keno Ticket.

x_i	$f_X(x_i)$
$0	0.9791658999
9	0.0183025856
85	0.0023667137
1,500	0.0001604552
18,000	0.0000043457

Note: The table shows the probability density of the discrete random $X(\omega) = \sum_{i=1}^{5} x_i I_{F_i}(\omega)$, where F_1 is the event "catch 4 or less spots," F_2 is the event "catch 5 spots," etc. Table 2.2 is derived from Tables 1.2 and 1.3.

An example of a discrete random variable with a countable image is the random variable X that gives the roll on which a place bet on the 4 in craps terminates. Its image is $X(\Omega) = \{1, 2, \ldots\}$. In Section 1.4, we determined that

$$P[\{\omega \in \Omega: X(\omega) = i\}] = \frac{1}{4}\left(\frac{3}{4}\right)^{i-1}.$$

Therefore,

$$f_X(i) = \frac{1}{4}\left(\frac{3}{4}\right)^{i-1}, \qquad i = 1, 2, \ldots.$$

2.3.2 *Bivariate Discrete Random Variables*

As with continuous random variables, there can be more than one discrete random variable defined on the sample space Ω. If there are two,

$$x_i = X(\omega)$$
$$y_j = Y(\omega),$$

then the representation is

$$[X(\omega), Y(\omega)] = \sum_{x_i \in X(\Omega)} \sum_{y_j \in Y(\Omega)} (x_i, y_j) I_{F_{ij}}(\omega),$$

where

$$F_{ij} = \{\omega \in \Omega: X(\omega) = x_i, Y(\omega) = y_j\},$$

and the *joint density* is

$$f_{X,Y}(x_i, y_j) = P(F_{ij}).$$

Probabilities are computed as

$$P_{X,Y}(A) = \sum_{(x_i, y_j) \in A} f_{X,Y}(x_i, y_j).$$

The joint density satisfies the consistency relationships

$$f_X(x_i) = \sum_{y_j \in Y(\Omega)} f_{X,Y}(x_i, y_j)$$

$$f_Y(y_j) = \sum_{x_i \in X(\Omega)} f_{X,Y}(x_i, y_j),$$

where $f_X(x_i)$ and $f_Y(y_j)$ are the densities of the random variables X and Y considered separately. When $f_X(x_i)$ and $f_Y(y_j)$ are derived from the joint density $f_{X,Y}(x, y)$ in this fashion they are called *marginal densities*.

As an example, consider the random variables X and Y, where X gives the catch on one 8-spot keno ticket and Y the catch on another. Assuming that the two tickets have no spots in common, the joint density is

$$f_{X,Y}(i, j) = \frac{\binom{8}{i}\binom{8}{j}\binom{64}{20-i-j}}{\binom{80}{20}}.$$

If there are S spots in common, then the joint density is

$$f_{X,Y}(i, j) = \sum_{k=0}^{\min(i,j,S)} \frac{\binom{S}{k}\binom{8-S}{i-k}\binom{8-S}{j-k}\binom{64+S}{20+k-i-j}}{\binom{80}{20}}.$$

In Section 1.6 we determined that the density of the random variable X is

$$f_X(i) = \frac{\binom{8}{i}\binom{72}{20-i}}{\binom{80}{20}}.$$

We can check the consistency claim by summing either of the joint densities above to see if we get a marginal density that agrees with f_X from Section 1.6. We will check the first. We know from Section 1.6 that

$$\sum_{j=0}^{8} \frac{\binom{8}{j}\binom{64}{20-i-j}}{\binom{72}{20-i}} = 1.$$

Therefore,

$$f_X(i) = \sum_{j=0}^{8} \frac{\binom{8}{i}\binom{8}{j}\binom{64}{20-i-j}}{\binom{80}{20}} = \frac{\binom{8}{i}\sum_{j=0}^{8}\binom{8}{j}\binom{64}{20-i-j}}{\binom{80}{20}} = \frac{\binom{8}{i}\binom{72}{20-i}}{\binom{80}{20}},$$

which agrees.

2.4 Unconditional Expectation

2.4.1 *Discrete Random Variables*

To compute the expected payoff of a \$1 wager on an 8-spot keno ticket we would proceed as shown in Table 2.3 to compute

$$\mathscr{E}X = \sum_{x_i \in X(\Omega)} x_i P(F_i) = \sum_{x_i \in X(\Omega)} x_i f_X(x_i) = \$0.68464,$$

where $F_i = \{\omega \in \Omega : X(\omega) = x_i\}$. Similarly, we would compute the expected number of rolls for a place bet on the 4 to be decided in craps as

$$\mathscr{E}X = \sum_{x_i \in X(\Omega)} x_i P(F_i) = \sum_{x_i \in X(\Omega)} x_i f_X(x_i)$$
$$= \sum_{i=1}^{\infty} i \frac{1}{4}\left(\frac{3}{4}\right)^{i-1} = 4 \text{ rolls},$$

TABLE 2.3
Average Payoff to a \$1 Wager on an 8-Spot Keno Ticket.

payoff x_i	*density* $f_X(x_i)$	$x_i \times f_X(x_i)$
\$0	0.9791658999	\$0.00000
9	0.0183025856	0.16457
85	0.0023667137	0.20117
1,500	0.0001604552	0.24068
18,000	0.0000043457	0.07822
		Total \$0.68464

Note: The table computes the expectation $\mathscr{E}X$ of the discrete random $X(\omega) = \sum_{i=1}^{5} x_i I_{F_i}(\omega)$, where F_i is the event "payoff=x_i." Table 2.3 is derived from Table 2.2.

where the probabilities are from Subsection 2.3.1 and the answer is obtained by direct computation on a computer.

Computing the *expected value* $\mathscr{E}X$ of a discrete random variable

$$X = \sum_{x_i \in X(\Omega)} x_i I_{F_i}(x_i)$$

is straightforward; the formula is

$$\mathscr{E}X = \sum_{x_i \in X(\Omega)} x_i P(F_i) = \sum_{x_i \in X(\Omega)} x_i f_X(x_i).$$

There is a caveat. If the discrete random variable takes on both positive and negative values, then we need either the sum $\sum_{x_i>0} x_i f_X(x_i)$ or the sum $\sum_{x_i<0} x_i f_X(x_i)$, or both, to be finite for expectation to be well defined.

2.4.2 *Continuous Random Variables*

It is less obvious how the expectation of a continuous random variable should be computed. One reasonable approach would be to approximate the continuous random variable X by a discrete random variable X_N and use the expectation of the discrete random variable $\mathscr{E}X_N$ to approximate the expectation of the continuous random variable $\mathscr{E}X$. Figure 2.4 shows an approximation of the random variable

$$X(\omega) = \log\left(\frac{\omega}{1-\omega}\right)$$

discussed in Section 2.2 by the discrete random variable

$$X_N(\omega) = \sum_{i=1}^{N} x_i I_{F_i}(\omega),$$

where the intervals $F_i = (a_i, b_i) \subset \Omega$ are chosen in such a way that both $\max_i(b_i - a_i) < 2/N$ and $\sum_{i=1}^{N}(b_i - a_i) = 1$. The points $x_i = X(\omega_i) \in \mathscr{X}$ are chosen so that both $a_i \leq \omega_i \leq b_i$ and $|X_N(\omega)| \leq |X(\omega)|$. The expectation of the discrete random variable is

$$\mathscr{E}X_N = \sum_{i=1}^{N} x_i P(F_i) = \sum_{i=1}^{N} X(\omega_i)(b_i - a_i).$$

Due to the restrictions that we have placed on the choice of the x_i and

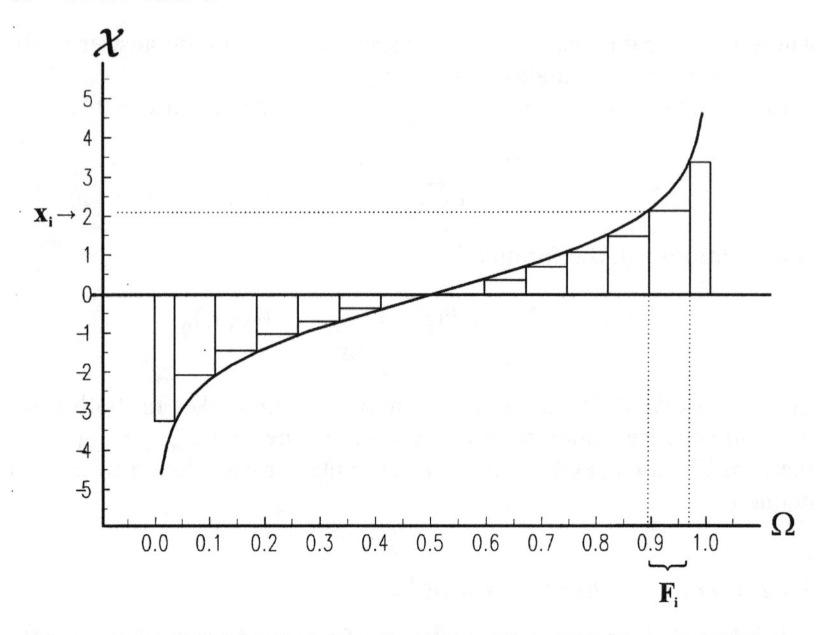

Figure 2.4. Approximation of a continuous random variable by a discrete random variable. The continuous random variable is $X(\omega) = \log[\omega/(1-\omega)]$. The discrete random variable is $X_N(\omega) = \sum_{i=1}^{N} x_i I_{F_i}(\omega)$. The horizontal axis is $\Omega = (0, 1)$ and the vertical axis is $\mathscr{X} = (-\infty, \infty)$.

F_i, the theory of integration implies that

$$\lim_{N\to\infty} \mathscr{E}X_N = \int_0^1 X(\omega)\, d\omega.$$

It seems reasonable, under these circumstances, to define

$$\mathscr{E}X = \int_0^1 X(\omega)\, d\omega. \tag{2.4}$$

Using the change of variable

$$x = \log\left(\frac{\omega}{1-\omega}\right), \qquad \omega = \frac{e^x}{1+e^x}, \qquad d\omega = \frac{e^x}{(1+e^x)^2}\, dx,$$

we have

$$\mathscr{E}X = \int_{-\infty}^{\infty} x f_X(x)\, dx,$$

where

$$f_X(x) = \frac{e^x}{(1+e^x)^2}.$$

Thus, $\mathscr{E}X = \int_{-\infty}^{\infty} x f_X(x)\,dx$ seems a reasonable definition of expectation for a continuous random variable. This is subject to the same caveat as above; we will need either $\int_0^{\infty} x f_X(x)\,dx$ or $\int_{-\infty}^{0} x f_X(x)\,dx$, or both, to be finite for expectation to be well defined.

2.4.3 *Bivariate Random Variables*

As we have seen, the expectation $\mathscr{E}X$ of a discrete random variable X with density f_X can be computed using

$$\mathscr{E}X = \sum_{x_i \in \mathscr{X}} x_i f_X(x_i),$$

where $\mathscr{X}$ is the set of points that X can assume. The expectation $\mathscr{E}X$ of a continuous random variable X with density f_X can be computed using

$$\mathscr{E}X = \int_{-\infty}^{\infty} x f_X(x)\,dx.$$

In either case, if one has the density function f_X, no knowledge of $(\Omega, \mathscr{F}, P)$ is required.

For a bivariate discrete random variable (X, Y), the formulas are

$$\mathscr{E}X = \sum_{x_i \in X(\Omega)} \sum_{y_j \in Y(\Omega)} x_i f_{X,Y}(x_i, y_j)$$

$$\mathscr{E}Y = \sum_{x_i \in X(\Omega)} \sum_{y_j \in Y(\Omega)} y_j f_{X,Y}(x_i, y_j).$$

For a bivariate continuous random variable, the formulas are

$$\mathscr{E}X = \int_{-\infty}^{\infty} \int_{-\infty}^{\infty} x f_{X,Y}(x, y)\,dx\,dy$$

$$\mathscr{E}Y = \int_{-\infty}^{\infty} \int_{-\infty}^{\infty} y f_{X,Y}(x, y)\,dx\,dy.$$

2.4.4 *General Random Variables*

Not all random variables are either discrete or continuous. Definitions of expectation that rely on an ability to construct the probability space $(\mathscr{X}, \mathscr{A}, P_X)$ can become awkward in these situations. We need a more primitive notion of expectation that applies when all that is available is $(\Omega, \mathscr{F}, P)$. That is the topic of this section.

There is no problem in computing the expectation of a discrete random variable of the form

$$X_N(\omega) = \sum_{i=1}^{N} x_i I_{F_i}(\omega).$$

Its expectation is

$$\mathscr{E} X_N = \sum_{i=1}^{N} x_i P(F_i).$$

No knowledge of $(\mathscr{X}, \mathscr{A}, P_X)$ is required.

For random variables that are not discrete, we mimic the recipe we followed above for continuous random variables and use approximation by discrete random variables to define expectation. There are three steps to the process:

1. For a nonnegative random variable X, that is, a random variable with $X(\omega) \geq 0$ for all $\omega \in \Omega$, define

$$\mathscr{E} X = \sup\left\{ \mathscr{E} X_N : X_N(\omega) = \sum_{i=1}^{N} x_i I_{F_i}(\omega), 0 \leq X_N(\omega) \leq X(\omega) \right\}.$$

   There are no restrictions on the choice of disjoint F_i other than membership in $\mathscr{F}$. Either the set

$$\left\{ \mathscr{E} X_N : X_N(\omega) = \sum_{i=1}^{N} x_i I_{F_i}(\omega), 0 \leq X_N(\omega) \leq X(\omega) \right\}$$

   has an upper bound, in which case $\mathscr{E} X$ is a finite nonnegative number, or it has no upper bound, in which case $\mathscr{E} X = \infty$.
2. Define the expectation of a nonpositive random variable X, that is, a random variable with $X(\omega) \leq 0$ for all $\omega \in \Omega$, to be $-\mathscr{E}(-X)$.

3. A random variable can be split into its nonnegative part $X^+ = XI_{[0,\infty)}(X)$ and its nonpositive part $X^- = XI_{(-\infty,0]}(X)$; they satisfy

$$X(\omega) = X^+(\omega) + X^-(\omega).$$

If either $\mathscr{E}X^+ \neq \infty$ or $\mathscr{E}X^- \neq -\infty$, then define

$$\mathscr{E}X = \mathscr{E}X^+ + \mathscr{E}X^-.$$

Otherwise, $\mathscr{E}X$ is left undefined.

We may illustrate using Figure 2.4. Figure 2.4 is a plot of the random variable $X(\omega) = \log[\omega/(1-\omega)]$ over the coin tossing probability space (Subsection 1.4.1) together with an approximating discrete random variable of the type required by the definition. As seen from the figure, $X^+(\omega)$ takes its nonzero values to the right of $\omega = 1/2$ and $X^-(\omega)$ takes its nonzero values to the left. Taking the limit of the expectation of the approximating discrete random variables, we have (Problem 8)

$$\mathscr{E}X^+ = \int_{1/2}^{1} \log\left(\frac{\omega}{1-\omega}\right) d\omega$$

$$\mathscr{E}X^- = \int_{0}^{1/2} \log\left(\frac{\omega}{1-\omega}\right) d\omega.$$

The sum of the positive and negative parts is

$$\mathscr{E}X = \mathscr{E}X^+ + \mathscr{E}X^- = \int_{0}^{1} \log\left(\frac{\omega}{1-\omega}\right) d\omega, \qquad (2.5)$$

which agrees with Equation (2.4).

2.4.5 *Expectation Viewed as Integration*

As Equation (2.5) suggests, expectation can be viewed as integration on $(\Omega, \mathscr{F}, P)$. The integral over the whole sample space Ω is defined as

$$\int X(\omega)\, dP(\omega) = \mathscr{E}X.$$

The integral over $A \in \mathscr{F}$ is defined as

$$\int_A X(\omega)\, dP(\omega) = \int I_A(\omega) X(\omega)\, dP(\omega) = \mathscr{E}(I_A X).$$

The integral on $(\Omega, \mathcal{F}, P)$ thus defined satisfies the standard properties of an integral, such as

1. $f(\omega) \leq g(\omega) \Rightarrow \int f(\omega)\,dP(\omega) \leq \int g(\omega)\,dP(\omega)$.
2. $f(\omega) \leq g(\omega)$ and $P\{\omega: f(\omega) \neq g(\omega)\} > 0 \Rightarrow \int f(\omega)\,dP(\omega) < \int g(\omega)\,dP(\omega)$.
3. $\int af(\omega) + bg(\omega)\,dP(\omega) = a\int f(\omega)\,dP(\omega) + b\int g(\omega)\,dP(\omega)$.
4. $A, B \in \mathcal{F}$ and $A \cap B = \emptyset \Rightarrow \int_{A\cup B} f(\omega)\,dP(\omega) = \int_A f(\omega)\,dP(\omega) + \int_B f(\omega)\,dP(\omega)$.

In addition, note that

$$P(A) = \int I_A(\omega)\,dP(\omega) = \mathcal{E}I_A.$$

2.4.6 *Expectation of Limits*

Two important convergence results that apply to expectation are the following.

Theorem 2.2 (Monotone Convergence Theorem). *If* $0 \leq f_n(\omega) \leq f_{n+1}(\omega)$ *for* $n = 1, 2, \ldots,$ *then*

$$\lim_{n\to\infty} \int f_n(\omega)\,dP(\omega) = \int \lim_{n\to\infty} f_n(\omega)\,dP(\omega).$$

Theorem 2.3 (Dominated Convergence Theorem). *If* $|f_n(\omega)| \leq g(\omega)$ *for* $n = 1, 2, \ldots,$ $\int g(\omega)\,dP(\omega) < \infty$, *and* $\lim_{n\to\infty} f_n(\omega) = f(\omega)$ *except for* $\omega \in E$ *with* $P(E) = 0$, *then*

$$\lim_{n\to\infty} \int f_n(\omega)\,dP(\omega) = \int f(\omega)\,dP(\omega).$$

2.5 Conditional Expectation

2.5.1 *General Random Variables*

Suppose there are two random variables X and Y defined on the same probability space $(\Omega, \mathcal{F}, P)$. If one is permitted to observe X, then what can one say about Y?

One might try to predict Y by some function $g(X)$. The most commonly used measure of the quality of a predictor g is its mean square error,

$$\mathrm{MSE}(g) = \mathcal{E}[Y - g(X)]^2 = \int \{Y(\omega) - g[X(\omega)]\}^2\,dP(\omega).$$

One then wants the best choice g^* in the sense of minimizing MSE(g). The *conditional expectation* of Y given X, denoted $\mathscr{E}(Y|X)$, turns out to be the solution of this problem; that is, $g^*(X) = \mathscr{E}(Y|X)$. This fact motivates the considerations of this section. Our plan is to first characterize $\mathscr{E}(Y|X)$, next deduce a few of its properties, and then verify that $g^*(X) = \mathscr{E}(Y|X)$.

We begin by noting what can be learned by observing X. The random variable X maps the probability space $(\Omega, \mathscr{F}, P)$ into a measurable space $(\mathscr{X}, \mathscr{A})$ as discussed in Section 2.1. If we are permitted to observe X, then we know whether or not any event $A \in \mathscr{A}$ has occurred. If we know whether or not any event $A \in \mathscr{A}$ has occurred, then we know whether or not any event in the sub-σ-algebra $\mathscr{F}_0 = X^{-1}(\mathscr{A}) = \{F \in \mathscr{F}: F = X^{-1}(A),\ A \in \mathscr{A}\}$ has occurred. Attention therefore focuses on $\mathscr{F}_0$.

The random variable Y maps $(\Omega, \mathscr{F}, P)$ into a measurable space $(\mathscr{Y}, \mathscr{B})$. The predictor g is a measurable mapping of $(\mathscr{X}, \mathscr{A})$ into $(\mathscr{Y}, \mathscr{B})$. If $B \in \mathscr{B}$, then $g^{-1}(B) \in \mathscr{A}$; hence $X^{-1}[g^{-1}(B)] \in \mathscr{F}_0$. We conclude that the composite function $g(X)$ is measurable $\mathscr{F}_0/\mathscr{B}$. This observation further directs our attention towards $\mathscr{F}_0$.

Not only does attention focus on the sub-σ-algebra $\mathscr{F}_0$, it is all that is actually needed to define conditional expectation; it is not necessary to mention X.

Definition 2.3. Let Y be a random variable mapping the probability space $(\Omega, \mathscr{F}, P)$ into the measurable space $(\mathscr{Y}, \mathscr{B})$ such that $\mathscr{E}|Y| < \infty$. Let $\mathscr{F}_0$ be a sub-σ-algebra of $\mathscr{F}$. The *conditional expectation* of Y given $\mathscr{F}_0$, denoted $\mathscr{E}(Y|\mathscr{F}_0)$, is an $\mathscr{F}_0$-measurable function $h^*(\omega)$ that satisfies

$$\int_F Y(\omega)\, dP(\omega) = \int_F h^*(\omega)\, dP(\omega)$$

for every $F \in \mathscr{F}_0$. Equivalently, $\mathscr{E}(Y|\mathscr{F}_0)$ is a random variable mapping $(\Omega, \mathscr{F}, P)$ into $(\mathscr{Y}, \mathscr{B})$ that is measurable $\mathscr{F}_0/\mathscr{B}$ and that satisfies $\mathscr{E}(I_F Y) = \mathscr{E}[I_F \mathscr{E}(Y|\mathscr{F}_0)]$ for every $F \in \mathscr{F}_0$.

If $\mathscr{F}_0 = X^{-1}(\mathscr{A})$ for some random variable X mapping $(\Omega, \mathscr{F})$ into $(\mathscr{X}, \mathscr{A})$, then one may write $\mathscr{E}(Y|X)$ for $\mathscr{E}(Y|\mathscr{F}_0)$. Although we will not prove it, it is nonetheless true that if a function $h(\omega)$ is $\mathscr{F}_0$-measurable and $\mathscr{F}_0 = X^{-1}(\mathscr{A})$, then h must be a composite function of the form $h(\omega) = g[X(\omega)]$, which justifies this notational convention. A proof that there exists an h^* that satisfies the definition is difficult. We will, however, show how to construct h^* for both continuous and discrete random variables below, which is adequate for our purposes. An h^* that satisfies the definition is not necessarily unique, but if h^* and h^{**} both satisfy the definition, then they agree except for $\omega \in E$ with $P(E) = 0$. Which h^* we choose for $\mathscr{E}(Y|\mathscr{F}_0)$ does not matter.

Also, note that $\mathscr{E}(Y|\mathscr{F}_0)$ and $\mathscr{E}(Y|X)$ are functions. Writing $\mathscr{E}(Y|\mathscr{F}_0)(\omega)$, $\mathscr{E}(Y|X)(x)$, or $\mathscr{E}(Y|X)[X(\omega)]$ calls attention to their arguments. If $\mathscr{F}_0 = X^{-1}(\mathscr{A})$, then the relation among them is

$$\mathscr{E}(Y|\mathscr{F}_0)(\omega) = \mathscr{E}(Y|X)(x)\big|_{x=X(\omega)} = \mathscr{E}(Y|X)[X(\omega)].$$

Example 2.1. We shall illustrate these ideas by computing the expectation of a general random variable $Y(\omega)$ conditional on a discrete random variable

$$X(\omega) = \sum_{i=0}^{N} x_i I_{F_i}(\omega).$$

We can require (i) that the F_i are mutually exclusive and exhaustive, (ii) that $P(F_0) = 0$, (iii) that $P(F_i) > 0$ for $i \neq 0$, and (iv) that the x_i are distinct, and we shall do so. It follows from these restrictions that $\mathscr{F}_0$ consists of the empty set and all possible unions of the F_i. To verify that this is true, we presume that, minimally, $\mathscr{A}$ contains all possible subsets of $\mathscr{X} = \{x_1, \ldots x_N\}$ plus the empty set. As we have noted earlier, the Borel sets satisfy this condition. All that matters in computing the inverse image $X^{-1}(A)$ of a subset A of $\mathscr{X}$ is which of the points $x_0, \ldots x_N$ are in A. If, for example, A contains only x_1 and x_3 then $X^{-1}(A) = F_1 \cup F_3$. Therefore, the inverse image $X^{-1}(A)$ of a subset A of $\mathscr{X}$ must either be the empty set or a union of the F_i. If h^* is to be $\mathscr{F}_0$-measurable, then it too must be of the form

$$h^*(\omega) = \sum_{i=0}^{N} h_i I_{F_i}(\omega),$$

although the h_i are not necessarily distinct (Problem 6). The definition of conditional expectation requires

$$\int_{F_i} Y(\omega)\, dP(\omega) = \int_{F_i} h^*(\omega)\, dP(\omega) = \sum_{j=1}^{N} h_j \int_{F_i} I_{F_j}(\omega)\, dP(\omega) = h_i P(F_i).$$

Thus (Problem 9),

$$h_i = \frac{1}{P(F_i)} \int_{F_i} Y(\omega)\, dP(\omega) = \int Y(\omega)\, dP(\omega|F_i),$$

where $P(\cdot|F_i)$ is the probability function defined for every $F \in \mathcal{F}$ by $P(F|F_i) = P(F \cap F_i)/P(F_i)$ that we discussed in Section 1.7.

This result makes a good deal of sense. It says that knowing that F_i has occurred, the best predictor of Y is the average value of Y over F_i, which is h_i. To write $h^*(\omega)$ in the form $h^*(\omega) = g[X(\omega)]$, put $g(x_i) = h_i$. This too makes sense. It says that upon observing x_i, the best predictor of Y is $g(x_i) = h_i$.

In summary, our results are

$$\mathscr{E}(Y|\mathcal{F}_0)(\omega) = \sum_{i=1}^{N}\left[\frac{1}{P(F_i)}\int_{F_i} Y(\tau)\,dP(\tau)\right] I_{F_i}(\omega) \tag{2.6}$$

$$\mathscr{E}(Y|X)(x) = \sum_{i=1}^{N}\left[\frac{1}{P(F_i)}\int_{F_i} Y(\omega)\,dP(\omega)\right] I_{\{x_i\}}(x). \tag{2.7}$$

The fact that N was finite played no role in the derivation; these results also hold when $N = \infty$.

As an illustration, for the single roll sample space

$$\Omega_p = \{(n_1, n_2): n_1 = 1, \ldots, 6,\ n_2 = 1, \ldots, 6\}$$

let the random variable $X = n_1$, which is the outcome on the first die, and $Y = n_1 + n_2$, which is the sum of the two dice. Then

$$X = \sum_{i=1}^{6} i I_{F_i}(x),$$

where

$$F_i = \{(n_1, n_2): n_1 = i,\ n_2 = 1, \ldots, 6\},$$

and

$$P(F_i) = \frac{6}{36}$$

$$\int_{F_i} Y(\omega)\,dP(\omega) = \frac{1}{36}[(1+i) + \cdots + (6+i)].$$

Equations (2.6) and (2.7) give

$$\mathscr{E}(Y|\mathcal{F}_0)(n_1, n_2) = 3.5 + n_1$$

$$\mathscr{E}(Y|X)(x) = 3.5 + x,$$

which is the obvious answer.

Conditional expectation, like unconditional expectation, is linear and preserves inequality.

Theorem 2.4. *If both $\mathscr{E}|Y|$ and $\mathscr{E}|Z|$ are finite, then*

$$\mathscr{E}(aZ + bY \mid \mathscr{F}_0) = a\mathscr{E}(Z|\mathscr{F}_0) + b\mathscr{E}(Y|\mathscr{F}_0).$$

If, in addition, $Z(\omega) \leq Y(\omega)$, then $\mathscr{E}(Z|\mathscr{F}_0) \leq \mathscr{E}(Y|\mathscr{F}_0)$. Because conditional expectation is not uniquely defined, these relationships may not hold for ω in some set E that has $P(E) = 0$.

The special properties of conditional expectation that we shall need to verify that $g^*(X) = \mathscr{E}(Y|X)$ minimizes $\text{MSE}(g) = \mathscr{E}[Y - g(X)]^2$ are stated in the next two theorems.

Theorem 2.5 (Law of Iterated Expectations). *If $\mathscr{E}|Y|$ is finite, $\mathscr{F}_0$ and $\mathscr{F}_1$ are sub-σ-algebras of $\mathscr{F}$, and $\mathscr{F}_0 \subset \mathscr{F}_1$, then*

$$\mathscr{E}(Y|\mathscr{F}_0)(\omega) = \mathscr{E}\big[\mathscr{E}(Y|\mathscr{F}_1)\big|\mathscr{F}_0\big](\omega),$$

except on an event E with $P(E) = 0$. In particular, $\mathscr{E}Y = \mathscr{E}[\mathscr{E}(Y|\mathscr{F}_0)]$.

Proof. We will take care of the easy case, which is $\mathscr{E}Y = \mathscr{E}[\mathscr{E}(Y|\mathscr{F}_0)]$, first. By the definition of conditional expectation,

$$\int_F Y(\omega)\, dP(\omega) = \int_F \mathscr{E}(Y|\mathscr{F}_0)(\omega)\, dP(\omega)$$

for all $F \in \mathscr{F}_0$. In particular, $\Omega \in \mathscr{F}_0$ so that

$$\mathscr{E}Y = \int_\Omega Y(\omega)\, dP(\omega) = \int_\Omega \mathscr{E}(Y|\mathscr{F}_0)(\omega)\, dP(\omega) = \mathscr{E}[\mathscr{E}(Y|\mathscr{F}_0)].$$

This proves that $\mathscr{E}Y = \mathscr{E}[\mathscr{E}(Y|\mathscr{F}_0)]$.

Put $h^*_{1,0}(\omega) = \mathscr{E}\big[\mathscr{E}(Y|\mathscr{F}_1) \mid \mathscr{F}_0\big](\omega)$. If we could show that

$$\int_F Y(\omega)\, dP(\omega) = \int_F h^*_{1,0}(\omega)\, dP(\omega)$$

for all $F \in \mathscr{F}_0$, then we would have the result by the remarks following Definition 2.3. Put $h^*_1(\omega) = \mathscr{E}(Y|\mathscr{F}_1)(\omega)$. By hypothesis $h^*_{1,0}(\omega) = \mathscr{E}(h^*_1|\mathscr{F}_0)$. Therefore,

$$\int_F h^*_1(\omega)\, dP(\omega) = \int_F h^*_{1,0}(\omega)\, dP(\omega)$$

for all $F \in \mathcal{F}_0$. Now $h_1^*(\omega)$ satisfies

$$\int_F Y(\omega)\,dP(\omega) = \int_F h_1^*(\omega)\,dP(\omega)$$

for all $F \in \mathcal{F}_1$. But if $F \in \mathcal{F}_0$, then $F \in \mathcal{F}_1$, because $\mathcal{F}_0 \subset \mathcal{F}_1$. Therefore,

$$\int_F Y(\omega)\,dP(\omega) = \int_F h_1^*(\omega)\,dP(\omega)$$

for all $F \in \mathcal{F}_0$. We have shown that

$$\int_F Y(\omega)\,dP(\omega) = \int_F h_{1,0}^*(\omega)\,dP(\omega)$$

for all $F \in \mathcal{F}_0$ as required. □

Theorem 2.6. *If Z is $\mathcal{F}_0$-measurable and both $\mathscr{E}|Y|$ and $\mathscr{E}|YZ|$ are finite, then*

$$\mathscr{E}(ZY|\mathcal{F}_0) = Z\mathscr{E}(Y|\mathcal{F}_0).$$

In particular, $\mathscr{E}(Z|\mathcal{F}_0) = Z$.

Proof. By assumption, Z and $\mathscr{E}(Y|\mathcal{F}_0)$ are $\mathcal{F}_0$-measurable. As remarked in Section 2.1, standard algebraic operations do not destroy measurability. Thus, $Z\mathscr{E}(Y|\mathcal{F}_0)$ is $\mathcal{F}_0$-measurable. Therefore, all we need to show is that

$$\int_F Z(\omega)\mathscr{E}(Y|\mathcal{F}_0)(\omega)\,dP(\omega) = \int_F Z(\omega)Y(\omega)\,dP(\omega)$$

for every $F \in \mathcal{F}_0$.

First consider the case when Z is a discrete random variable

$$Z(\omega) = \sum_{i=1}^{N} z_i I_{F_i}(\omega)$$

with $F_i \in \mathcal{F}_0$. If $F \in \mathcal{F}_0$, then $F \cap F_i \in \mathcal{F}_0$, so that

$$\begin{aligned}\int_F Z(\omega)\mathscr{E}(Y|\mathcal{F}_0)(\omega)\,dP(\omega) &= \int_F \left[\sum_{i=1}^{N} z_i I_{F_i}(\omega)\right]\mathscr{E}(Y|\mathcal{F}_0)(\omega)\,dP(\omega)\\ &= \sum_{i=1}^{N} z_i \int_{F\cap F_i} \mathscr{E}(Y|\mathcal{F}_0)(\omega)\,dP(\omega)\end{aligned}$$

$$= \sum_{i=1}^{N} z_i \int_{F \cap F_i} Y(\omega)\, dP(\omega)$$

$$= \int_F \left[\sum_{i=1}^{N} z_i I_{F_i}(\omega) \right] Y(\omega)\, dP(\omega)$$

$$= \int_F Z(\omega) Y(\omega)\, dP(\omega).$$

Thus, the result holds if Z is discrete.

Now suppose that both Z and Y are nonnegative random variables. Let Z_N be a discrete random variable as above such that $0 \le Z_N(\omega) \le Z(\omega)$ and $\lim_{N\to\infty} Z_N(\omega) = Z(\omega)$ (Problem 10). By the monotone convergence theorem (Theorem 2.2) and the result above,

$$\int_F Z(\omega) \mathscr{E}(Y|\mathscr{F}_0)(\omega)\, dP(\omega) = \lim_{N\to\infty} \int_F Z_N(\omega) \mathscr{E}(Y|\mathscr{F}_0)(\omega)\, dP(\omega)$$

$$= \lim_{N\to\infty} \int_F Z_N(\omega) Y(\omega)\, dP(\omega)$$

$$= \int_F Z(\omega) Y(\omega)\, dP(\omega).$$

Thus, the result holds if Y and Z are nonnegative.

The remainder of the proof is accomplished by breaking both Z and Y into their nonnegative and nonpositive parts, writing

$$ZY = (Z^+ + Z^-)(Y^+ + Y^-)$$

$$= Z^+Y^+ - (-Z^-)Y^+ - Z^+(-Y^-) + (-Z^-)(-Y^-),$$

and applying the result above to each piece. The details are not interesting and we omit them.

The particular result is obtained by noting that if we put $h^*(\omega) = Z(\omega)$, then h^* is an $\mathscr{F}_0$-measurable function that satisfies the definition of conditional expectation trivially. □

Note, in passing, that if $\mathscr{F}_0 \subset \mathscr{F}_1$, then $\mathscr{E}(Y|\mathscr{F}_0)(\omega)$ is $\mathscr{F}_1$-measurable. Therefore Theorem 2.6 implies that $\mathscr{E}(Y|\mathscr{F}_0) = \mathscr{E}\left[\mathscr{E}(Y|\mathscr{F}_0) \,\middle|\, \mathscr{F}_1\right]$.

We are now in a position to verify that $g^*(X) = \mathscr{E}(Y|X)$ minimizes $\text{MSE}(g)$. Now

$$\text{MSE}(g)$$

$$= \mathscr{E}[Y - g(X)]^2$$

$$= \mathscr{E}[Y - \mathscr{E}(Y|X) + \mathscr{E}(Y|X) - g(X)]^2$$
$$= \mathscr{E}[Y - \mathscr{E}(Y|X)]^2 + \mathscr{E}[\mathscr{E}(Y|X) - g(X)]^2$$
$$+ 2\,\mathscr{E}\{[\mathscr{E}(Y|X) - g(X)][Y - \mathscr{E}(Y|X)]\} \quad \text{[Theorem 2.4]}$$
$$= \mathscr{E}[Y - \mathscr{E}(Y|X)]^2 + \mathscr{E}[\mathscr{E}(Y|X) - g(X)]^2$$
$$+ 2\,\mathscr{E}(\mathscr{E}\{[\mathscr{E}(Y|X) - g(X)][Y - \mathscr{E}(Y|X)]|\mathscr{F}_0\}) \quad \text{[Theorem 2.5]}$$
$$= \mathscr{E}[Y - \mathscr{E}(Y|X)]^2 + \mathscr{E}[\mathscr{E}(Y|X) - g(X)]^2$$
$$+ 2\mathscr{E}([\mathscr{E}(Y|X) - g(X)]\mathscr{E}\{[Y - \mathscr{E}(Y|X)]|\mathscr{F}_0\}) \quad \text{[Theorem 2.6]}$$
$$= \mathscr{E}[Y - \mathscr{E}(Y|X)]^2 + \mathscr{E}[\mathscr{E}(Y|X) - g(X)]^2$$
$$+ 2\,\mathscr{E}([\mathscr{E}(Y|X) - g(X)][\mathscr{E}(Y|X) - \mathscr{E}(Y|X)]) \quad \text{[Theorem 2.6]}$$
$$= \mathscr{E}[Y - \mathscr{E}(Y|X)]^2 + \mathscr{E}[\mathscr{E}(Y|X) - g(X)]^2.$$

We now have that in general

$$\text{MSE}(g) = \mathscr{E}[Y - \mathscr{E}(Y|X)]^2 + \mathscr{E}[\mathscr{E}(Y|X) - g(X)]^2,$$

whereas if we put $g^*(X) = \mathscr{E}(Y|X)$ we have

$$\text{MSE}(g^*) = \mathscr{E}[Y - \mathscr{E}(Y|X)]^2.$$

This implies $g^*(X) = \mathscr{E}(Y|X)$ minimizes MSE(g).

2.5.2 *Discrete Random Variables*

If (X, Y) is a discrete random variable with values (x_i, y_j) in $\mathscr{X} \times \mathscr{Y}$ and joint density $f_{X,Y}(x_i, y_j)$, then

$$\mathscr{E}(Y|X)(x_i) = \sum_{y_j \in \mathscr{Y}} y_j\, f_{Y|X}(y_j|x_i),$$

where

$$f_{Y|X}(y_j|x_i) = \frac{f_{Y,X}(x_i, y_j)}{f_X(x_i)}$$

and

$$f_X(x_i) = \sum_{y_j \in \mathscr{Y}} f_{Y,X}(x_i, y_j).$$

In the case where $f_X(x_i) = 0$, put $f_{Y|X}(y_j|x_i) = 0$. The density $f_{Y|X}(y_j|x_i)$ is called the *conditional density* of Y given X and $f_X(x_i)$ is called the *marginal density* of X. This result is actually a special case of Example 2.1 with $F_i = X^{-1}(\{x_i\})$.

Consider the density f_{XY} from Subsection 2.3.2 where X is the catch on one 8-spot keno ticket and Y the catch on another when the two tickets have no spots in common. Subsection 2.3.2 gives joint density as

$$f_{X,Y}(i,j) = \frac{\binom{8}{i}\binom{8}{j}\binom{64}{20-i-j}}{\binom{80}{20}}$$

and marginal density as

$$f_X(i) = \frac{\binom{8}{i}\binom{72}{20-i}}{\binom{80}{20}}.$$

Division gives the conditional density

$$f_{Y|X}(j|i) = \frac{\binom{8}{j}\binom{64}{20-i-j}}{\binom{72}{20-i}}.$$

The answer makes sense. Knowing that exactly i of eight numbers excluded from consideration have been drawn is like playing keno with 72 numbers in total instead of 80 and with $20 - i$ numbers drawn instead of 20.

The conditional expectation is

$$\begin{aligned}
\mathscr{E}(Y|X)(i) &= \sum_{j=0}^{8} j f_{Y|X}(j|i) \\
&= \sum_{j=1}^{8} j \frac{\binom{8}{j}\binom{64}{20-i-j}}{\binom{72}{20-i}} \\
&= \sum_{j=1}^{8} j \frac{8!}{j!\,(8-j)!} \frac{\binom{64}{20-i-j}}{\binom{72}{20-i}} \\
&= \sum_{j=1}^{8} \frac{8!}{(j-1)!\,(8-j)!} \frac{\binom{64}{20-i-j}}{\binom{72}{20-i}} \\
&= 8 \sum_{j=1}^{8} \frac{7!}{(j-1)!\,[7-(j-1)]!} \frac{\binom{64}{19-i-(j-1)}}{\binom{72}{20-i}}
\end{aligned}$$

$$= 8\frac{\sum_{j=0}^{7}\binom{7}{j}\binom{64}{19-i-j}}{\binom{72}{20-i}}$$

$$= 8\frac{\binom{71}{19-i}}{\binom{72}{20-i}}$$

$$= 8\frac{71!\,(20-i)!(52+i)!}{72!\,(19-i)!(52+i)!}$$

$$= 8\frac{(20-i)}{72}$$

This answer

$$\mathscr{E}(Y|X)(i) = 8\,\frac{(20-i)}{72}$$

also makes sense. The larger the catch i on the first card, the less likely a catch on the second because the two cards have no spots in common. Thus, the expected catch on the second card should decline as the catch on the first increases.

2.5.3 *Continuous Random Variables*

If (X, Y) is a continuous random variable with joint density $f_{X,Y}(x, y)$, then

$$\mathscr{E}(Y|X)(x) = \int_{-\infty}^{\infty} y\, f_{Y|X}(y|x)\, dy,$$

where

$$f_{Y|X}(y|x) = \frac{f_{X,Y}(x, y)}{f_X(x)}$$

and

$$f_X(x_i) = \int_{-\infty}^{\infty} f_{X,Y}(x, y)\, dy.$$

Again, the density $f_{Y|X}(y|x)$ is called the *conditional density* of Y given X and $f_X(x)$ is called the *marginal density* of X. Again, put $f_{Y|X}(y|x) = 0$ if $f_X(x) = 0$.

To verify that $\mathscr{E}(Y|X)(x)$ satisfies the definition is straightforward. Recall that if $F \in \mathscr{F}_0$, then $F = X^{-1}(A)$ for some $A \in \mathscr{A}$ and $I_F(\omega) = I_A[X(\omega)]$. Therefore,

$$
\begin{aligned}
&\int_F \mathscr{E}(Y|X)[X(\omega)]\,dP(\omega) \\
&\quad = \int I_A[X(\omega)]\,\mathscr{E}(Y|X)[X(\omega)]\,dP(\omega) \\
&\quad = \int_{-\infty}^{\infty}\int_{-\infty}^{\infty} I_A(x)\,\mathscr{E}(Y|X)(x)\,f_{X,Y}(y,x)\,dy\,dx \\
&\quad = \int_{-\infty}^{\infty}\int_{-\infty}^{\infty} I_A(x)\int_{-\infty}^{\infty} u f_{Y|X}(u|x)\,du\,f_{X,Y}(y,x)\,dy\,dx \\
&\quad = \int_{-\infty}^{\infty} I_A(x)\int_{-\infty}^{\infty} u f_{Y|X}(u|x)\,du\,f_X(x)\,dx \\
&\quad = \int_{-\infty}^{\infty} I_A(x)\int_{-\infty}^{\infty} u f_{Y,X}(u,x)\,du\,dx \\
&\quad = \int_{-\infty}^{\infty}\int_{-\infty}^{\infty} I_A(x)\,y\,f_{Y,X}(y,x)\,dy\,dx \\
&\quad = \int I_A[X(\omega)]\,Y(\omega)\,dP(\omega) \\
&\quad = \int_F Y(\omega)\,dP(\omega).
\end{aligned}
$$

2.5.4 *Conditional Expectation of Limits*

There are versions of the monotone and dominated convergence theorems that apply to conditional expectation.

Theorem 2.7 (Monotone Convergence Theorem). *If* $0 \le Y_n(\omega) \le Y_{n+1}(\omega)$ *and* $\mathscr{E}|Y_n| < \infty$ *for* $n = 1, 2, \ldots,$ *then*

$$\lim_{n\to\infty} \mathscr{E}(Y_n|\mathscr{F}_0)(\omega) = \mathscr{E}\Big(\lim_{n\to\infty} Y_n \,\Big|\, \mathscr{F}_0\Big)(\omega)$$

except for ω *in some event* E *with* $P(E) = 0$.

Theorem 2.8 (Dominated Convergence Theorem). *If* $|Y_n(\omega)| \le Z(\omega)$ *for* $n = 1, 2, \ldots,$ $\mathscr{E}|Z| < \infty$, *and* $\lim_{n\to\infty} Y_n(\omega) = Y(\omega)$ *except for* $\omega \in F$ *with* $P(F) = 0$, *then*

$$\lim_{n\to\infty} \mathscr{E}(Y_n|\mathscr{F}_0)(\omega) = \mathscr{E}(Y|\mathscr{F}_0)(\omega)$$

except for ω *in some event* E *with* $P(E) = 0$.

This is, no doubt, the hardest section in the book, and it is probably the most important. It is likely worth whatever time it takes to make sense of it. The reader who should like to pursue these ideas further should see Billingsley 1995 or Chung 1974.

2.6 Problems

1. If A and B are subsets of $\mathscr{X}$, and $A_1, A_2, \ldots$ is a sequence of subsets from $\mathscr{X}$, show that the inverse image satisfies these properties: (i) If $A \subset B$, then $X^{-1}(A) \subset X^{-1}(B)$. (ii) $X^{-1}(A \cup B) = X^{-1}(A) \cup X^{-1}(B)$. (iii) $X^{-1}(A \cap B) = X^{-1}(A) \cap X^{-1}(B)$. (iv) $X^{-1}(\bigcup_{i=1}^{\infty} A_i) = \bigcup_{i=1}^{\infty} X^{-1}(A_i)$. (v) $X^{-1}(\bigcap_{i=1}^{\infty} A_i) = \bigcap_{i=1}^{\infty} X^{-1}(A_i)$. (vi) If $h(\omega) = g[X(\omega)]$, then $h^{-1}(B) = X^{-1}[g^{-1}(B)]$ (see Problem 2). Show that (ii) and (iii) imply $\Omega = X^{-1}(A \cup \tilde{A}) = X^{-1}(A) \cup X^{-1}(\tilde{A})$ and $\emptyset = X^{-1}(A \cap \tilde{A}) = X^{-1}(A) \cap X^{-1}(\tilde{A})$. Use these two results to show that (vii) $X^{-1}(\sim A) = \sim X^{-1}(A)$.
2. Let $\Omega = (0, 1)$, $X(\omega) = 2\omega^2$, and $g(x) = \log x$. Then X maps Ω into $\mathscr{X} = (0, 2)$ and g maps $\mathscr{X}$ into $\mathscr{Y} = (-\infty, \log 2)$. The composite function $h(\omega) = g[X(\omega)]$ is $h(\omega) = \log 2 + 2 \log \omega$, which maps Ω into $\mathscr{Y}$. Let $B = (-1, 0)$. Find $A = g^{-1}(B)$ and $F = X^{-1}(A)$. Find $h^{-1}(B)$. Why must $F = h^{-1}(B)$?
3. Let X be a random variable that maps the sample space Ω onto $\mathscr{X}$. Let $\mathscr{A}$ be a σ-algebra of subsets of $\mathscr{X}$. Show that the collection of sets $\mathscr{F}_0$ that consists of all preimages of sets A from $\mathscr{A}$ is a σ-algebra. That is, show that $\mathscr{F}_0 = \{F : F = X^{-1}(A),\ A \in \mathscr{A}\}$ is a σ-algebra.
4. Let X be a random variable mapping the probability space $(\Omega, \mathscr{F}, P)$ into a measurable space $(\mathscr{X}, \mathscr{A})$, and let $P_X(A) = P\left[X^{-1}(A)\right]$ for $A \in \mathscr{A}$. Show that $(\mathscr{X}, \mathscr{A}, P_X)$ is a probability space; that is, show that P_X satisfies the axioms of probability.
5. Referring to Table 1.2, compute the MGM Grand's take as a percentage of the wager on a 6-spot keno ticket.
6. Let $\mathscr{F}_0$ consist of the empty set plus all possible unions of the mutually exclusive and exhaustive sequence of sets $F_0, \ldots, F_N$. Show that any random variable Z that is $\mathscr{F}_0$-measurable must be of the form $Z(\omega) = \sum_{i=0}^{N} z_i I_{F_i}(\omega)$, where the z_i are not necessarily distinct.
7. For the joint density

$$f_{X,Y}(i, j) = \frac{\binom{8}{i}\binom{8}{j}\binom{64}{20-i-j}}{\binom{80}{20}}$$

with marginal densities

$$f_X(i) = \frac{\binom{8}{i}\binom{72}{20-i}}{\binom{80}{20}}, \qquad f_Y(j) = \frac{\binom{8}{j}\binom{72}{20-j}}{\binom{80}{20}}$$

we derived the conditional expectation

$$\mathscr{E}(Y|X)(i) = 8\,\frac{(20-i)}{72}.$$

Direct computation gives

$$\mathscr{E}Y = \sum_{j=0}^{8} j f_Y(j) = 2.$$

Theorem 2.5 states that

$$\mathscr{E}Y = \mathscr{E}[\mathscr{E}(Y|X)] = \sum_{i=0}^{8} \mathscr{E}(Y|X)(i) f_X(i).$$

Compute this sum and compare.

8. At first glance, it is not clear that taking the limit of the expectation of the approximating discrete random variables shown in Figure 2.4 is the same as taking the supremum as required by the definition of expectation. The verification that this is so proceeds as follows. What is shown in the figure is a lower approximation of X^+ by a discrete random variable $X_N(\omega) = \sum_{i=1}^{N} x_i I_{F_i}(\omega)$, where the F_i are nonoverlapping intervals. The definition permits F_i to be any measurable set so it is always possible to find a better lower approximation $X^*(\omega) = \sum_{j=1}^{J} x_j^* I_{F_j^*}(\omega)$, $J \geq N$, where the F_j^* are not so restricted (Why?). Therefore, $\mathscr{E}X^+ = \sup \mathscr{E}X^* \geq \lim_{N\to\infty} \mathscr{E}X_N$ (Why?). By adjusting the x_i of X_N we can obtain an upper approximation $X_N^+(\omega) = \sum_{i=1}^{N} x_i^+ I_{F_i}(\omega) \geq X^+(\omega)$, where we leave the F_i unchanged. Moreover, for any N and J we have $X_N^+(\omega) \geq X^*(\omega)$ (Why?). Therefore, $\lim_{N\to\infty} \mathscr{E}X_N^+ \geq \sup \mathscr{E}X^*$ (Why?). But

$$\lim_{N\to\infty} \mathscr{E}X_N^+ = \int_{1/2}^{1} \log[\omega(1-\omega)]\, d\omega = \lim_{N\to\infty} \mathscr{E}X_N$$

(Why?). Therefore, $\mathscr{E}X^+ = \int_{1/2}^{1} \log[\omega(1-\omega)]\, d\omega$ (Why?).

9. Start with the probability space $(\Omega, \mathcal{F}, P)$ and let $P(\cdot|B)$ be the probability function defined by $P(F|B) = P(F \cap B)/P(B)$, which was discussed in Section 1.7. Because $[\Omega, \mathcal{F}, P(\cdot|B)]$ is a probability space, the integral $\int X(\omega)\, dP(\omega|B)$ is defined. Another common notation for this integral is $\mathscr{E}(X|B)$. Show that

$$\int X(\omega)\, dP(\omega|B) = \frac{1}{P(B)} \int I_B(\omega) Y(\omega)\, dP(\omega).$$

Hint: First verify that the formula works when X is a discrete random variable. Why does this imply that it must work for every random variable?

10. Let $Z \geq 0$. Put

$$Z_N(\omega) = \sum_{i=0}^{N^2} \frac{i}{N} I_{F_i}(\omega),$$

where

$$F_i = \left\{\omega\colon \frac{i}{N} \leq Z(\omega) < \frac{i+1}{N}\right\}.$$

Show that if Z is $\mathcal{F}_0/\mathcal{B}$-measurable, where $\mathcal{B}$ denotes the Borel sets, then $F_i \in \mathcal{F}_0$. Given $\omega^o \in \Omega$, show that $\lim_{N\to\infty} Z_N(\omega^o) = Z(\omega^o)$.

11. Show that conditional expectation is an orthogonal projection in the sense that it satisfies the Pythagorean identity

$$\mathscr{E}(Y^2) = \mathscr{E}\{[\mathscr{E}(Y|\mathcal{F})]^2\} + \mathscr{E}\{[Y - \mathscr{E}(Y|\mathcal{F})]^2\}$$

and the random variables $\mathscr{E}(Y|\mathcal{F})$ and $[Y - \mathscr{E}(Y|\mathcal{F})]$ are orthogonal,

$$\mathscr{E}\{\mathscr{E}(Y|\mathcal{F})[Y - \mathscr{E}(Y|\mathcal{F})]\} = 0.$$

3

Distributions, Transformations, and Moments

3.1 Distribution Functions

3.1.1 *Univariate Distribution Functions*

We have seen that it can be helpful to move from the sample space to the real line and solve problems by means of summation or integration of density functions. On the real line, discussions of σ-algebras and such like can be dismissed because it is hard to go wrong. The standard rules one learned in first-year calculus apply and considerations beyond that usually do not arise. In fact, not only is it helpful to move to the real line $\mathscr{X} = (-\infty, \infty)$, it would be better yet to be able to start there and dispense with any consideration of an underlying probability space $(\Omega, \mathscr{F}, P)$. This can be done. With many problems it is only necessary to write down the density function and set to work. Consider some examples.

1. Suppose one has a shipment of N objects of which D are defective. One samples n of them without replacement, counts the number of defectives x in the sample, and estimates the proportion of defectives D/N by the ratio x/n. To determine how large n should be for good accuracy, it is necessary to know how x behaves.

   To determine the density of the random X, the reasoning is the same as for the game of keno in Section 1.6. There are $\binom{N}{n}$ possible samples. There are $\binom{D}{x}$ ways to obtain x defectives and there are $\binom{N-D}{n-x}$ ways to fill out the rest of the sample. The density is

$$f_X(x) = \frac{\binom{D}{x}\binom{N-D}{n-x}}{\binom{N}{n}},$$

   which is called the *hypergeometric* density. It is positive when x is an integer between $\max(0, D+n-N)$ and $\min(n, D)$. The parameters of the density are n, D, and N; they are positive integers that satisfy $n, D \leq N$.

2. Another discrete example is tossing a coin n times that has probability p of landing heads and observing the number of heads x in the n tosses. Any specific sequence of x heads and $(n-x)$ tails, for instance (H, T, H, T, T), occurs with probability $p^x(1-p)^{n-x}$. There are $\binom{n}{x}$ such sequences that have x heads. Thus,

$$f_X(x) = \binom{n}{x} p^x (1-p)^{n-x},$$

which is called the *binomial* density. The density is positive for $x = 0, \ldots, n$. The parameters of the density are n, which is a positive integer, and $0 \leq p \leq 1$.

3. It is often reasonable to assume that a random variable is normally distributed. The central limit theorem, which will be discussed in a later chapter, states that the average of a large number of random variables will be approximately normally distributed in most circumstances. As many phenomena are the sum of a small number of random or chaotic influences, much data is approximately normally distributed. For instance, the flight of a projectile is influenced by small gusts of wind, encounters with small particles, etc. The *normal* density function is

$$f_X(x) = \frac{1}{\sigma\sqrt{2\pi}} e^{-(1/2)[(x-\mu)/\sigma]^2}.$$

The density is positive for $-\infty < x < \infty$. The parameters of the density are $-\infty < \mu < \infty$ and $\sigma > 0$. When $\mu = 0$ and $\sigma = 1$, the density is called the *standard normal* density. The normal density is also known as the *Gaussian* density.

4. Another standard continuous density is the *uniform*, which is the density for the coin tossing example of Subsection 1.1.3. It is

$$f_X(x) = (b-a)^{-1} I_{(a,b]}(x).$$

The domain of the uniform density is either $-\infty < x < \infty$ or $a < x \leq b$, depending on one's point of view. It is positive for $a < x \leq b$. The parameters are $-\infty < a < b < \infty$.

Additional examples are listed in the Appendix. From the examples, we see that it is possible to arrive at a density without a detailed description of the underlying probability space $(\Omega, \mathcal{F}, P)$.

For problems in which a density function is not available, it would be desirable to have some similarly convenient mechanism for specifying probabilities on the real line. The distribution function is such a mechanism.

Definition 3.1. The *distribution function* F_X of a random variable X is defined by

$$F_X(x) = P\{\omega: X(\omega) \leq x\} = P_X(-\infty, x].$$

Rather than writing $P\{\omega: X(\omega) \leq x\}$ or $P_X(-\infty, x]$ as above, it is common to write $P(X \leq x)$ to mean either as determined by context. In this notation, $P(a < X \leq b) = P\{\omega: a < X(\omega) \leq b\} = P_X(a, b]$, $P(a < X < b) = P\{\omega: a < X(\omega) < b\} = P_X(a, b)$, and so on.

For a discrete random variable with density f_X, the distribution function is computed as

$$F_X(x) = \sum_{x_i \leq x} f_X(x_i).$$

For a continuous random variable with density f_X, the distribution function is computed as

$$F_X(x) = \int_{-\infty}^{x} f_X(t)\, dt.$$

From $F_X(x) = \int_{-\infty}^{x} f_X(t)\, dt$ we have that

$$f_X(t) = \frac{d}{dx} F_X(x)$$

for continuous random variables.

The distribution functions for the four examples above—normal, uniform, hypergeometric, and binomial—are plotted in Figure 3.1. The normal, uniform, and binomial distributions are commonly denoted by $N(x|\mu, \sigma^2)$, $U(x|a, b)$, and $B(x|n, p)$, respectively. Often the argument x is suppressed: $N(\mu, \sigma^2)$, $U(a, b)$, and $B(n, p)$. The corresponding densities are denoted by lowercase equivalents: $n(x|\mu, \sigma^2)$, $u(x|a, b)$, $h(x|n, D, N)$, and $b(x|n, p)$. The standard normal distribution, $N(x|0, 1)$, is often denoted by $\Phi(x)$ and its density by $\phi(x)$.

The distribution function satisfies the following properties.

Proposition 3.1. *If F_X is a distribution function, then*

1. $\lim_{x\to-\infty} F_X(x) = 0$ *and* $\lim_{x\to\infty} F_X(x) = 1$.
2. $F_X(x)$ *is a nondecreasing function of x. That is, if $s < t$, then* $F_X(s) \leq F_X(t)$.
3. $F_X(x)$ *is right continuous. That is, for every* x_0,

$$\lim_{\substack{h\to 0\\ h>0}} F_X(x_0 + h) = F_X(x_0).$$

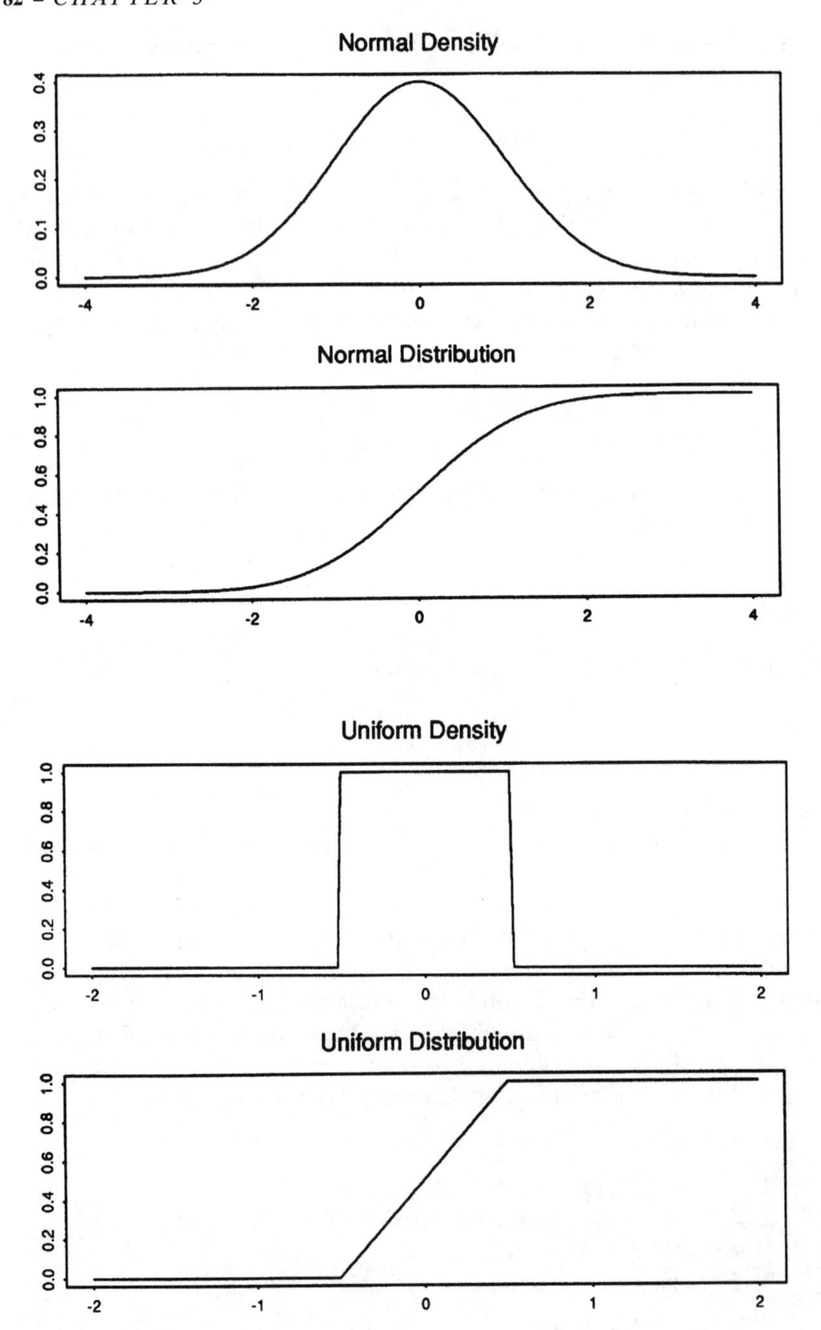

Figure 3.1. Density and distribution functions. Parameters are as follows: Normal, $\mu = 0$, $\sigma^2 = 1$; uniform, $a = -1/2$, $b = 1/2$; hypergeometric, $N = 15$, $D = 5$, $n = 5$; and binomial, $p = 1/3$, $n = 5$.

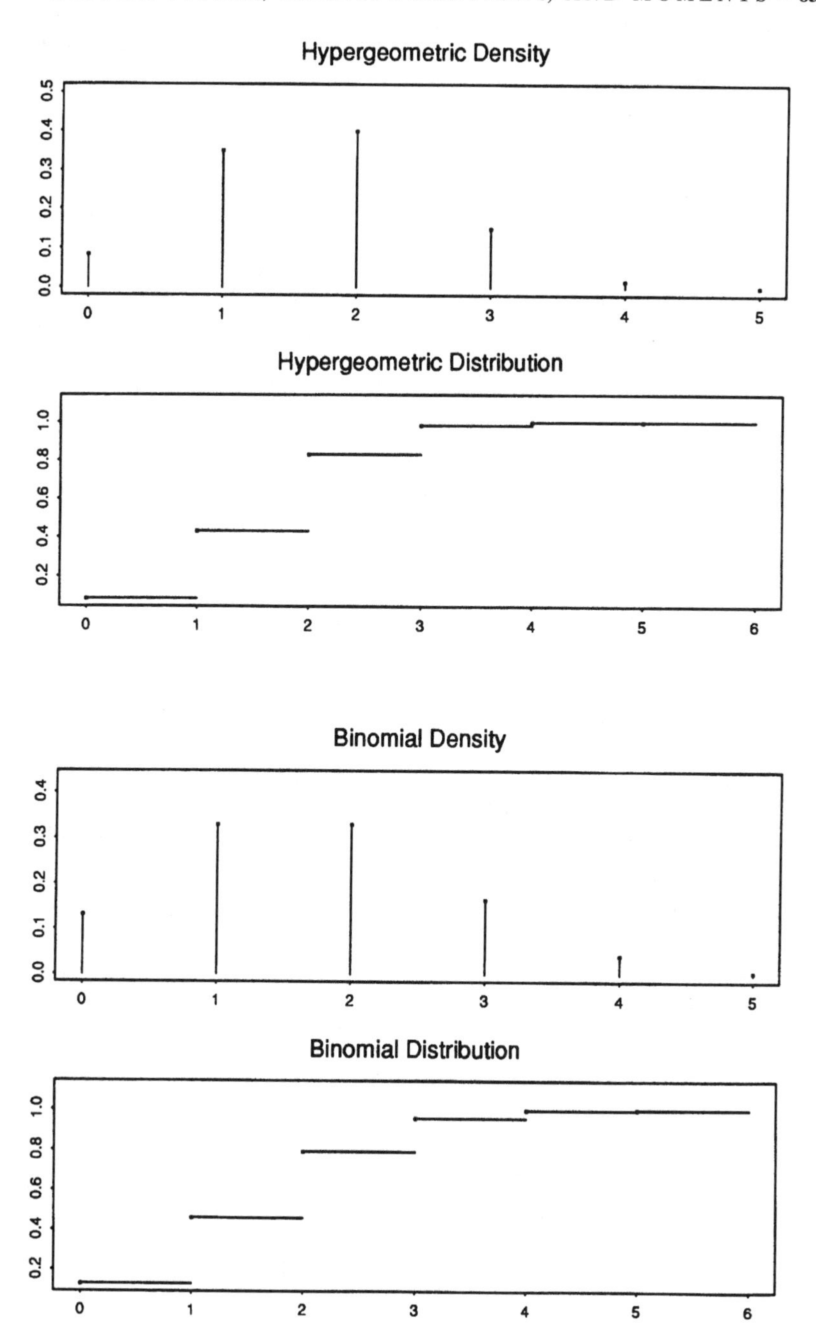

Figure 3.1. (*Continued*).

More interesting, from our perspective, is that if $F_X(x)$ is a function that satisfies the three properties listed in Proposition 3.1, then there is a probability space $(\Omega^*, \mathcal{F}^*, P^*)$ and a random variable X such that $F_X(x) = P(X \le x)$. The proof is not difficult and proceeds exactly along the same lines as in Section 1.4: One puts $\Omega^* = (-\infty, \infty)$ and takes $\mathcal{F}^*$ to be the Borel sets. For each A of the form $A = \bigcup_{i=1}^{\infty}(a_i, b_i]$ where the $(a_i, b_i]$ are disjoint, one puts $P^*(A) = \sum_{i=1}^{\infty}[F_X(b_i) - F_X(a_i)]$. The probability of $F \in \mathcal{F}^*$ is the infimum of the probabilities of all such sets A that contain F. The requisite random variable is $X(\omega) = \omega$. With this construction, there is no difference between $(\Omega^*, \mathcal{F}^*, P^*)$ and $(\mathcal{X}, \mathcal{A}, P_X)$ given by Theorem 2.1; one is just a copy of the other.

We could continue with this development exactly as in Subsection 2.4.4 and construct the integral $\int g(\omega)\, dP^*(\omega)$ on $(\Omega^*, \mathcal{F}^*, P^*)$, which is also the integral $\int g(x)\, dP_X(x)$ on $(\mathcal{X}, \mathcal{A}, P_X)$ because $(\mathcal{X}, \mathcal{A}, P_X)$ is a copy of $(\Omega^*, \mathcal{F}^*, P^*)$. A common notation for $\int g(x)\, dP_X(x)$ is $\int g(x)\, dF_X(x)$. It is called the *Lebesque-Stieltjes integral*. In fact, even if we start with $(\Omega, \mathcal{F}, P)$, get P_X from Theorem 2.1, and get F_X from P_X using Definition 3.1, we can still construct $(\Omega^*, \mathcal{F}^*, P^*)$ and thereby define $\int g(x)\, dF_X(x)$. The interpretation of the integral is that $Y = g(X)$ is a random variable defined on $(\mathcal{X}, \mathcal{A}, P_X)$ and the integral is its expectation: $\mathcal{E}Y = \int g(x)\, dF_X(x)$. A common notation for $\mathcal{E}Y$ is $\mathcal{E}g(X)$. As a practical matter, the details of the construction of $\int g(x)\, dF_X(x)$ can be ignored because $\int g(x)\, dF_X(x)$ is usually computed using density functions as described below. These results mean that we need not bother with $(\Omega, \mathcal{F}, P)$. We can start a problem by writing down a distribution function F_X that satisfies the three properties of Proposition 3.1 and the entire structure described in Chapters 1 and 2 becomes available automatically. This is the convenience we were looking for.

Regardless of how we got F_X—by specifying F_X or f_X directly or by starting from a probability space $(\Omega, \mathcal{F}, P)$—if X is a discrete random variable with density f_X, then

$$\mathcal{E}g(X) = \int g(x)\, dF_X(x) = \sum_{i=1}^{N} g(x_i) f_X(x_i).$$

Similarly, regardless of how we got F_X, if X is a continuous random variable with density f_X, then

$$\mathcal{E}g(X) = \int g(x)\, dF_X(x) = \int_{-\infty}^{\infty} g(x) f_X(x)\, dx.$$

If X is a general random variable with a distribution function F_X such as is shown in Figure 3.2, then it is necessary to decompose F_X into a

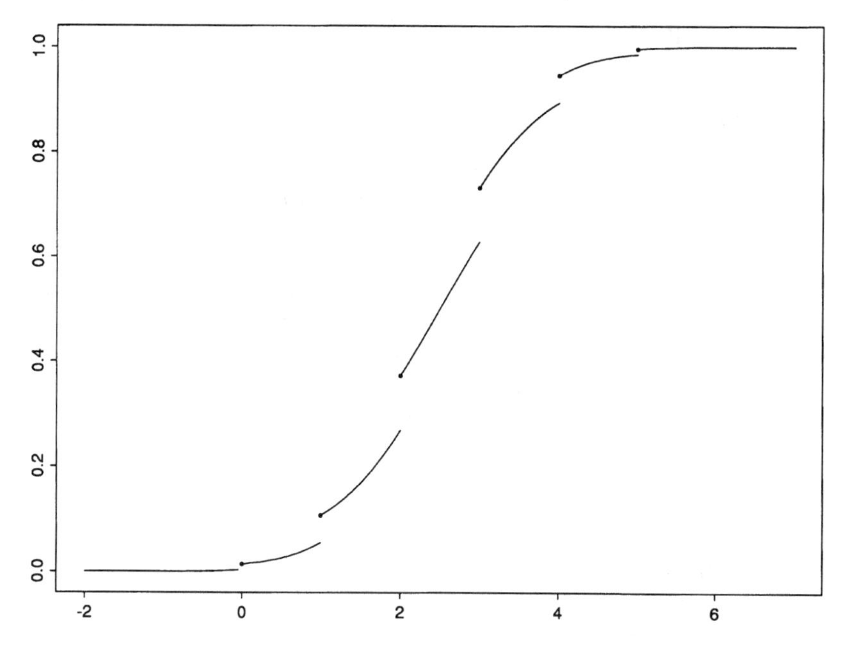

Figure 3.2. Distribution function of a general random variable. The distribution shown is a mixture of a normal distribution with parameters $\mu = 2.5$ and $\sigma^2 = 1$ and a binomial distribution with parameters $p = 1/2$, $n = 5$. The mixing proportions are 0.34 binomial, 0.66 normal.

discrete and a continuous part, apply the two formulas above, and then average the two results using weights that reflect the contribution of the discrete and continuous parts of the distribution. We can illustrate using Figure 3.2. In the figure, jumps occur at $x_i = 0, 1, \ldots, 5$. Let p_i for $i = 1, \ldots, N$ be the heights of the jumps, set $p = \sum_{i=1}^{N} p_i$, and put $f_d(x_i) = p_i/p$. In Figure 3.2, the p_i are 0.01, 0.05, 0.11, 0.11, 0.05, 0.01, and their sum is $p = 0.34$. Remove the jumps from F_X using the formula $F_c(x) = [F_X(x) - \sum_{x_i \le x} p_i]/(1 - p)$. Assuming that $F_c(x)$ is differentiable, put $f_c(x) = (d/dx)F_c(x)$. Then

$$\begin{aligned} \mathscr{E}g(X) &= \int g(x)\, dF_X(x) \\ &= p\sum_{i=1}^{N} g(x_i) f_d(x_i) + (1-p)\int_{-\infty}^{\infty} g(x) f_c(x)\, dx. \end{aligned}$$

Often $F_c(x)$ is differentiable except at the points x_i where the distribution jumps. In this case, break the region of integration up into pieces and compute the integral using the formula

$$\int_{-\infty}^{\infty} g(x)f_c(x)\,dx$$

$$= \int_{-\infty}^{x_1} g(x)f_c(x)\,dx + \sum_{i=1}^{N-1} \int_{x_i}^{x_{i+1}} g(x)f_c(x)\,dx + \int_{x_N}^{\infty} g(x)f_c(x)\,dx.$$

The points where the distribution is not differentiable do not necessarily have to occur at jump points. This method of breaking the region of integration up into pieces will work regardless of where they occur. Also, N above does not have to be finite, the ideas extend to the case where there are a countable number of isolated jumps.

3.1.2 *Mixtures*

A random variable X with distribution such as is shown in Figure 3.2 can be generated by tossing a coin that lands heads with probability p then sampling f_d if the coin lands heads and sampling f_c if it lands tails. Distributions of this sort are called *mixtures*.

Another example of a mixture is the random variable U with density $f_U(u) = \int_{-\infty}^{\infty} f_X(u-y)f_Y(y)\,dy$, where f_X and f_Y are densities of continuous random variables. Similarly, $f_V(v) = \sum_{j=1}^{N}(1/y_j)f_X(v/y_j)f_Y(y_j)$ is a mixture where f_X is a continuous density and f_Y is discrete with $y_j > 0$. All mixtures have this flavor: sample one density and then conditionally upon the outcome sample another. U would be generated by sampling Y to get y and then sampling $f_{U|Y}(u|y) = f_X(u-y)$ to get u. V would be generated by sampling Y to get y_j and then sampling $f_{V|Y}(v|y) = (1/y_j)f_X(v/y_j)$ to get v.

3.1.3 *Quantiles*

The αth *quantile* is the solution x_α of the equation $F_X(x) = \alpha$. If the equation $F_X(x) = \alpha$ has more than one solution, then the infimum of the set of solutions is taken as the quantile. If the equation $F_X(x) = \alpha$ has no solution, then define $x_\alpha = \inf\{x: \alpha \le F_X(x)\}$. Notice that the definition $x_\alpha = \inf\{x: \alpha \le F_X(x)\}$ also gives the correct result when the equation $F_X(x) = \alpha$ has one or more solutions. The function $x_\alpha = Q_X(\alpha)$ defined by this recipe is called the *quantile function* of the random variable X:

$$Q_X(\alpha) = \inf\{x: \alpha \le F_X(x)\}.$$

The quantile function $Q_X(\alpha)$ is sometimes denoted by $F_X^{-1}(\alpha)$ and $Q_X(\alpha)$ does agree with the standard definition of an inverse function when the inverse function exists.

The *median* is the 0.5 quantile. It divides the population that F_X represents in half if $F_X(x) = \alpha$ has a solution, and nearly does so if not. The *quartiles* are the quantiles 0.25, 0.5, and 0.75. The *interquartile range* is $x_{.75} - x_{.25}$.

3.1.4 *Multivariate Distribution Functions*

For multivariate random variables, the development is analogous to Subsection 3.1.1.

The distribution function of a bivariate random variable is defined by $F_{X,Y}(x, y) = P(X \le x, Y \le y)$. If X and Y are discrete with joint density $f_{X,Y}(x_i, y_j)$, then $F_{X,Y}(x, y) = \sum_{x_i \le x} \sum_{y_j \le y} f_{X,Y}(x_i, y_j)$. If X and Y are continuous with joint density $f_{X,Y}(x, y)$, then $F_{X,Y}(x, y) = \int_{-\infty}^{x} \int_{-\infty}^{y} f_{X,Y}(s, t)\, ds\, dt$ and $f_{X,Y}(x, y) = (\partial^2/\partial x\, \partial y) F_{X,Y}(x, y)$. The formula for the probability of a rectangle is $P(a_x < X \le b_x, a_y < Y \le b_y) = F_{X,Y}(b_x, b_y) - F_{X,Y}(a_x, b_y) - F_{X,Y}(b_x, a_y) + F_{X,Y}(a_x, a_y)$.

In general we have the following definition.

Definition 3.2. The *joint distribution function* $F_{X_1,\ldots,X_n}$ of a finite sequence of random variables $X_1, X_2, \ldots, X_n$ is defined by

$$\begin{aligned} F_{X_1,\ldots,X_n}(x_1, \ldots, x_n) &= P\left(\bigcap_{i=1}^{n} \{\omega : X_i(\omega) \le x_i\}\right) \\ &= P_{X_1,\ldots,X_n}(-\infty, x_1] \times \cdots \times (-\infty, x_n]. \end{aligned}$$

The joint distribution satisfies properties that are analogous to those listed in Proposition 3.1. And, if a function satisfies these properties, then, as above, there exists a probability space $(\Omega^*, \mathcal{F}^*, P^*)$ with $\Omega^* = \Re^n$ and random variables $X_1, X_2, \ldots, X_n$ for which it is the distribution.

3.2 Independent Random Variables

The conditional density $f_{Y|X}(y|x)$ represents what is known about Y when one is permitted to observe X. Among other things, it can be used to compute the conditional expectation of Y given X, which is the optimal predictor of Y as we saw in Section 2.5. For $f_{Y|X}(y|x)$ to contain information about Y it must depend upon x. Otherwise, for instance, the conditional expectation of Y given X would not depend upon x and would be useless for prediction. If Y independent of X is taken to mean that we learn nothing about Y when we observe X, then we are led to conclude that Y independent of X means that the conditional density does not upon x. Thus, independence means $f_{Y|X}(y|x) = g(y)$ for some function $g(y)$.

If $f_{Y|X}(y|x) = g(y)$, then the joint density factors as

$$f_{X,Y}(x, y) = g(y) f_X(x) \tag{3.1}$$

because $f_{Y|X}(y|x) = f_{X,Y}(x, y)/f_X(x)$. We know that $g(y)$ is the marginal density of Y because upon integrating or summing both sides of Equation (3.1), whichever is appropriate, we get $f_Y(y) = g(y)$. Therefore, independence implies that the joint density factors into the product of the marginal densities. Conversely, if the joint density factors into the product of the marginal densities, then $f_{Y|X}(y|x)$ does not depend on x because $f_{Y|X}(y|x) = f_{X,Y}(x, y)/f_X(x) = f_Y(y)f_X(x)/f_X(x) = f_Y(y)$. We adopt this factorization result as our formal definition of independence.

Definition 3.3. Two random variables X and Y are *independent* if and only if their joint distribution function factors into the product of the marginal distributions

$$F_{X,Y}(x, y) = F_X(x) F_Y(y).$$

If the random variables possess densities, then X and Y are *independent* if and only if their joint density function factors into the product of the marginal densities

$$f_{X,Y}(x, y) = f_X(x) f_Y(y).$$

To show independence for continuous random variables, according to this definition, one is obligated to show that (i) $f_{X,Y}(x, y) = f_X(x) f_Y(y)$, (ii) $\int_{-\infty}^{\infty} f_{X,Y}(x, y)\, dx = f_Y(y)$, and (iii) $\int_{-\infty}^{\infty} f_{X,Y}(x, y)\, dy = f_X(x)$. Similarly for discrete random variables.

As an example, consider the uniform distribution on the unit square with density

$$f_{X,Y}(x, y) = I_{(0,1]\times(0,1]}(x, y).$$

This is the density for tossing two different coins that was discussed in Section 1.4. Because

(i) $I_{(0,1]\times(0,1]}(x, y) = I_{(0,1]}(x)I_{(0,1]}(y)$,
(ii) $\int_{-\infty}^{\infty} I_{(0,1]\times(0,1]}(x, y)\,dy = I_{(0,1]}(x)$,
(iii) $\int_{-\infty}^{\infty} I_{(0,1]\times(0,1]}(x, y)\,dx = I_{(0,1]}(y)$,

the random variables X and Y are independent. Knowing the outcome of the first toss tells us nothing about the outcome of the second toss.

Consider the density f_{XY} from Subsection 2.3.2 where X is the catch on one 8-spot keno ticket and Y the catch on another when the two tickets have no spots in common. Subsection 2.3.2 gives the joint density as

$$f_{X,Y}(i, j) = \frac{\binom{8}{i}\binom{8}{j}\binom{64}{20-i-j}}{\binom{80}{20}}$$

and the marginal densities as

$$f_X(i) = \frac{\binom{8}{i}\binom{72}{20-i}}{\binom{80}{20}}, \qquad f_Y(j) = \frac{\binom{8}{j}\binom{72}{20-j}}{\binom{80}{20}}.$$

Now

$$f_{X,Y}(i, j) = \frac{\binom{8}{i}\binom{8}{j}\binom{64}{20-i-j}}{\binom{80}{20}} \neq \frac{\binom{8}{i}\binom{72}{20-i}}{\binom{80}{20}} \frac{\binom{8}{j}\binom{72}{20-j}}{\binom{80}{20}} = f_X(i)f_Y(j)$$

because

$$\binom{80}{20}\binom{64}{20-i-j} \neq \binom{72}{20-i}\binom{72}{20-j}.$$

For instance, put $i = j = 0$ and the inequality is seen at sight. Thus, the two random variables X and Y are not independent. If we get to look at the catch of one of the tickets, then we know something about the catch of the other.

Theorem 3.1. *If X and Y are independent, then $\mathscr{E}[g(X)h(Y)] = \mathscr{E}g(X)\mathscr{E}h(Y)$ and $\mathscr{E}[h(Y)|X] = \mathscr{E}h(Y)$ provided the expectations exist.*

Proof. We will consider the case when X and Y are continuous random variables with joint density $f_{XY} = f_X f_Y$. In that case

$$\begin{aligned}
\mathscr{E}[h(Y)|X] &= \int h(y) f_{Y|X}(y,x)\,dy = \int h(y)\frac{f_{XY}(x,y)}{f_X(x)}\,dy \\
&= \int h(y)\frac{f_X(x)f_Y(y)}{f_X(x)}\,dy = \int h(y)f_Y(y)\,dy \\
&= \mathscr{E}h(Y) \\
\mathscr{E}[g(X)h(Y)] &= \int\int g(x)h(y)f_X(x)f_Y(y)\,dx\,dy \\
&= \int g(x)f_X(x)\,dx \int h(y)f_Y(y)\,dy \\
&= \mathscr{E}g(X)\mathscr{E}h(Y).
\end{aligned}$$

□

Definition 3.4. The random variables $X_1, X_2, \ldots, X_n$ are *independent* if and only if their joint distribution function factors into the product of the marginal distribution functions

$$F_{X_1,\ldots,X_n}(x_1,\ldots,x_n) = \prod_{i=1}^{n} F_{X_i}(x_i).$$

If the random variables possess densities, then the random variables $X_1, X_2, \ldots, X_n$ are independent if and only if their joint density function factors into the product of the marginal density functions

$$f_{X_1,\ldots,X_n}(x_1,\ldots,x_n) = \prod_{i=1}^{n} f_{X_i}(x_i).$$

3.3 Transformations

In this section we discuss the situation where we have a random variable X with density f_X and should like to find the density f_Y of a random variable Y defined by $Y = g(X)$, where $g(x)$ is some function such as $\log(x)$. Actually, this situation is no different than that described in Section 2.1 where we transferred considerations from the probability space $(\Omega, \mathscr{F}, P)$ to the probability space $(\mathscr{X}, \mathscr{A}, P_X)$ by means of Theorem 2.1. Here, effectively what we shall be doing is transferring considerations from the probability space $(\mathscr{X}, \mathscr{A}, P_X)$ to the probability space

$(\mathcal{Y}, \mathcal{B}, P_Y)$ by means of Theorem 2.1, although we shall be somewhat less formal and shall rely upon examples to present the ideas.

3.3.1 *Discrete Univariate*

For a discrete random variable X with density f_X, finding the density f_Y of the random variable $Y = g(X)$ is primarily a bookkeeping problem. Let $\mathcal{X} = \{x_1, x_2, \ldots\}$ be the set of points for which $f_X(x_i)$ is positive, which is either finite or countable. The image of $\mathcal{X}$ under g is

$$\mathcal{Y} = g(\mathcal{X}) = \{y_j \colon y_j = g(x_i), x_i \in \mathcal{X}\},$$

which is the set of points on which f_Y is positive. For each y_j in $\mathcal{Y}$,

$$f_Y(y_j) = \sum_{x_i \in g^{-1}\{y_j\}} f_X(x_i).$$

Thus, what is required is to determine the set $\mathcal{Y}$ and then to determine the inverse image $g^{-1}\{y_j\}$ for each y_j in $\mathcal{Y}$.

As an example, consider the binomial density

$$f_X(x) = \binom{n}{x} p^x (1-p)^{n-x}$$

with parameters n and p which is positive on the set

$$\mathcal{X} = \{0, 1, \ldots, n\}.$$

If $g(x) = n - x$ and $Y = g(X)$, then

$$\mathcal{Y} = g(\mathcal{X}) = \{0, 1, \ldots, n\}.$$

For each $y \in \mathcal{Y}$ the inverse image is the single point $x = n - y$ so that

$$f_Y(y) = \binom{n}{n-y} p^{n-y} (1-p)^y = \binom{n}{y} q^y (1-q)^{n-y}$$

where $q = 1 - p$. Thus, the random variable Y has the binomial density with parameters n and q.

3.3.2 *Discrete Bivariate*

We will use the *Poisson density* to construct a bivariate example. The Poisson density has a variety of applications, one of which is modelling the number of occurrences per unit time. For example, one might use it to model the number of passengers that arrive in a given hour at a bus stop when λ passengers are expected to arrive per hour on average. The density is

$$f_X(x) = \frac{e^{-\lambda}\lambda^x}{x!}.$$

The density is positive for the integers $x = 0, 1, \ldots$. The parameter of the density is λ, which is a positive real number.

Let X and Y be independent Poisson random variables with parameters θ and λ, respectively. The joint density is

$$f_{X,Y}(x, y) = \frac{e^{-\theta}\theta^x}{x!}\frac{e^{-\lambda}\lambda^y}{y!}.$$

The set of points where the density is positive is

$$\mathscr{D} = \{(x, y): x = 0, 1, \ldots; y = 0, 1, \ldots\}.$$

Consider the random variables $U = X + Y$ and $V = Y$. That is, $(U, V) = g(X, Y)$, where $g_1(x, y) = x + y$ and $g_2(x, y) = y$. If (x, y) is in $\mathscr{D}$, then $(u, v) = (x + y, y)$ so $u \geq v$ and the image of $\mathscr{D}$ under g is

$$\mathscr{R} = g(\mathscr{D}) = \{(u, v): u \geq v; u = 0, 1, \ldots; v = 0, 1, \ldots\}.$$

For $(u, v) \in \mathscr{R}$, $g^{-1}\{(u, v)\}$ consists of the single point $(x, y) = (u - v, v)$. The density of (U, V) is therefore

$$f_{U,V}(u, v) = \frac{e^{-\theta}\theta^{u-v}}{(u - v)!}\frac{e^{-\lambda}\lambda^v}{v!}.$$

The marginal density $f_U(u)$, which is the density function of the sum of two independent Poisson random variables, is of interest. It is obtained by summing $f_{U,V}(u, v)$ over v. For each fixed u, v ranges over the points $v = 0, \ldots, u$. Therefore,

$$f_U(u) = \sum_{v=0}^{u} \frac{e^{-\theta}\theta^{u-v}}{(u - v)!}\frac{e^{-\lambda}\lambda^v}{v!} = e^{-\lambda-\theta} \sum_{v=0}^{u} \frac{\theta^{u-v}\lambda^v}{(u - v)!v!}.$$

We can evaluate the sum by means of the *binomial theorem* which states that

$$(x+y)^m = \sum_{i=0}^{m} \binom{m}{i} x^i y^{m-i}.$$

Multiplying and dividing by $u!$, we have

$$f_U(u) = \frac{e^{-\lambda-\theta}}{u!} \sum_{v=0}^{u} \binom{u}{v} \theta^{u-v} \lambda^v = \frac{e^{-(\lambda+\theta)}(\theta+\lambda)^u}{u!}.$$

We see that the sum of two independent Poisson random variables with parameters θ and λ, respectively, is a Poisson random variable with parameter $\theta+\lambda$.

3.3.3 *Continuous Univariate*

If a continuous random variable X is transformed by an increasing, differentiable function g to obtain the random variable $Y = g(X)$, then

$$F_Y(y) = P(Y \le y) = P[g(X) \le y] = P[X \le g^{-1}(y)] = F_X[g^{-1}(y)].$$

Differentiating, we obtain

$$f_Y(y) = \frac{d}{dx} F_X[g^{-1}(y)] \frac{d}{dy} g^{-1}(y) = f_X[g^{-1}(y)] \frac{d}{dy} g^{-1}(y).$$

The region $\mathscr{X}$ where f_X is positive is called the *support* of the density f_X. The support of the density f_Y is the image $\mathscr{Y} = g(\mathscr{X})$ of $\mathscr{X}$ under g.

If a continuous random variable X is transformed by a decreasing, differentiable function g to obtain the random variable $Y = g(X)$, then

$$\begin{aligned} F_Y(y) = P(Y \le y) = P[g(X) \le y] &= P[X \ge g^{-1}(y)] \\ &= 1 - F_X[g^{-1}(y)]. \end{aligned}$$

Differentiating, we obtain

$$f_Y(y) = -\frac{d}{dx} F_X[g^{-1}(y)] \frac{d}{dy} g^{-1}(y) = -f_X[g^{-1}(y)] \frac{d}{dy} g^{-1}(y).$$

These results may also be obtained by using Theorem 2.1 and the change of variable formula as in Subsection 2.2. Suppose $g(x)$ is an increasing function. Then

$$P_Y(B) = P_X[g^{-1}(B)] = \int_{\mathscr{X}} I_B[g(x)] f_X(x)\, dx.$$

Applying the change of variable formula

$$x = g^{-1}(y) \qquad dx = \left[\frac{d}{dy} g^{-1}(y)\right] dy \qquad \mathscr{Y} = g(\mathscr{X}),$$

we have

$$\begin{aligned} P_Y(B) &= \int_{\mathscr{X}} I_B[g(x)] f_X(x)\, dx \\ &= \int_{\mathscr{Y}} I_B(y) f_X[g^{-1}(y)] \frac{d}{dy} g^{-1}(y)\, dy, \end{aligned}$$

which implies

$$f_Y(y) = f_X[g^{-1}(y)] \frac{d}{dy} g^{-1}(y)$$

as above.

To illustrate, let X have the uniform density $f_X(x) = I_{(0,1)}(x)$ and let $Y = g(X)$ where $g(x) = -\beta \log(x)$ and $\beta > 0$, which is a decreasing function. Then

$$x = e^{-y/\beta} \qquad dx = -\frac{1}{\beta} e^{-y/\beta} \qquad \mathscr{Y} = (0, \infty)$$

and

$$\begin{aligned} P_Y(B) &= \int_0^1 I_B[g(x)]\, dx = -\int_\infty^0 I_B(y) \frac{1}{\beta} e^{-y/\beta}\, dy \\ &= \int_0^\infty I_B(y) \frac{1}{\beta} e^{-y/\beta}\, dy. \end{aligned}$$

The density $f_Y(y) = \beta^{-1} e^{-y/\beta}$, which has support $0 < y < \infty$, is called the *exponential* density with parameter β.

If $g(x)$ is neither an increasing nor decreasing function, then computations become more tedious. What one must do is break the support of f_X up into pieces upon which $g(x)$ is either increasing or decreasing and then apply the change of variable formula to each piece. For example, let X have the standard normal density

$$f_X(x) = (2\pi)^{-(1/2)}e^{-(1/2)x^2}$$

and let $Y = X^2$. The transformation $y = x^2$ is decreasing with inverse $x = -\sqrt{y}$ on the interval $-\infty < x < 0$ and is increasing with inverse $x = \sqrt{y}$ on the interval $0 < x < \infty$. Therefore,

$$\begin{aligned}
P_Y(B) &= \int_{-\infty}^{\infty} I_B(x^2)\, f_X(x)\, dx \\
&= \int_{-\infty}^{0} I_B(x^2)\, f_X(x)\, dx + \int_{0}^{\infty} I_B(x^2)\, f_X(x)\, dx \\
&= \int_{\infty}^{0} I_B(y)\, f_X(-\sqrt{y}) \frac{-1}{2\sqrt{y}}\, dy \\
&\quad + \int_{0}^{\infty} I_B(y)\, f_X(\sqrt{y}) \frac{1}{2\sqrt{y}}\, dy \\
&= \int_{0}^{\infty} I_B(y) \frac{e^{-y/2}}{\sqrt{2\pi}} \frac{1}{2\sqrt{y}}\, dy \\
&\quad + \int_{0}^{\infty} I_B(y) \frac{e^{-y/2}}{\sqrt{2\pi}} \frac{1}{2\sqrt{y}}\, dy \\
&= \int_{0}^{\infty} I_B(y) \frac{e^{-y/2}}{\sqrt{2\pi y}}\, dy.
\end{aligned}$$

The density of Y is $f_Y(y) = e^{-y/2}/\sqrt{2\pi y}$ with support $0 < y < \infty$. This is the density of a chi-squared random variable with one degree of freedom; see the Appendix.

3.3.4 *Continuous Bivariate*

Consider a bivariate transformation

$$\begin{pmatrix} u \\ v \end{pmatrix} = g(x, y) = \begin{pmatrix} g_1(x, y) \\ g_2(x, y) \end{pmatrix}$$

that is a one-to-one mapping of $\mathscr{D}$ onto $\mathscr{R} = g(\mathscr{D})$ with inverse

$$\begin{pmatrix} x \\ y \end{pmatrix} = h(u, v) = \begin{pmatrix} h_1(u, v) \\ h_2(u, v) \end{pmatrix}.$$

The Jacobian of the inverse transformation is defined as

$$J(u, v) = \begin{pmatrix} \dfrac{\partial}{\partial u} h_1(u, v) & \dfrac{\partial}{\partial v} h_1(u, v) \\ \dfrac{\partial}{\partial u} h_2(u, v) & \dfrac{\partial}{\partial v} h_2(u, v) \end{pmatrix}$$

Its determinant is

$$\det J(u, v) = \frac{\partial}{\partial u} h_1(u, v) \frac{\partial}{\partial v} h_2(u, v) - \frac{\partial}{\partial v} h_1(u, v) \frac{\partial}{\partial u} h_2(u, v).$$

We assume that $\det J(u, v)$ is not identically zero on $\mathcal{D}$. The change of variable formula for the transformation g is

$$\int\int_{\mathcal{D}} f(x, y)\, dx\, dy = \int\int_{\mathcal{R}} f[h_1(u, v), h_2(u, v)]\, |\det J(u, v)|\, du\, dv.$$

For a proof see Bartle 1976, Section 45.

As in the univariate case, the bivariate change of variable formula may be used to deduce the density of the random variables $(U, V) = g(X, Y)$. Theorem 2.1 implies

$$P_{U,V}(B) = P_{X,Y}[g^{-1}(B)] = \int\int_{\mathcal{D}} I_B[g(x, y)]\, f_{X,Y}(x, y)\, dx\, dy.$$

Applying the change of variable formula

$$(x, y) = h(u, v) \qquad dx\, dy = |\det J(u, v)|\, du\, dv \qquad \mathcal{R} = g(\mathcal{D}),$$

we have

$$\begin{aligned} P_{U,V}(B) &= \int\int_{\mathcal{D}} I_B[g(x, y)]\, f_{X,Y}(x, y)\, dx\, dy \\ &= \int\int_{\mathcal{R}} I_B(u, v)\, f_{X,Y}[h(u, v)]\, |\det J(u, v)|\, du\, dv \end{aligned}$$

which implies

$$f_{U,V}(u, v) = f_{X,Y}[h(u, v)]\, |\det J(u, v)|.$$

As an example, let X and Y be independent standard normal random variables. The density is $f_{X,Y}(x, y) = (2\pi)^{-1} e^{-(x^2+y^2)/2}$ with support $\mathcal{D} = \{(x, y): -\infty < x < \infty, -\infty < y < \infty\}$. Consider the transformation

$$\begin{aligned} U &= X + Y \\ V &= X - Y, \end{aligned}$$

which is a one-to-one mapping of $\mathscr{D}$ onto $\mathscr{R} = \{(u, v): -\infty < u < \infty, -\infty < v < \infty\}$ with inverse

$$X = \frac{1}{2}(U + V)$$
$$Y = \frac{1}{2}(U - V),$$

Jacobian

$$J(u, v) = \begin{pmatrix} \frac{1}{2} & \frac{1}{2} \\ \frac{1}{2} & -\frac{1}{2} \end{pmatrix},$$

and $\det J(u, v) = -\frac{1}{2}$. Then

$$\begin{aligned} f_{U,V}(u, v) &= \frac{1}{2} f_{X,Y}[(u + v)/2, (u - v)/2] \\ &= (4\pi)^{-1} e^{-[(u+v)^2 + (u-v)^2]/8} \\ &= (4\pi)^{-1} e^{-(u^2 + 2uv + v^2 + u^2 - 2uv + v^2)/8} \\ &= (4\pi)^{-1} e^{-(2u^2 + 2v^2)/8} \\ &= \left[(4\pi)^{-1/2} e^{-u^2/4}\right]\left[(4\pi)^{-1/2} e^{-v^2/4}\right]. \end{aligned}$$

U and V are independent normal random variables, each with mean zero and variance 2.

If the function g is not one-to-one, we must break $\mathscr{D}$ into subregions $\mathscr{D}_1, \mathscr{D}_2, \ldots, \mathscr{D}_N$ on which for each i the mapping $g: \mathscr{D}_i \to \mathscr{R}_i$ is one-to-one and onto. Let $h_i(u, v): \mathscr{R}_i \to \mathscr{D}_i$ denote the inverse mapping on subregion $\mathscr{R}_i$. If $\det J_i(u, v)$ does not vanish on $\mathscr{R}_i$, then

$$\begin{aligned} P_{U,V}(B) &= \sum_{i=1}^{N} \int\int_{\mathscr{D}_i} I_B[g(x, y)] f_{X,Y}(x, y)\, dx\, dy \\ &= \sum_{i=1}^{N} \int\int_{\mathscr{R}_i} I_B(u, v) f_{X,Y}[h_i(u, v)]\, |\det J_i(u, v)|\, du\, dv \\ &= \int\int I_B(u, v) \sum_{i=1}^{N} I_{\mathscr{R}_i}(u, v) f_{X,Y}[h_i(u, v)]\, |\det J_i(u, v)|\, du\, dv \end{aligned}$$

and we conclude that the density is

$$f_{U,V}(u,v) = \sum_{i=1}^{N} I_{\mathcal{R}_i}(u,v)\, f_{X,Y}[h_i(u,v)]\,|\det J_i(u,v)|.$$

3.3.5 *Special Functions*

We conclude this section by applying the change of variable formula to establish some miscellaneous results that are useful later. Specifically, we shall show that the normal density integrates to 1, deduce some properties of the *gamma function*

$$\Gamma(\alpha) = \int_0^\infty t^{\alpha-1} e^{-t}\, dt, \qquad \alpha > 0,$$

and introduce two densities that depend on it.

Consider the integral $\int_{-\infty}^{\infty} e^{-z^2/2}\, dz$. Because $f(z) = e^{-z^2/2}$ is an even function, that is, $f(z) = f(-z)$, we have

$$\int_{-\infty}^{\infty} e^{-z^2/2}\, dz = 2 \int_0^\infty e^{-z^2/2}\, dz.$$

Further,

$$\begin{aligned}\left(\int_0^\infty e^{-z^2/2}\, dz\right)^2 &= \int_0^\infty e^{-x^2/2}\, dx \int_0^\infty e^{-y^2/2}\, dy \\ &= \int_0^\infty \int_0^\infty e^{-(x^2+y^2)/2}\, dx\, dy.\end{aligned}$$

We shall apply the change of variable formula using the transform

$$\begin{aligned} r &= \sqrt{x^2 + y^2} \\ \theta &= \arctan(y/x), \end{aligned}$$

with domain $\mathcal{D} = \{(x, y): 0 < x < \infty, 0 < y < \infty\}$, range $\mathcal{R} = \{(r, \theta): 0 < r < \infty, 0 < \theta < \pi/2\}$, inverse transform

$$\begin{aligned} x &= r\cos\theta \\ y &= r\sin\theta, \end{aligned}$$

Jacobian

$$J(r,\theta)=\begin{pmatrix}\cos\theta & -r\sin\theta\\ \sin\theta & r\cos\theta\end{pmatrix},$$

and $\det J(\theta,r)=r(\cos^2\theta+\sin^2\theta)=r$ to get

$$\begin{aligned}\int_0^\infty\int_0^\infty e^{-(x^2+y^2)/2}\,dx\,dy &= \int_0^{\pi/2}\int_0^\infty re^{-r^2/2}\,dr\,d\theta\\ &=\frac{\pi}{2}(-e^{-r^2/2}|_0^\infty)=\frac{\pi}{2}.\end{aligned}$$

Thus

$$\int_0^\infty e^{-z^2/2}\,dz=\sqrt{\frac{\pi}{2}} \tag{3.2}$$

and

$$\int_{-\infty}^\infty e^{-z^2/2}\,dz=\sqrt{2\pi}. \tag{3.3}$$

Using the change of variable $x=\sigma z+\mu$, $z=(x-\mu)/\sigma$, $dz=(1/\sigma)\,dx$, we obtain

$$\frac{1}{\sigma\sqrt{2\pi}}\int_{-\infty}^\infty e^{-(1/2)[(x-\mu)/\sigma]^2}\,dx=1.$$

We now deduce some facts regarding the gamma function. Using Equation (3.2) and the change of variable $t=z^2/2$, $z=\sqrt{2t}$, $dz=1/\sqrt{2t}\,dt$, we obtain

$$\Gamma\left(\frac{1}{2}\right)=\int_0^\infty t^{-1/2}e^{-t}\,dt=\sqrt{\pi}.$$

Integration by parts

$$\begin{aligned}\int_0^\infty t^\alpha e^{-t}\,dt &= t^\alpha(-e^{-t})|_0^\infty-\int_0^\infty \alpha t^{\alpha-1}(-e^{-t})\,dt\\ &=\alpha\int_0^\infty t^{\alpha-1}e^{-t}\,dt\end{aligned}$$

gives

$$\Gamma(\alpha+1)=\alpha\Gamma(\alpha),\qquad \alpha>0.$$

Thus, if n is a positive integer, we have $\Gamma(n) = (n-1)(n-2)\cdots(2)\Gamma(1)$. Because $\Gamma(1) = \int_0^\infty e^{-t}\,dt = 1$, this implies

$$\Gamma(n) = (n-1)!\,.$$

If n is odd, then

$$\Gamma\left(\frac{n}{2}\right) = \left(\frac{n}{2}-1\right)\left(\frac{n}{2}-2\right)\cdots\left(\frac{3}{2}\right)\left(\frac{1}{2}\right)\sqrt{\pi}.$$

The values $\Gamma(n)$ and $\Gamma(n/2)$ are those most commonly required in statistical applications.

The *gamma* density is

$$f_X(x) = \frac{1}{\Gamma(\alpha)\beta^\alpha} x^{\alpha-1} e^{-x/\beta}.$$

The support of the density is $0 < x < \infty$. The parameters are $\alpha > 0$ and $\beta > 0$. A special case of the gamma density is the *chi-squared* density

$$f_X(x) = \frac{1}{\Gamma(p/2)2^{p/2}} x^{p/2-1} e^{-x/2},$$

where $p = 1, 2, \ldots$ is the parameter, which is usually referred to as the degrees of freedom parameter. Above, we deduced that if X has the standard normal density, then $Y = X^2$ has the density, $f_Y(y) = e^{-y/2}/\sqrt{2\pi y}$, which is a chi-squared density with one degree of freedom.

The *beta density* is

$$f_X(x) = \frac{\Gamma(\alpha+\beta)}{\Gamma(\alpha)\Gamma(\beta)} x^{\alpha-1}(1-x)^{\beta-1}.$$

The support of the density is $0 < x < 1$. The parameters are $\alpha > 0$ and $\beta > 0$.

3.4 Moments and Moment Generating Functions

Definition 3.5. The ith *moment* of the random variable X is

$$\mu_i' = \mathscr{E}(X^i).$$

The ith *central moment* of the random variable X is

$$\mu_i = \mathscr{E}[(X - \mathscr{E}X)^i].$$

The first moment $\mathscr{E}X$ is called the *mean* and is often denoted by μ. The second central moment $\mathscr{E}(X - \mu)^2$ is called the *variance* and is denoted by σ^2 or $\mathrm{Var}(X)$. Its square root is called the *standard deviation* and is denoted by σ. Thus

$$\mu = \mathscr{E}X, \qquad \mathrm{Var}(X) = \mathscr{E}(X - \mu)^2, \qquad \sigma^2 = \mathrm{Var}(X), \qquad \sigma = \sqrt{\mathrm{Var}(X)}.$$

When more than one random variable is under discussion, which is meant is often indicated by a subscript:

$$\mu_Y = \mathscr{E}Y, \qquad \sigma_Y^2 = \mathrm{Var}(Y), \qquad \sigma_Y = \sqrt{\mathrm{Var}(Y)}.$$

It is useful to note that $\mathscr{E}(Y - \mu_Y)^2 = \mathscr{E}[Y(Y - \mu_Y)] - \mu_Y \mathscr{E}(Y - \mu_Y) = \mathscr{E}[Y(Y - \mu_Y)] = \mathscr{E}Y^2 - \mu_Y^2$, which gives the computational formula

$$\mathrm{Var}(Y) = \mathscr{E}(Y^2) - (\mathscr{E}Y)^2.$$

Also, $\mathscr{E}[aY + b - \mathscr{E}(aY + b)]^2 = \mathscr{E}[aY - \mathscr{E}(aY)]^2 = a^2\mathscr{E}[Y - \mathscr{E}(Y)]^2$, which implies

$$\mathrm{Var}(aY + b) = a^2\,\mathrm{Var}(Y).$$

The mean can be interpreted as the best predictor of Y by a constant. That is, $\alpha^* = \mu_Y$ minimizes $\mathrm{MSE}(\alpha) = \mathscr{E}(Y - \alpha)^2$. This is proved by noting that

$$\begin{aligned}
\mathrm{MSE}(\alpha) &= \mathscr{E}(Y - \mu_Y + \mu_Y - \alpha)^2 \\
&= \mathscr{E}(Y - \mu_Y)^2 + \mathscr{E}(\mu_Y - \alpha)^2 + 2\mathscr{E}(Y - \mu_Y)(\mu_Y - \alpha) \\
&= \sigma_Y^2 + (\mu_Y - \alpha)^2 + 2(\mu_Y - \alpha)\mathscr{E}(Y - \mu_Y) \\
&= \sigma_Y^2 + (\mu_Y - \alpha)^2.
\end{aligned}$$

Now $(\mu_Y - \alpha)^2$ is positive except when $\alpha = \mu_Y$. Therefore, $\alpha^* = \mu_Y$ minimizes $\mathrm{MSE}(\alpha)$. The mean squared error of the prediction is $\mathrm{MSE}(\alpha^*) = \sigma_Y^2$. For the normal density, using the change of variable $z = (x - \mu)/\sigma$, $x = \sigma z + \mu$, $dx = \sigma\, dz$, we have

$$\begin{aligned}
\mathscr{E}X &= \int_{-\infty}^{\infty} x(2\pi\sigma^2)^{-(1/2)} e^{-(1/2)[(x-\mu)/\sigma]^2}\, dx \\
&= \int_{-\infty}^{\infty} (\sigma z + \mu)(2\pi)^{-(1/2)} e^{-(1/2)z^2}\, dz.
\end{aligned}$$

Now

$$\int_{-\infty}^{\infty} ze^{-(1/2)z^2}\,dz = -e^{-(1/2)z^2}\Big|_{-\infty}^{\infty} = 0$$

and, from Section 3.3,

$$\int_{-\infty}^{\infty} e^{-(1/2)z^2}\,dz = \sqrt{2\pi}.$$

Thus, $\mathscr{E}X = \mu$ as the notation suggests. Similarly,

$$\begin{aligned}\mathscr{E}(X-\mu)^2 &= \int_{-\infty}^{\infty} (x-\mu)^2(2\pi\sigma^2)^{-1/2}e^{-(1/2)[(x-\mu)/\sigma]^2}\,dx \\ &= \sigma^2(2\pi)^{-1/2}\int_{-\infty}^{\infty} z^2e^{-(1/2)z^2}\,dz.\end{aligned}$$

Using integration by parts,

$$\begin{aligned}\int_{-\infty}^{\infty} z^2e^{-(1/2)z^2}\,dz &= -\int_{-\infty}^{\infty} z(-ze^{-(1/2)z^2})\,dz \\ &= -ze^{-(1/2)z^2}\Big|_{-\infty}^{\infty} + \int_{-\infty}^{\infty} e^{-(1/2)z^2}\,dz = \sqrt{2\pi}.\end{aligned}$$

Thus, $\mathscr{E}(X-\mu)^2 = \sigma^2$. The mean μ changes the location of the normal and the standard deviation σ changes the scale as seen in Figure 3.3.

The first moment of the binomial distribution is computed as follows:

$$\begin{aligned}\mathscr{E}X &= \sum_{x=0}^{n} x\binom{n}{x}p^xq^{n-x} \qquad (q = 1-p) \\ &= \sum_{x=1}^{n} x\frac{n!}{x!(n-x)!}p^xq^{n-x} \\ &= \sum_{x=1}^{n} np\frac{(n-1)!}{(x-1)!(n-x)!}p^{x-1}q^{n-x} \\ &= np\sum_{t=0}^{n-1}\frac{(n-1)!}{t!(n-1-t)!}p^tq^{n-1-t} \\ &= np\sum_{t=0}^{n-1}\binom{n-1}{t}p^tq^{n-1-t} \\ &= np\end{aligned}$$

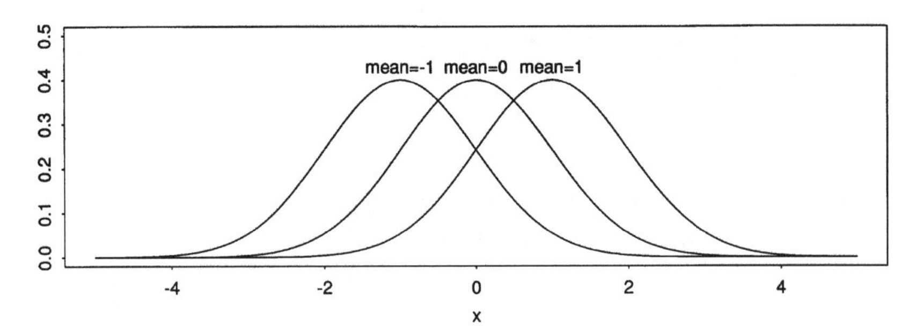

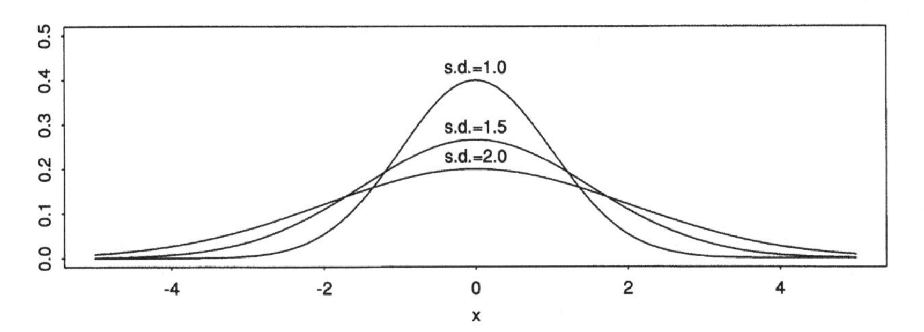

Figure 3.3. The normal density. The upper panel plots the normal density for $\mu = -1, 0, 1$ and $\sigma = 1$. The lower panel plots the normal density for $\mu = 0$ and $\sigma = 1.0, 1.5, 2.0$.

because $\sum_{t=0}^{n-1} \binom{n-1}{t} p^t q^{n-1-t} = 1$. The second moment is computed similarly:

$$
\begin{aligned}
\mathscr{E}X^2 &= \sum_{x=0}^{n} x^2 \binom{n}{x} p^x q^{n-x} \\
&= \sum_{x=1}^{n} x^2 \frac{n!}{x!(n-x)!} p^x q^{n-x} \\
&= \sum_{x=1}^{n} npx \frac{(n-1)!}{(x-1)!(n-x)!} p^{x-1} q^{n-x} \\
&= np \sum_{t=0}^{n-1} (t+1) \frac{(n-1)!}{t!(n-1-t)!} p^t q^{n-1-t} \\
&= np \sum_{t=0}^{n-1} t \binom{n-1}{t} p^t q^{n-1-t} + np \sum_{t=0}^{n-1} \binom{n-1}{t} p^t q^{n-1-t}
\end{aligned}
$$

$$= np(n-1)p + np$$
$$= n^2p^2 - np^2 + np$$
$$= (np)^2 + npq$$

because $\sum_{t=0}^{n-1} t\binom{n-1}{t} p^t q^{n-1-t} = (n-1)p$ and $\sum_{t=0}^{n-1} \binom{n-1}{t} p^t q^{n-1-t} = 1$. Using $\text{Var}(X) = \mathscr{E}X^2 - (\mathscr{E}X)^2 = \mathscr{E}X^2 - (np)^2$, we have $\text{Var}(X) = npq$. In summary, the mean and variance of the binomial distribution are

$$\mathscr{E}X = np, \qquad \text{Var}(X) = npq.$$

From $0 \le \mathscr{E}(X - \mathscr{E}X)^2 = \mathscr{E}X^2 - (\mathscr{E}X)^2$ we have the inequality $(\mathscr{E}X)^2 \le \mathscr{E}X^2$. The generalization of this inequality is *Jensen's inequality* which states that if g is a convex function, then

$$g(\mathscr{E}X) \le \mathscr{E}g(X).$$

A function is convex if $g[\lambda x^o + (1-\lambda)x] \le \lambda g(x^o) + (1-\lambda)g(x)$ for all x, x^o, and $0 < \lambda < 1$. Some examples are x^2, $-\log x$, and e^x. The property of a convex function that gives rise to the inequality is the fact that a convex function plots above any tangent line. For convenience, we will verify Jensen's inequality under the additional assumption that g is differentiable at $\mathscr{E}X$ so that the tangent line at the point $x^o = \mathscr{E}X$ is $y = g(x^o) + g'(x^o)(x - x^o)$. Because $g(x)$ plots above the tangent line we have the inequality

$$g(x^o) + g'(x^o)(X - x^o) \le g(X).$$

Taking expectations of both sides, we have

$$g(x^o) + g'(x^o)\mathscr{E}(X - x^o) \le \mathscr{E}g(X).$$

Because $\mathscr{E}(X - x^o) = \mathscr{E}X - \mathscr{E}X = 0$ we have $g(x^o) \le \mathscr{E}g(X)$, which is Jensen's inequality. The same argument will work using conditional expectation. Thus, if g is a convex function, then

$$g[\mathscr{E}(Y|X)] + g'[\mathscr{E}(Y|X)][Y - \mathscr{E}(Y|X)] \le g(Y)$$

whence

$$g[\mathscr{E}(Y|X)] \le \mathscr{E}[g(Y)|X].$$

The moment generating function, as the name suggests, can be used to calculate moments. It is also useful as an alternative to the methods of Section 3.3 for finding the distribution of a function of a random variable. It is defined as follows.

Definition 3.6. The *moment generating function* of a random variable X is

$$M_X(t) = \mathscr{E}e^{tX}$$

provided that the expectation is finite in some neighborhood of zero; that is, provided $\mathscr{E}e^{tX} < \infty$ for all t in the interval $(-h, h)$ for some small h. The moment generating function of a random vector $X = (X_1, X_2, \ldots, X_n)'$ is

$$M_X(t) = \mathscr{E}e^{t'X}$$

where $t = (t_1, \ldots, t_n)'$ and $t'X = \sum_{i=1}^n t_i X_i$. Again there is the proviso that $\mathscr{E}e^{t'X} < \infty$ for all $(t_1, \ldots, t_n)$ in $(-h, h) \times \cdots \times (-h, h)$ for some small h.

The moment generating function gets its name from the series expansion

$$e^{tX} = 1 + tX + \frac{1}{2!}t^2X^2 + \frac{1}{3!}t^3X^3 + \cdots$$

which suggests that

$$\begin{aligned}
\left.\frac{d^j}{dt^j}M_X(t)\right|_{t=0} &= \left.\mathscr{E}\frac{d^j}{dt^j}e^{tX}\right|_{t=0} \\
&= \mathscr{E}X^j + \left.t\mathscr{E}X^{(j+1)}\right|_{t=0} + \left.t^2\mathscr{E}\frac{1}{2!}X^{(j+2)}\right|_{t=0} + \cdots \\
&= \mathscr{E}X^j + 0\mathscr{E}X^{(j+1)} + 0\frac{1}{2!}\mathscr{E}X^{(j+2)} + \cdots \\
&= \mathscr{E}X^j.
\end{aligned}$$

When the interchange of order of differentiation and expectation $(d^j/dt^j)M_X(t) = \mathscr{E}(d^j/dt^j)e^{tX}$ can be justified, the result

$$\left.\frac{d}{dt^j}M_X(t)\right|_{t=0} = \mathscr{E}X^j$$

can be proved rigorously.

A more general concept than the moment generating function is the *characteristic function*, which is defined as $\phi(t) = \mathscr{E}e^{\iota tX} = \mathscr{E}\cos tX + \iota\mathscr{E}\sin tX$ where ι is the imaginary unit; that is, $\iota^2 = -1$. It has all the properties of the moment generating function that we shall describe below plus the advantage of always existing because the sine and cosine functions are bounded by 1. However, the moment generating function will be adequate for our purposes and it does not require experience with the calculus on the complex plane.

The moment generating function of the normal can be calculated by completing the square as follows:

$$\begin{aligned} M_X(t) &= (2\pi\sigma^2)^{-1/2}\int_{-\infty}^{\infty} e^{tx}e^{-(1/2)(\frac{x-\mu}{\sigma})^2}\,dx \\ &= (2\pi\sigma^2)^{-1/2}\int_{-\infty}^{\infty} e^{-(1/2\sigma^2)(x^2-2\mu x+\mu^2-2\sigma^2 tx)}\,dx \\ &= (2\pi\sigma^2)^{-(1/2)}\int_{-\infty}^{\infty} e^{-(1/2\sigma^2)[x^2-2(\mu+\sigma^2 t)x+(\mu+\sigma^2 t)^2-(\mu+\sigma^2 t)^2+\mu^2]}\,dx \\ &= e^{-(1/2\sigma^2)(-\mu^2-2\mu\sigma^2 t-\sigma^4 t^2+\mu^2)}(2\pi\sigma^2)^{-1/2}\int_{-\infty}^{\infty} e^{-(1/2\sigma^2)[x-(\mu+\sigma^2 t)]^2}\,dx \\ &= e^{\mu t+(1/2)\sigma^2 t^2}. \end{aligned}$$

One can check that $(d/dt)M_X(0) = \mu$ and $(d^2/dt^2)M_X(0) = \mu^2 + \sigma^2$.

The moment generating function of the binomial can be calculated using the binomial theorem as follows:

$$M_X(t) = \sum_{x=0}^{n} e^{tx}\binom{n}{x}p^x q^{n-x} = \sum_{x=0}^{n}\binom{n}{x}(pe^t)^x q^{n-x} = (pe^t + q)^n.$$

The moment generating functions of other common distributions are listed in the Appendix.

The value of the moment generating function stems from the following theorem. The proof is incredibly tedious and will be omitted.

Theorem 3.2. *Let X and Y be two random variables with distribution functions F_X and F_Y that possess moment generating functions M_X and M_Y. If $M_X(t) = M_Y(t)$ in some small neighborhood of zero, then $F_X(u) = F_Y(u)$ for all u.*

In addition, let $X_1, X_2, \ldots$ be a sequence of random variables with distribution functions F_{X_i} and moment generating functions M_{X_i}. If $\lim_{i\to\infty} M_{X_i}(t) = M_Y(t)$ for each t in some small neighborhood of zero, then $\lim_{i\to\infty} F_{X_i}(u) = F_Y(u)$ for all u.

We can illustrate the value of Theorem 3.2 by deriving the distribution of the sum $Z = X + Y$ of two independent chi-squared random variables X and Y with degrees of freedom m and n, respectively. The moment generating function of the chi-squared distribution is $M_X(t) = (1-2t)^{-n/2}$, which exists for $|t| < 1/2$. Now,

$$M_Z(t) = \mathscr{E}e^{t(X+Y)} = \mathscr{E}e^{tX}\mathscr{E}e^{tY} = M_X(t)M_Y(t)$$

by Theorem 3.1. Therefore,

$$M_X(t)M_Y(t) = (1-2t)^{-n/2}(1-2t)^{-m/2} = (1-2t)^{-(m+n)/2}.$$

$M_Z(t) = (1-2t)^{-(m+n)/2}$ is the moment generating function of a chi-squared random variable with degrees of freedom $m + n$. One should attempt to derive this result using the methods of Section 3.3 to see what a labor-saving device moment generating functions can be.

3.5 Covariance and Correlation

Covariance and correlation are measures of linear association between two random variables. They are defined as follows.

Definition 3.7. The *covariance* between the random variables X and Y is

$$\text{Cov}(X, Y) = \mathscr{E}[(X - \mathscr{E}X)(Y - \mathscr{E}Y)].$$

The *correlation* between the random variables X and Y is

$$\rho_{XY} = \frac{\text{Cov}(X, Y)}{\sigma_X \sigma_Y}$$

provided $\sigma_X > 0$ and $\sigma_Y > 0$. It is undefined if $\sigma_X = 0$ or $\sigma_Y = 0$.

From $\mathscr{E}[(X - \mathscr{E}X)(Y - \mathscr{E}Y)] = \mathscr{E}[(X - \mathscr{E}X)Y] = \mathscr{E}XY - \mathscr{E}X\mathscr{E}Y$ we obtain the computational formula

$$\text{Cov}(X, Y) = \mathscr{E}(XY) - (\mathscr{E}X)(\mathscr{E}Y).$$

A common notation for $\text{Cov}(X, Y)$ is σ_{XY}. Note that the covariance of a random variable with itself is the variance: $\text{Var}(X) = \text{Cov}(X, X)$ or $\sigma_X^2 = \sigma_{XX}$. If X and Y are independent, then $\mathscr{E}XY = (\mathscr{E}X)(\mathscr{E}Y)$ by Theorem 3.1, which implies $\text{Cov}(X, Y) = 0$. The converse is not true: $\text{Cov}(X, Y) = 0$ does not imply independence. Panel (c) of Figure 3.4

shows an example of two random variables that are not independent but for which $\text{Cov}(X, Y) = 0$.

The variance of a sum of two random variables is $\mathscr{E}(X + Y - \mu_X - \mu_Y)^2 = \mathscr{E}[(X - \mu_X)^2 + 2(X - \mu_X)(Y - \mu_Y) + (Y - \mu_Y)^2]$, which implies

$$\text{Var}(X + Y) = \text{Var}(X) + 2\,\text{Cov}(X, Y) + \text{Var}(Y).$$

More generally,

$$\text{Cov}\left(\sum_{i=1}^{n} a_i X_i, \sum_{j=1}^{m} b_j Y_j\right) = \sum_{i=1}^{n}\sum_{j=1}^{m} a_i b_j \,\text{Cov}(X_i, Y_j),$$

which implies

$$\begin{aligned}\text{Var}\left(\sum_{i=1}^{n} a_i X_i\right) &= \sum_{i=1}^{n}\sum_{j=1}^{n} a_i a_j \,\text{Cov}(X_i, X_j)\\ &= \sum_{i=1}^{n} a_i^2 \,\text{Var}(X_i) + 2\sum_{i<j} a_i a_j \,\text{Cov}(X_i, X_j).\end{aligned}$$

In Section 2.5 we determined that the best predictor of Y using X was the conditional expectation $\mathscr{E}(Y|X)(x)$. That is, $g^*(x) = \mathscr{E}(Y|X)(x)$ minimizes

$$\text{MSE}(g) = \mathscr{E}[Y - g(X)]^2.$$

Suppose that instead of trying to minimize $\text{MSE}(g)$ over all functions of X, we only consider linear predictors $g(x) = \alpha + \beta x$ and try to minimize

$$\text{MSE}(\alpha, \beta) = \mathscr{E}(Y - \alpha - \beta X)^2.$$

Rewriting this equation as

$$\begin{aligned}\text{MSE}(\alpha, \beta) &= \mathscr{E}[(Y - \mu_Y) - \beta(X - \mu_X) - (\alpha - \mu_Y + \beta\mu_X)]^2\\ &= \sigma_Y^2 + \beta^2\sigma_X^2 + (\alpha - \mu_Y + \beta\mu_X)^2 - 2\beta\,\text{Cov}(X, Y),\end{aligned}$$

we see that $\text{MSE}(\alpha, \beta)$ is a quadratic function of α and β that can be minimized by setting the partial derivatives

$$\frac{\partial}{\partial\alpha}\text{MSE}(\alpha, \beta) = 2(\alpha - \mu_Y + \beta\mu_X)$$

$$\frac{\partial}{\partial\beta}\text{MSE}(\alpha, \beta) = 2\beta\sigma_X^2 + 2(\alpha - \mu_Y + \beta\mu_X)\mu_X - 2\,\text{Cov}(X, Y)$$

to zero and solving for α and β. The solution is

$$\alpha^* = \mu_Y - \beta\mu_X, \qquad \beta^* = \frac{\operatorname{Cov}(X, Y)}{\sigma_X^2}.$$

The prediction equation is

$$Y = \mu_Y + \beta^*(X - \mu_X).$$

The slope of this line, $\beta^* = \sigma_{XY}/\sigma_{XX}$, is called the (population) *regression coefficient*.

The mean squared error of the prediction is

$$\operatorname{MSE}(\alpha^*, \beta^*) = \sigma_Y^2 - (\beta^*)^2\sigma_X^2 = \sigma_Y^2(1 - \rho_{XY}^2). \tag{3.4}$$

Because $0 \le \operatorname{MSE}(\alpha^*, \beta^*)$, we have $0 \le \sigma_Y^2(1 - \rho_{XY}^2)$. Because we require $\sigma_Y > 0$ for ρ_{XY} to be defined, this implies

$$-1 \le \rho_{XY} \le 1.$$

Equation (3.4) defines the sense in which ρ_{XY} is a measure of linear association. If the error from a linear prediction is small, then ρ_{XY} will be close to ± 1 with sign the same as β^*. If $\rho_{XY} = \pm 1$, then the linear fit is perfect because $0 = \operatorname{MSE}(\alpha^*, \beta^*) = \mathscr{E}(Y - \alpha^* - \beta^* X)^2$ implies $0 = P_{X,Y}[(Y - \alpha^* - \beta^* X)^2 > 0] = P_{X,Y}(Y \neq \alpha^* + \beta^* X)$. If the linear prediction is useless in the sense that knowing X is of no more value for predicting Y than knowing $\mathscr{E}Y$, then $\operatorname{MSE}(\alpha^*, \beta^*) = \sigma_Y^2$ and $\rho_{XY} = 0$.

As an aside, one might note that there is no reason to stop with linear prediction. One could also consider quadratic approximation

$$\operatorname{MSE}(\alpha_0, \alpha_1, \alpha_2) = \mathscr{E}\left(Y - \alpha_0 - \alpha_1 X - \alpha_2 X^2\right)^2$$

and find the best quadratic predictor. If one kept this up indefinitely and found the best polynomial predictor $P_N(x) = \sum_{i=1}^N a_i x^i$ for each N, then the limit would be the conditional expectation of Y given X; that is, $\lim_{N\to\infty} P_N(x) = \mathscr{E}(Y|X)(x)$ (Gallant 1980). We shall now illustrate these ideas with an example.

Example 3.1. Consider the random variables

$$Y = g(X) + Z$$
$$X = X,$$

where $g(X)$ is some differentiable function as yet unspecified. Let X and Z be independent random variables where X is distributed uniformly on (0,10) and Z is distributed uniformly on $(-\epsilon, +\epsilon)$.

The domain of the transformation $y = g(x) + z$, $x = x$ is $\mathscr{D} = \{(x, z): 0 < x < 10, -\epsilon < z < \epsilon\}$ and its image is $\mathscr{R} = \{(x, y): g(x) - \epsilon < y < g(x) + \epsilon, 0 < x < 10\}$. The inverse transformation is $z = y - g(x)$, $x = x$ and the determinant of the Jacobian is $\det J(y, x) = 1$ so that $dz\,dx = dy\,dx$. Therefore,

$$f_{XY}(x, y) = \frac{1}{10} I_{(0,10)}(x) \frac{1}{2\epsilon} I_{(-\epsilon, \epsilon)}[y - g(x)].$$

The equation $Y = g(X) + Z$ is an example of a (nonlinear) regression equation, although it is more customary to assume that Z is normally distributed than to assume that it is uniformly distributed. The advantage of the uniform assumption is twofold: (i) The support of $f_{XY}(x, y)$ is bounded and can therefore be plotted and inspected. (ii) The equation $Y = g(X) + Z$ is directly interpretable in that if one is permitted to observe X and knows $g(x)$, then one can predict Y to within $\pm\epsilon$. Figure 3.4 plots the support of $f_{XY}(x, y)$ for three cases: (i) $g(x)$ linear and ϵ small, (ii) $g(x)$ linear and ϵ moderately large, and (iii) $g(x)$ quadratic and ϵ small. Comparing cases (i) and (ii), one can see that ρ_{XY} is a measure of linear association: if there is a linear relationship, then ρ_{XY} is near 1 when the prediction error is small and ρ_{XY} is near zero when the prediction error is large. Looking at case (iii), one can see that ρ_{XY} is not a general measure of association: ρ_{XY} can be zero even when Y is nearly perfectly predictable by using $\mathscr{E}(Y|X)(x)$ as the prediction equation.

We will now compute the correlation coefficient. This computation is somewhat tedious because we are attempting to compute ρ_{XY} for a general function g rather than a specific choice such as $g(x) = x$, which would simplify matters considerably. From the joint density f_{XY} and error density f_Z we compute the following quantities:

$$\mu_Z = \int_{-\epsilon}^{\epsilon} z \frac{1}{2\epsilon} I_{(-\epsilon, \epsilon)}(z)\, dz = z^2/(4\epsilon)\Big|_{-\epsilon}^{\epsilon} = 0$$

$$\sigma_Z^2 = \int_{-\epsilon}^{\epsilon} z^2 \frac{1}{2\epsilon} I_{(-\epsilon, \epsilon)}(z)\, dz = z^3/(6\epsilon)\Big|_{-\epsilon}^{\epsilon} = \frac{\epsilon^2}{3}$$

$$f_X(x) = \int_{g(x)-\epsilon}^{g(x)+\epsilon} \frac{1}{10} I_{(0,10)}(x) \frac{1}{2\epsilon} I_{(-\epsilon, \epsilon)}[y - g(x)]\, dy$$

$$= \frac{1}{10} I_{(0,10)}(x) \int_{-\epsilon}^{\epsilon} \frac{1}{2\epsilon} I_{(-\epsilon, \epsilon)}(z)\, dz = \frac{1}{10} I_{(0,10)}(x)$$

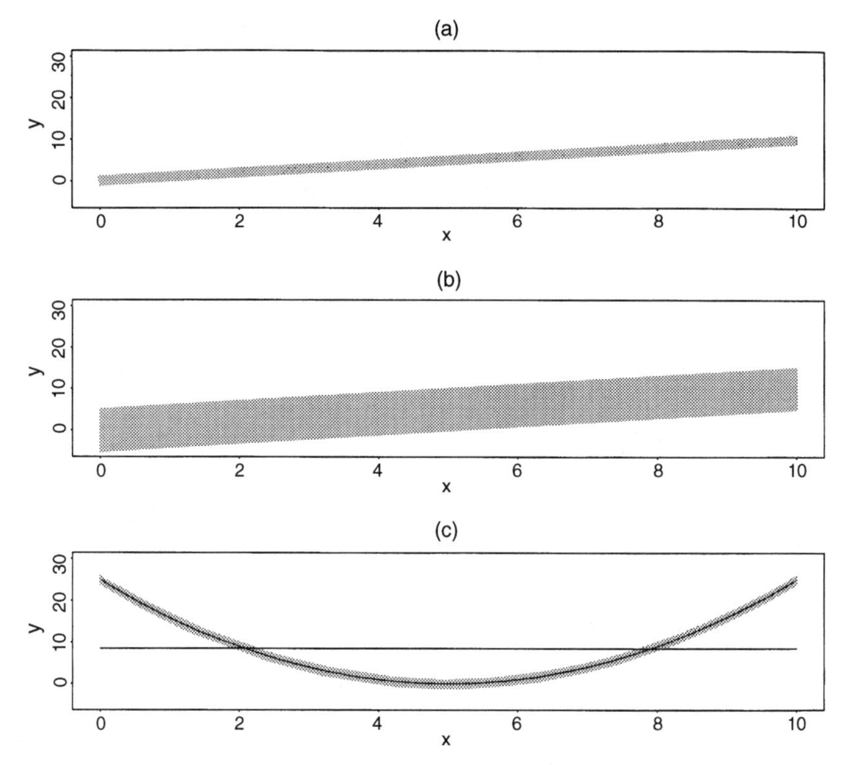

Figure 3.4. Support of the density f_{XY} of Example 3.1. Panel (a) shows the support for $g(x) = x$ and $\epsilon = 1$, which implies $\rho_{XY} = 0.98$. Panel (b) shows the support for $g(x) = x$ and $\epsilon = 5$, which implies $\rho_{XY} = 0.71$. Panel (c) shows the support for $g(x) = (x - 5)^2$ and $\epsilon = 1$, which implies $\rho_{XY} = 0.0$. The horizontal line in panel (c) is the linear predictor $y = \mu_Y + \beta^*(x - \mu_X)$; the line within the shaded region is a plot of the conditional expectation $y = \mathscr{E}(Y|X)(x)$.

$$f_{Y|X}(y|x) = f_{XY}(x, y)/f_X(x) = \frac{1}{2\epsilon} I_{(-\epsilon,\, \epsilon)}[y - g(x)]$$

$$\mu_X = \int_0^{10} x \frac{1}{10} I_{(0,\, 10)}(x)\, dx = x^2/20 \Big|_0^{10} = 5$$

$$\sigma_X^2 = \int_0^{10} x^2 \frac{1}{10} I_{(0,\, 10)}(x)\, dx - \mu_X^2 = x^3/30 \Big|_0^{10} - 25 = \frac{25}{3}$$

$$\mathscr{E}(Y|X)(x) = \int_{g(x)-\epsilon}^{g(x)+\epsilon} y \frac{1}{2\epsilon} I_{(-\epsilon,\, \epsilon)}[y - g(x)]\, dy$$

$$= \int_{-\epsilon}^{\epsilon} [g(x) + z] \frac{1}{2\epsilon} I_{(-\epsilon,\, \epsilon)}(z)\, dz = g(x)$$

$$\mu_Y = \int_0^{10} \mathscr{E}(Y|X)(x)\frac{1}{10}I_{(0,\,10)}(x)\,dx = \frac{1}{10}\int_0^{10} g(x)\,dx$$

$$= \mathscr{E}[g(X)] = \mu_G$$

$$\sigma_Y^2 = \int_0^{10}\int_{g(x)-\epsilon}^{g(x)+\epsilon} [y - g(x) + g(x) - \mu_Y]^2 f_{Y|X}(y|x)\,dy\,f_X(x)\,dx$$

$$= \int_0^{10} \mathrm{Var}(Z) + [g(x) - \mu_Y)]^2 f_X(x)\,dx$$

$$= \mathrm{Var}(Z) + \int_0^{10} [g(x) - \mu_g)]^2 f_X(x)\,dx$$

$$= \mathrm{Var}(Z) + \mathrm{Var}[g(X)] = \sigma_Z^2 + \sigma_G^2$$

$$\sigma_{XY} = \int_0^{10}\int_{g(x)-\epsilon}^{g(x)+\epsilon} (x - \mu_X)(y - \mu_Y) f_{Y|X}(y|x)\,dy\,f_X(x)\,dx$$

$$= \int_0^{10} (x - \mu_X)[g(x) - \mu_Y]\,f_X(x)\,dx$$

$$= \int_0^{10} (x - \mu_X)[g(x) - \mu_G]\,f_X(x)\,dx$$

$$= \mathrm{Cov}[g(X), X] = \sigma_{GX}$$

$$\rho_{XY} = \frac{\sigma_{XY}}{\sigma_X\sigma_Y} = \frac{\sigma_{GX}}{\sigma_X\sqrt{\sigma_Z^2 + \sigma_G^2}} = \frac{\sigma_{GX}}{\sigma_X\sqrt{\epsilon^2/3 + \sigma_G^2}}.$$

If $g(x)$ is the linear function $g(x) = x$, then $\sigma_{GX} = \sigma_{XX} = \sigma_X^2$ and $\sigma_G^2 = \sigma_X^2$ so that

$$\rho_{XY} = \frac{\sigma_X}{\sqrt{\epsilon^2/3 + \sigma_X^2}} = \frac{5}{\sqrt{\epsilon^2 + 25}}.$$

The smaller is ϵ the closer is ρ_{XY} to 1.

If $g(x)$ is the quadratic function $g(x) = (x - 5)^2$, then

$$\sigma_{GX} = \int_0^{10} (x - 5)^2(x - 5)\frac{1}{10}I_{(0,\,10)}(x)\,dx = \int_{-5}^{5} u^3\frac{1}{10}I_{(-5,\,5)}(u)\,du = 0.$$

Regardless of the value of ϵ, ρ_{XY} is zero.

3.6 The Bivariate Normal Distribution

The density function of the bivariate normal is

$$f_{X,Y}(x, y) = \left(2\pi\sigma_X\sigma_Y\sqrt{1-\rho^2}\right)^{-1} \times \exp\left\{-\frac{1}{2(1-\rho^2)}\left[\left(\frac{x-\mu_X}{\sigma_X}\right)^2 - 2\rho\left(\frac{x-\mu_X}{\sigma_X}\right)\left(\frac{y-\mu_Y}{\sigma_Y}\right) + \left(\frac{y-\mu_Y}{\sigma_Y}\right)^2\right]\right\},$$

which looks formidable, and is. Its appearance can be considerably simplified by introducing a matrix notation, as in Section 3.8. However, to accomplish our objective, which is to gain a qualitative understanding of conditional densities, it will take less time to slog through the algebra than to introduce the requisite matrix concepts and notations. The density is plotted in Figure 3.5. If we put

$$u = \frac{y-\mu_Y}{\sigma_Y}, \qquad v = \frac{x-\mu_X}{\sigma_X},$$

the density can be rewritten

$$f_{X,Y}(x, y) = \left(2\pi\sigma_X\sigma_Y\sqrt{1-\rho^2}\right)^{-1} \exp\left\{-\frac{1}{2(1-\rho^2)}\left[u^2 - 2\rho uv + v^2\right]\right\}.$$

Completing the square

$$u^2 - 2\rho uv + v^2 = u^2 - 2\rho vu + \rho^2 v^2 + v^2 - \rho^2 v^2 = (u-\rho v)^2 + (1-\rho^2)v^2,$$

we have

$$\begin{aligned} f_{X,Y}(x, y) &= \left(2\pi\sigma_X\sigma_Y\sqrt{1-\rho^2}\right)^{-1} \times \exp\left\{-\frac{1}{2(1-\rho^2)}\left[(u-\rho v)^2 + (1-\rho^2)v^2\right]\right\} \\ &= \left(\sqrt{2\pi}\sigma_Y\sqrt{1-\rho^2}\right)^{-1} \exp\left\{-\frac{1}{2(1-\rho^2)}(u-\rho v)^2\right\} \\ &\quad \times \left(\sqrt{2\pi}\sigma_X\right)^{-1} \exp\left\{-\frac{1}{2}v^2\right\}. \end{aligned}$$

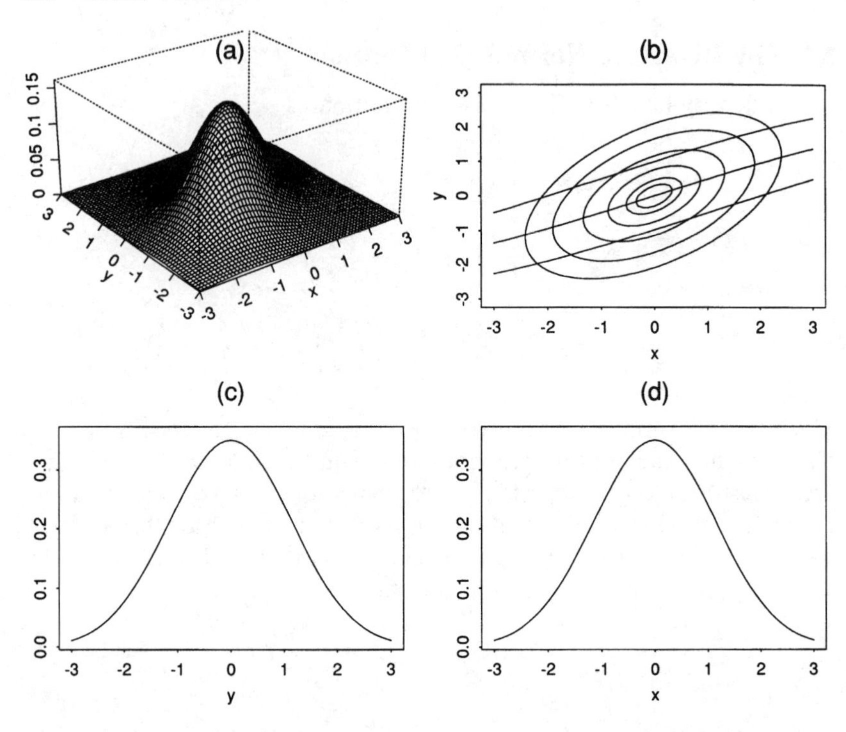

Figure 3.5. Bivariate normal distribution function. The parameters are $\mu_X = 0$, $\mu_Y = 0$, $\sigma_X^2 = 1$, $\sigma_Y^2 = 1$, and $\rho = 0.5$. Panel (a) is a perspective plot of $f_{X,Y}(x, y)$. Panel (b) is a contour plot of $f_{X,Y}(x, y)$. The lines shown in panel (b) are $\mathscr{E}(Y|X)(x)$ (center), $\mathscr{E}(Y|X)(x)$ plus one standard deviation of $f_{Y|X}(y|x)$ (top), and $\mathscr{E}(Y|X)(x)$ minus one standard deviation of $f_{Y|X}(y|x)$ (bottom). Panel (c) is a plot of $f_Y(y)$. Panel (d) is a plot of $f_X(x)$.

Thus, the bivariate normal density factors into the conditional density

$$f_{Y|X}(y|x) = \left(\sqrt{2\pi}\sigma_Y\sqrt{1-\rho^2}\right)^{-1} \times \exp\left\{-\frac{1}{2(1-\rho^2)\sigma_Y^2}\left[y - \mu_Y - \frac{\rho\sigma_Y}{\sigma_X}(x - \mu_X)\right]^2\right\}$$

and the marginal density

$$f_X(x) = \left(\sqrt{2\pi}\sigma_X\right)^{-1} \exp\left\{-\frac{1}{2}\left(\frac{y - \mu_Y}{\sigma_Y}\right)^2\right\}.$$

The conditional density $f_{Y|X}(y|x)$ is normal with mean and variance

$$\mu_{Y|X} = \mu_Y + \frac{\rho\sigma_Y}{\sigma_X}(x - \mu_X)$$
$$\sigma^2_{Y|X} = (1 - \rho^2)\sigma^2_Y.$$

The marginal density $f_X(x)$ is normal with mean μ_X and variance σ^2_X. The covariance is

$$\sigma_{YX} = \int\int (y - \mu_Y) f_{Y|X}(y|x)\, dy\, (x - \mu_X) f_X(x)\, dx$$

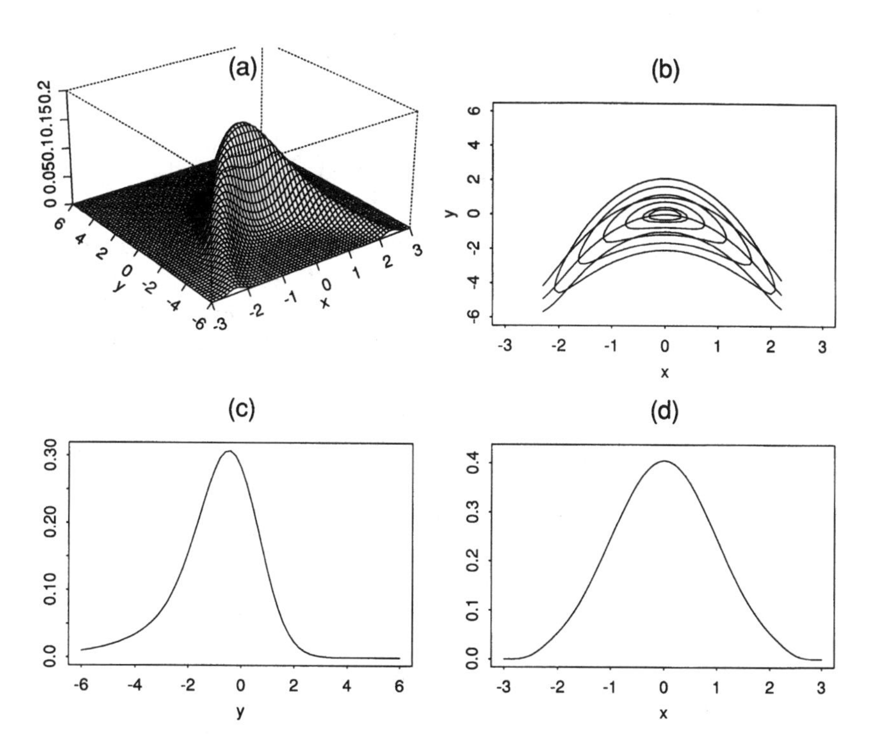

Figure 3.6. The distribution of a quadratic regression with normal errors. The density is $f_{X,Y}(x, y) = f_{Y|X}(y|x) f_X(x)$, where $f_{Y|X}(y|x)$ is normal with mean $g(x) = -x^2$ and variance $\sigma^2_{Y|X} = 1$, and $f_X(x)$ is normal with mean $\mu_X = 0$ and $\sigma^2_X = 1$. Panel (a) is a perspective plot of $f_{X,Y}(x, y)$. Panel (b) is a contour plot of $f_{X,Y}(x, y)$. The lines shown in panel (b) are $\mathscr{E}(Y|X)(x)$ (center), $\mathscr{E}(Y|X)(x)$ plus one standard deviation of $f_{Y|X}(y|x)$ (top), and $\mathscr{E}(Y|X)(x)$ minus one standard deviation of $f_{Y|X}(y|x)$ (bottom). Panel (c) is a plot of $f_Y(y)$. Panel (d) is a plot of $f_X(x)$.

$$= \int \left[\mu_Y + \frac{\rho\sigma_Y}{\sigma_X}(x - \mu_X) - \mu_Y \right](x - \mu_X) f_X(x)\, dx$$

$$= \frac{\rho\sigma_Y}{\sigma_X} \int (x - \mu_X)^2 f_X(x)\, dx$$

$$= \rho\sigma_Y\sigma_X.$$

The mean of $f_{Y|X}(y|x)$, which is the conditional expectation of Y given X, is the linear function $g(x) = \mu_Y + \beta^*(x - \mu_X)$, where $\beta^* = (\rho\sigma_Y/\sigma_X) = \sigma_{YX}/\sigma_X^2$, and the conditional variance $\sigma_{Y|X}^2$ is constant. The functions $g(x)$, $g(x)+\sigma_{Y|X}$, and $g(x)+\sigma_{Y|X}$ are plotted in Panel (d) of Figure 3.5. The second moment concepts of Section 3.5 characterize the bivariate normal.

Example 3.2. We can modify the bivariate normal by putting the conditional mean of $f_{Y|X}(y|x)$ to $g(x)$ as follows:

$$f_{Y|X}(y|x) = \left(\sigma_{Y|X}\sqrt{2\pi}\right)^{-1} \exp\left[-\frac{1}{2}\left(\frac{y - g(x)}{\sigma_{Y|X}} \right)^2 \right].$$

This is a (nonlinear) regression with normal errors which can be compared to the regression with uniform errors of Example 3.1. Plots of the density $f_{X,Y}(x, y) = f_{Y|X}(y|x) f_X(x)$ for $g(x) = -x^2$ are shown in Figure 3.6. In particular, compare Panel (b) of Figure 3.6 to Panel (b) of Figure 3.4.

3.7 Matrix Notation for Moments

Formulas such as

$$\mathscr{E}\left(\sum_{i=1}^{r} a_i X_i \right) = \sum_{i=1}^{r} a_i \mathscr{E} X_i$$

$$\mathrm{Cov}\left(\sum_{i=1}^{r} a_i X_i, \sum_{j=1}^{c} b_j Y_j \right) = \sum_{i=1}^{r} \sum_{j=1}^{c} a_i b_j \,\mathrm{Cov}(X_i, Y_j)$$

$$\mathrm{Var}\left(\sum_{i=1}^{r} a_i X_i \right) = \sum_{i=1}^{r} \sum_{j=1}^{r} a_i a_j \,\mathrm{Cov}(X_i, X_j)$$

$$= \sum_{i=1}^{r} a_i^2 \,\mathrm{Var}(X_i) + 2 \sum_{i<j} a_i a_j \,\mathrm{Cov}(X_i, X_j)$$

can be represented more compactly and manipulated more easily if they are given a matrix representation.

For a vector $X = (X_1, \ldots, X_r)'$ whose elements are random variables, define $\mathscr{E}X = (\mathscr{E}X_1, \ldots, \mathscr{E}X_r)'$; that is, $\mathscr{E}X$ is the r-vector whose elements are $\mathscr{E}X_i$. Often $\mathscr{E}X$ is denoted by μ or μ_X with typical element denoted by μ_i or μ_{X_i}. According to the rules of matrix algebra, if a is an r-vector of constants, then

$$\mathscr{E}(a'X) = \mathscr{E}\left(\sum_{i=1}^{r} a_i X_i\right) = \sum_{i=1}^{r} a_i \mathscr{E}(X_i) = a'\mathscr{E}(X) = a'\mu.$$

For an $r \times c$ matrix $U = [U_{ij}]$ whose elements U_{ij} are random variables, define $\mathscr{E}U = [\mathscr{E}U_{ij}]$; that is, $\mathscr{E}U$ is the $r \times c$ matrix whose elements are $\mathscr{E}U_{ij}$. As above, if a is an r-vector of constants and b is a c-vector of constants , then

$$\mathscr{E}(a'U) = a'\mathscr{E}(U), \qquad \mathscr{E}(Ub) = \mathscr{E}(U)b, \qquad \text{and} \qquad \mathscr{E}(a'Ub) = a'\mathscr{E}(U)b.$$

For instance,

$$\mathscr{E}(a'Ub) = \mathscr{E}\left(\sum_{i=1}^{r}\sum_{j=1}^{c} a_i b_j U_{ij}\right) = \sum_{i=1}^{r}\sum_{j=1}^{c} a_i b_j \mathscr{E}(U_{ij}) = a'\mathscr{E}(U)b.$$

If X is a random vector of length r and Y is a random vector of length c, then define $\mathscr{C}(X, Y')$ to be the $r \times c$ matrix with typical element $\mathrm{Cov}(X_i, Y_j)$. Various equivalent expressions for $\mathscr{C}(X, Y')$ are the following:

$$\begin{aligned}
&\mathscr{C}(X, Y') \\
&\quad = \begin{pmatrix} \mathscr{C}(X_1, Y_1) & \cdots & \mathscr{C}(X_1, Y_c) \\ \vdots & & \vdots \\ \mathscr{C}(X_r, Y_1) & \cdots & \mathscr{C}(X_r, Y_c) \end{pmatrix} \\
&\quad = \begin{pmatrix} \mathscr{E}(X_1 - \mathscr{E}X_1)(Y_1 - \mathscr{E}Y_1) & \cdots & \mathscr{E}(X_1 - \mathscr{E}X_1)(Y_c - \mathscr{E}Y_c) \\ \vdots & & \vdots \\ \mathscr{E}(X_r - \mathscr{E}X_r)(Y_1 - \mathscr{E}Y_1) & \cdots & \mathscr{E}(X_r - \mathscr{E}X_r)(Y_c - \mathscr{E}Y_c) \end{pmatrix} \\
&\quad = \mathscr{E}\begin{pmatrix} (X_1 - \mathscr{E}X_1)(Y_1 - \mathscr{E}Y_1) & \cdots & (X_1 - \mathscr{E}X_1)(Y_c - \mathscr{E}Y_c) \\ \vdots & & \vdots \\ (X_r - \mathscr{E}X_r)(Y_1 - \mathscr{E}Y_1) & \cdots & (X_r - \mathscr{E}X_r)(Y_c - \mathscr{E}Y_c) \end{pmatrix}
\end{aligned}$$

$$= \mathscr{E}\left[\begin{pmatrix} X_1 - \mathscr{E}X_1 \\ \vdots \\ X_r - \mathscr{E}X_r \end{pmatrix}(Y_1 - \mathscr{E}Y_1, \cdots, Y_c - \mathscr{E}Y_c)\right]$$

$$= \mathscr{E}(X - \mathscr{E}X)(Y - \mathscr{E}Y)'.$$

Common notations for the $r \times r$ matrix $\mathscr{C}(X, X')$ are $\text{Var}(X)$ and Σ. A typical element of Σ is usually denoted by either σ_{ij} or $\sigma_{X_i X_j}$. Sometimes one sees Σ_{XY} for the matrix $\mathscr{C}(X, Y')$ with typical element denoted by σ_{X_i, Y_j}. According to the rules of matrix algebra,

$$\begin{aligned}
\text{Cov}(a'X, b'Y) &= \text{Cov}\left(\sum_{i=1}^{r} a_i X_i, \sum_{j=1}^{c} b_j Y_j\right) \\
&= \mathscr{E}\left[\sum_{i=1}^{r} a_i (X_i - \mu_{X_i})\right]\left[\sum_{j=1}^{c} b_j (Y_j - \mu_{Y_j})\right] \\
&= \sum_{i=1}^{r}\sum_{j=1}^{c} a_i b_j \mathscr{E}(X_i - \mu_{X_i})(Y_j - \mu_{Y_j}) \\
&= \sum_{i=1}^{r}\sum_{j=1}^{c} a_i b_j \sigma_{X_i, Y_j} \\
&= a'\Sigma_{XY} b \\
&= a'\mathscr{C}(X, Y')b
\end{aligned}$$

and

$$\begin{aligned}
\text{Var}(a'X) &= \mathscr{E}\left[\left(\sum_{i=1}^{r} a_i X_i\right)^2\right] \\
&= \mathscr{E}\left[\sum_{i=1}^{r} a_i (X_i - \mu_i)\right]\left[\sum_{i=1}^{r} a_i (X_i - \mu_i)\right] \\
&= \sum_{i=1}^{r}\sum_{j=1}^{r} a_i a_j \mathscr{E}(X_i - \mu_i)(X_j - \mu_j) \\
&= \sum_{i=1}^{r}\sum_{j=1}^{r} a_i a_j \sigma_{ij} \\
&= a'\Sigma a \\
&= a' \text{Var}(X) b.
\end{aligned}$$

In this notation it becomes easy to obtain, for instance, $\text{Var}[a'(X+Y)]$ where X and Y are random vectors with the same length. Applying the rules of matrix algebra, we have

$$\begin{aligned}\text{Var}(X+Y) &= \mathscr{E}[(X-\mu_X)+(Y-\mu_Y)][(X-\mu_X)+(Y-\mu_Y)]' \\ &= \mathscr{E}(X-\mu_X)(X-\mu_X)' + \mathscr{E}(Y-\mu_Y)(Y-\mu_Y)' \\ &\quad + \mathscr{E}(X-\mu_X)(Y-\mu_Y)' + \mathscr{E}(Y-\mu_Y)(X-\mu_X)' \\ &= \Sigma_{XX} + \Sigma_{YY} + \Sigma_{XY} + \Sigma_{YX}\end{aligned}$$

and

$$\begin{aligned}\text{Var}[a'(X+Y)] &= a'(\Sigma_{XX} + \Sigma_{YY} + \Sigma_{XY} + \Sigma_{YX})a \\ &= a'\Sigma_{XX}a + a'\Sigma_{YY}a + 2a'\Sigma_{XY}a.\end{aligned}$$

Note that while $\Sigma_{XY} \neq \Sigma_{YX}$ it is nonetheless true that $a'\Sigma_{XY}a = a'\Sigma_{YX}a$.

If R is a matrix, then similar algebra gives

$$\begin{aligned}\mathscr{E}(RX) &= R\mathscr{E}(X) = R\mu \\ \text{Var}(RX) &= \mathscr{E}[R(X-\mu_X)(X-\mu_X)'R'] \\ &= \mathscr{E}R[(X-\mu_X)(X-\mu_X)']R' \\ &= R\Sigma R'.\end{aligned}$$

3.8 The Multivariate Normal Distribution

We shall need a few facts regarding the multivariate normal distribution for use in later sections, namely, the density function, the first and second moments, and the moment generating function. We shall derive these here using an approach that gets what we need as quickly as possible. The multivariate normal distribution will be extensively studied in later econometrics courses so that omissions here will eventually be remedied. What that later study will consist of is essentially rederiving the results of Section 3.6 in a matrix notation.

Let $Z = (Z_1, \ldots, Z_m)'$ be a vector of independent normal random variables each with mean zero and variance 1. The density of Z is

$$f_Z(z) = \prod_{i=1}^{m} (2\pi)^{-1/2} e^{-z_i^2/2} = (2\pi)^{-m/2} e^{-\sum_{i=1}^{m} z_i^2/2} = (2\pi)^{-m/2} e^{-z'z/2}$$

where $z = (z_1, \ldots, z_m)'$. The moment generating function is

$$M_Z(s) = \mathscr{E}e^{s'Z} = \mathscr{E}e^{\sum_{i=1}^{m} s_i Z_i}$$
$$= \mathscr{E}\prod_{i=1}^{m} e^{s_i Z_i} = \prod_{i=1}^{m} \mathscr{E}e^{s_i Z_i} = \prod_{i=1}^{m} e^{s_i^2/2} = e^{\sum_{i=1}^{m} s_i^2/2} = e^{s's/2}$$

where $s = (s_1, \ldots, s_m)'$. The moments of Z are $\mathscr{E}Z = 0$ and $\text{Var}(Z) = I$, where I denotes the identity matrix of order m.

Consider the transformation

$$Y = RZ + \mu$$

where R is an m by m, full rank matrix. Define

$$\Sigma = RR'$$

and note that

$$\Sigma^{-1} = (R')^{-1}(R)^{-1} \quad \text{and} \quad \det(R) = [\det(\Sigma)]^{1/2}.$$

A matrix that has the representation $\Sigma = RR'$ is called *positive semidefinite* or *nonnegative definite*; if R is nonsingular, it is called *positive definite*. We have immediately from the results of Section 3.7 that

$$\mathscr{E}Y = \mathscr{E}(RZ + \mu) = R\mathscr{E}(Z) + \mu = \mu$$

and

$$\text{Var}(X) = \mathscr{E}RZZ'R' = R\mathscr{E}(ZZ')R' = RIR' = RR' = \Sigma.$$

The inverse transformation of $y = Rz + \mu$ is $z = R^{-1}(y - \mu)$ with Jacobian $J(z) = R^{-1}$ so that

$$\det[J(z)] = \det(R^{-1}) = [\det(R)]^{-1} = [\det(\Sigma)]^{-1/2}.$$

Thus, using the change of variable formula of Section 3.3, the density of X is

$$f_X(x) = [\det(\Sigma)]^{-1/2} f_Z[R^{-1}(y - \mu)]$$
$$= [\det(\Sigma)]^{-1/2}(2\pi)^{-m/2} e^{-(x-\mu)'\Sigma^{-1}(x-\mu)/2}.$$

The density is often denoted as $n(x; \mu, \Sigma)$ and the distribution as $N(x; \mu, \Sigma)$ or $N(\mu, \Sigma)$. Put $s = t'R$ where $t = (t_1, \ldots, t_m)'$. Then the moment generating function of X is

$$\begin{aligned} M_X(t) &= \mathscr{E} e^{t'(RZ+\mu)} = e^{t'\mu} \mathscr{E} e^{s'Z} \\ &= e^{t'\mu} M_Z(s) = e^{t'\mu} M_Z(t'R) = e^{t'\mu} e^{t'RR't/2} = e^{t'\mu + t'\Sigma t/2}. \end{aligned}$$

In summary, the multivariate normal density function is

$$n(x; \mu, \Sigma) = (2\pi)^{-m/2} [\det(\Sigma)]^{-1/2} e^{-(1/2)(x-\mu)'\Sigma^{-1}(x-\mu)}.$$

If X has the $N(\mu, \Sigma)$ distribution, then the first and second moments are

$$\mathscr{E} X = \mu \quad \text{and} \quad \operatorname{Var}(X) = \Sigma$$

and the moment generating function is

$$M_X(t) = e^{t'\mu + (1/2)t'\Sigma t}.$$

3.9 Problems

1. Show that a distribution function satisfies the following properties: (i) $\lim_{x \to \infty} F_X(x) = 1$ and $\lim_{x \to -\infty} F_X(x) = 0$. (ii) $F_X(x)$ is a non-decreasing function of x. (iii) $F_X(x)$ is right continuous. You may use without proof the fact that if $A_{n+1} \subset A_n$, then $\lim_{n \to \infty} P(A_n) = P(\bigcap_{n=1}^{\infty} A_n)$.
2. Draw a diagram upon which are superimposed the sets $(-\infty, b_x] \times (-\infty, b_y]$, $(-\infty, a_x] \times (-\infty, b_y]$, $(-\infty, b_x] \times (-\infty, a_y]$, and $(-\infty, a_x] \times (-\infty, a_y]$. Label the vertices of the figures as (a_x, b_y), (a_x, b_y), etc. Use Proposition 1.1 to show that

$$\begin{aligned} &P(a_x < X \le b_x, a_y < Y \le b_y) \\ &\quad = F_{X,Y}(b_x, b_y) - F_{X,Y}(a_x, b_y) - F_{X,Y}(b_x, a_y) + F_{X,Y}(a_x, a_y). \end{aligned}$$

3. If X and Y are independent random variables, show that

$$\begin{aligned} &F_{X,Y}(b_x, b_y) - F_{X,Y}(a_x, b_y) - F_{X,Y}(b_x, a_y) + F_{X,Y}(a_x, a_y) \\ &\quad = [F_X(b_x) - F_X(a_x)][F_Y(b_y) - F_Y(a_y)]. \end{aligned}$$

4. Prove the binomial theorem which states that for any real numbers x and y and any integer $m > 0$,

$$(x+y)^m = \sum_{i=0}^{m} \binom{m}{i} x^i y^{m-i}.$$

Two proofs are possible. The first is to write

$$(x+y)^m = (x+y)(x+y)\cdots(x+y)$$

and consider how the right hand would be calculated. One can use the results of Section 1.6 to determine that each monomial $x^i y^j$ in the product must occur exactly $\binom{m}{i}$ times. The other is to use induction. One assumes that

$$(x+y)^m = \sum_{i=0}^{m} \binom{m}{i} x^i y^{m-i}$$

is correct and proves that

$$(x+y)(x+y)^m = \sum_{i=0}^{m+1} \binom{m+1}{i} x^i y^{m+1-i}.$$

5. Let $F_X(x) = (1/4)F_d(x) + (3/4)F_c(x)$ where $F_d(x)$ is the Poisson distribution with parameter $\lambda = 1/2$ and $F_c(x)$ is the standard normal distribution. Graph $F_X(x)$. Compute $P(-1 < X \le 5)$.
6. Suppose the location parameter μ of the normal distribution is obtained by sampling the uniform $(0, 1)$ distribution and then the normal $(\mu, 1)$ distribution is sampled to get a value for X. Derive the distribution of the random variable X.
7. Prove Theorem 3.1 when X and Y are discrete random variables.
8. Compute the first four central moments of the normal distribution using the moment generating function.
9. Compute the first four central moments of the binomial distribution using the moment generating function.
10. Find α_0, α_1, α_2 that minimize

$$\text{MSE}(\alpha_0, \alpha_1, \alpha_2) = \mathscr{E}(Y - \alpha_0 - \alpha_1 X - \alpha_2 X^2)^2.$$

11. Compute σ_{XY} for Example 3.2 by mimicking the computations for Example 3.1.

12. Let the random variable X have the multivariate $N(\mu, \Sigma)$ distribution. Compute the moment generating function of the random variable $Y = (X - \mu)'\Sigma^{-1}(X - \mu)$. What is the distribution of Y?
13. Consider the random variable X with density

$$f(x) = \begin{cases} A(1 - x^2) & -1 \le x \le 1, \\ 0 & \text{otherwise.} \end{cases}$$

(i) Compute A. (ii) Compute the mean of X. (iii) Compute $P(1/2 \le X \le 1)$. (iv) Compute the variance of X. (v) Find the density of the random variable $Y = X^3$.
14. Consider the jointly distributed random variables X and Y with density

$$f(x, y) = \begin{cases} A(x^2 + y) & 0 \le x \le 1,\ 0 \le y \le 1, \\ 0 & \text{otherwise.} \end{cases}$$

(i) Compute A. (ii) Compute the marginal density $f(x)$. (iii) Compute the conditional density $f(y|x)$. (iv) Compute the covariance between X and Y. (v) Are X and Y independent? (vi) Compute $P(1/2 \le X \le 1,\ 1/2 \le Y \le 1)$.
15. Let X be a continuous random variable with distribution function $F_X(x)$ and let Y be a continuous random variable with distribution $F_Y(y)$. Assume that both F_X and F_Y are strictly increasing. (i) What is the transformation $g(x)$ such that the random variable $W = g(X)$ has the uniform distribution? (ii) What is the transformation $g(x)$ such that the random variable $W = g(X)$ is distributed as the normal? (iii) What is the transformation $g(x)$ such that the random variable $W = g(X)$ is distributed as F_Y?
16. Consider a random experiment that consists of independent tosses of a coin that comes up heads (H) with probability 1/3 or tails (T) with probability 2/3. Define the random variable $X(\omega)$ as the binary expansion that results from recording a 1 for H and a 0 for T. That is, if the outcome ω is

$$\omega = (H, T, H, T, T, \ldots),$$

then

$$\begin{aligned} X(\omega) &= 0.10100\ldots_2 \\ &= 1\frac{1}{2} + 0\frac{1}{4} + 1\frac{1}{8} + 0\frac{1}{16} + 0\frac{1}{32} + \ldots \end{aligned}$$

is recorded. (i) Compute $P(X > 0.101_2)$ where 0.101_2 is binary, that is, $0.101_2 = 1/2 + 1/8$. (ii) Using $P(X \le x) = 1 - P(X > x)$, evaluate the distribution function of X at the points 0, 1/8, 1/4, 3/8, 1/2, 5/8, 3/4, 7/8, 1 and plot it. (iii) Explain why the ability to compute $P(X \le x)$ for every x with a binary expansion that terminates, for example 0.101_2, implies the ability to compute the distribution function at any point in theory and to arbitrary accuracy in practice.

17. Find the mean and variance of the hypergeometric distribution.
18. Suppose $f_X(x)$ is a density with mean μ and standard deviation σ. Find the density $f_Y(y)$ of the random variable $Y = (X - \mu)/\sigma$. What is the mean and variance of the random variable Y?
19. Find the distribution F_Y of $Y = -\log(X)$ when the density f_X of X is uniform over $[1, 2]$. Show that $\mathcal{E}Y = \mathcal{E}[-\log(X)]$ by direct computation, using f_Y and f_X, respectively, to compute $\mathcal{E}$.
20. Show that if X and Y are independent $N(0, 1)$ random variables, then the vector $(U, V) = (a + bX + cY, d + eY)$ has the bivariate normal distribution. What choice of a, b, c, d, e will give $\mu_U = \mu_V = 0$, $\sigma_U = \sigma_V = 1$, and $\rho = 1/2$?
21. What is the density of the random variable $Y = e^X$ if X has the normal density with mean μ and standard deviation σ?
22. Show that the following functions are distribution functions. (i) $F_X(x) = 1/2 + (1/\pi)\arctan(x)$. (ii) $F_X(x) = (1 + e^{-x})^{-1}$. (iii) $F_X(x) = (1 - e^{-x})I_{(0,\infty)}(x)$.
23. Find the constant A that makes $f(x)$ a density. (i) $f(x) = A\sin x$, $\mathcal{X} = (0, \pi/2)$. (ii) $f(x) = Ae^{-|x|}$, $\mathcal{X} = (-\infty, \infty)$.
24. For each density f_X, support $\mathcal{X}$, and transformation $Y = g(X)$ listed below, find the density f_Y and support $\mathcal{Y}$ of the random variable Y. Check your work by verifying that $\int_{\mathcal{Y}} f_Y(y)\,dy = 1$. (i) $f_X(x) = 42x^5(1 - x)$, $\mathcal{X} = \{x{:}\,0 < x < 1\}$, $Y = X^3$. (ii) $f_X(x) = 7e^{-7x}$, $\mathcal{X} = \{x{:}\,0 < x < \infty\}$, $Y = 4X + 3$. (iii) $f_X(x) = (2\pi)^{-1/2}e^{-x^2/2}$, $\mathcal{X} = \{x{:}\,-\infty < x < \infty\}$, $Y = 4X + 3$. (iv) $f_X(x) = (2\pi)^{-1/2}e^{-x^2/2}$, $\mathcal{X} = \{x{:}\,-\infty < x < \infty\}$, $Y = e^X$. (v) $f_X(x) = (2\pi)^{-1/2}e^{-x^2/2}$, $\mathcal{X} = \{x{:}\,-\infty < x < \infty\}$, $Y = |X|$.
25. For each density f_X, support $\mathcal{X}$, and transformation $Y = g(X)$ listed below, find the density f_Y and support $\mathcal{Y}$ of the random variable Y. Check your work by verifying that $\int_{\mathcal{Y}} f_Y(y)\,dy = 1$. (i) $f_X(x) = (1/2)e^{-|x|}$, $\mathcal{X} = \{x{:}\,-\infty < x < \infty\}$, $Y = |X|^3$. (ii) $f_X(x) = (3/8)(x+1)^2$, $\mathcal{X} = \{x{:}\,-1 < x < 1\}$, $Y = 1 - X^2$. (iii) $f_X(x) = (3/8)(x + 1)^2$, $\mathcal{X} = \{x{:}\,-1 < x < 1\}$, $Y = (1 - X^2)I_{(-\infty,0]}(x) + (1 - X)I_{(0,\infty)}(x)$.
26. Let X have the geometric density $f_X(x) = (1/3)(2/3)^x$, which has support $\mathcal{X} = \{x{:}\,x = 0, 1, \ldots\}$. Find the density $f_Y(y)$ and support $\mathcal{Y}$ of the random variable $Y = X/(X + 1)$.

27. Let the random variable X have density $f_X(x) = (x-1)/2$ with support $\mathscr{X} = \{x: 1 < x < 3\}$. Find a transformation $u(x)$ such that the random variable $Y = u(X)$ is distributed $U(0, 1)$.
28. Let the random variable X have the standard normal distribution. Compute $\mathscr{E}X^2$. In Section 3.3 we obtained the density of $Y = X^2$ and found it to be $f_Y(y) = e^{-y/2}/\sqrt{2\pi y}$. Compute $\mathscr{E}Y$ and compare to your answer for $\mathscr{E}X^2$. Should they be the same? Why?
29. A coin that lands heads with probability p is tossed and the number of times the first outcome repeats is the value assigned to the random variable Y. For instance, if $\omega = (H, H, H, H, T)$, then $Y(\omega) = 4$; if $\omega = (T, T, H)$, then $Y(\omega) = 2$. Derive the density of the random variable Y, and find $\mathscr{E}Y$.
30. Find the median of the following densities. (i) $f_X(x) = 3x^2$, $\mathscr{X} = \{x: 0 < x < 1\}$. (ii) $f_X(x) = [\pi(1+x^2)]^{-1}$, $\mathscr{X} = \{x: -\infty < x < \infty\}$. (iii) $f_X(x) = 1/N$: $\mathscr{X} = \{x: x = 1, 2, \ldots, N\}$, $\Theta = \{N: N = 1, 2, \ldots\}$. (iv) $f_X(x) = (3/2)(x-1)^2$, $\mathscr{X} = \{x: 0 < x < 2\}$.
31. Show that the median minimizes $\mathscr{E}|X - m|$.
32. Compute $\mathscr{E}X$ and $\operatorname{Var} X$ for each of the following. (i) $f_X(x) = \alpha x^{\alpha-1}$, $\mathscr{X} = \{x: 0 < x < 1\}$, $\Theta = \{\alpha: 0 < \alpha < \infty\}$. (ii) $f_X(x) = 1/N$, $\mathscr{X} = \{x: x = 1, 2, \ldots, N\}$, $\Theta = \{N: N = 1, 2, \ldots\}$. (iii) $f_X(x) = (3/2)(x-1)^2$, $\mathscr{X} = \{x: 0 < x < 2\}$.
33. Find the moment generating functions of the following densities. (i) $f_X(x) = 1/c$, $\mathscr{X} = \{x: 0 < x < c\}$. (ii) $f_X(x) = 2x/c^2$, $\mathscr{X} = \{x: 0 < x < c\}$. (iii) The negative binomial; see the Appendix. (iv) The double exponential; see the Appendix.
34. Let the random variable (X, Y) have density

$$f_{X,Y}(x, y) = \frac{1}{4} I_{\{(x,y):\ -1 \le x \le 1,\ -1 \le y \le 1\}}(x, y).$$

Compute the following probabilities. (i) $P(X^2 + Y^2 < 1)$. (ii) $P(2X - Y > 0)$. (iii) $P(|X + Y| > 0)$.

35. Let U and V be independent uniform random variables. Show that

$$X = \cos(2\pi U)\sqrt{-2\log V}$$
$$Y = \sin(2\pi U)\sqrt{-2\log V}$$

are independent $N(0, 1)$ random variables.

36. If $\mathscr{E}\log X = 0$, is $\mathscr{E}X$ greater than, less than, or equal to 0?
37. Prove Jensen's inequality for conditional expectation.

4

Convergence Concepts

4.1 Random Samples

In this chapter we will discuss four modes of convergence: almost sure convergence, convergence in probability, convergence in distribution, and L_p convergence. These are the basic tools used to establish the asymptotic properties of estimators and test statistics. When an analysis is based on a well-developed economic model, estimators and test statistics are usually too complex for us to be able determine their exact, finite sample properties using the methods discussed in Chapter 3. In these cases, asymptotic properties are studied instead. Asymptotic methods can also provide approximations to exact, finite sample results whose accuracy improves as the number of observations available for analysis increases. To illustrate the application of these tools, we will apply them to the average of a random sample.

Definition 4.1. The random variables $X_1, \ldots, X_n$ are a *random sample* of size n from the distribution $F(x)$ if $X_1, \ldots, X_n$ are independent and the marginal distribution of each X_i is $F(x)$.

A random sample from F is, therefore, a sequence of random variables $X_1, \ldots, X_n$ whose joint distribution is

$$F_{X_1, \ldots, X_n}(x_1, \ldots, x_n) = \prod_{i=1}^{n} F(x_i).$$

If F has a density f, then the joint density of the random sample is

$$f_{X_1, \ldots, X_n}(x_1, \ldots, x_n) = \prod_{i=1}^{n} f(x_i).$$

Because the density of the first is the density of them all, one also sees this condition expressed as

$$f_{X_1, \ldots, X_n}(x_1, \ldots, x_n) = \prod_{i=1}^{n} f_{X_1}(x_i).$$

Another term for a random sample is *independent and identically distributed*, which is abbreviated iid.

The simplest example of a random sample is drawing balls from an urn with replacement. If an urn contains pN red balls and qN green balls, where $0 \leq p \leq 1$ and $p + q = 1$, if the urn is mixed thoroughly before drawing each ball, if a drawn ball is replaced in the urn before the next draw, and if $x_i = 1$ is recorded when the ball on draw i is red and 0 when green, then

$$f_{X_1, \ldots, X_n}(x_1, \ldots, x_n) = \prod_{i=1}^{n} p^{x_i} q^{1-x_i}.$$

The term *simple random sample* is used when the n balls are drawn without replacement. When N is large relative to n, the joint density of a simple random sample is close enough to the joint density of a random sample that the distinction can be disregarded.

In econometrics, much data can be considered to be a random sample from the empirical distribution of a population. If $x_1, \ldots, x_N$ is a sequence of numbers—these numbers might be the taxable income of each worker in a state—the *empirical distribution* of the sequence is

$$F_N(x) = \frac{1}{N} \sum_{j=1}^{N} I_{(\infty, x]}(x_j);$$

that is, $F_N(x)$ is computed by counting how many members of the sequence $x_1, \ldots, x_N$ are less than or equal to x and then dividing that count by N.

If balls on which are painted the numbers $j = 1, \ldots, N$ are placed in an urn, if n of them are drawn with replacement, and if x_j from the sequence above is recorded as the outcome of the random variable X_i when ball j is the outcome of draw i, then $X_1, \ldots, X_n$ is a random sample from $F_N(x)$. This is the customary way of drawing a random sample in practice, although the urn might be mimicked by some electronic or physical device.

The empirical distribution $F_N(x)$ is a step function. If the numbers $x_1, \ldots, x_N$ do not repeat, then each jump of this step function is located at one of the x_j and is of size $1/N$. Usually N is large enough that $F_N(x)$ can be accurately approximated by a smooth, differentiable curve $F(x)$. In this case, $X_1, \ldots, X_n$ can be assumed to be a random sample from $f(x) = (d/dx)F(x)$.

A *statistic* is a function of random variables that does not depend on any unknown parameters of the distribution of these random variables.

For example, if $X_1, X_2, \ldots, X_n$ is a random sample from F, then $T = \max(X_1, X_2, \ldots, X_n)$ is a statistic. Incidentally, because $X_1, \ldots, X_n$ is a random sample and therefore iid,

$$\begin{aligned} F_T(t) &= P[\max(X_1, \ldots, X_n) \le t] \\ &= P[X_1 < t, \ldots, X_n \le t] = \prod_{i=1}^{n} P(X_i \le t) = [F(t)]^n. \end{aligned}$$

On the other hand, if $X_1, \ldots, X_n$ is a random sample from a normal (μ, σ^2) distribution, then $U = (n^{-1}\sum_{i=1}^n X_i - \mu)/\sigma$ is not a statistic because one would have to know μ and σ to compute U.

As mentioned above, our intent is to study the four modes of convergence—almost sure, in probability, in distribution, and L_p—and to illustrate by application to the average of a random sample. Specifically, we will consider the *sample mean*

$$\bar{X}_n = \frac{1}{n}\sum_{i=1}^{n} X_i$$

and, incidentally, the *sample variance*

$$S_n^2 = \frac{1}{n-1}\sum_{i=1}^{n}(X_i - \bar{X}_n)^2.$$

The *sample standard deviation* is $S = \sqrt{S^2}$.

To be precise, we should use the notation $\bar{X}_n$ and S_n^2 to refer to random variables and use $\bar{x}_n$ and s_n^2 to refer to data. That is, $\bar{X}_n$ and S_n^2 are function of random variables and are therefore ultimately functions of the form $\bar{X}_n(\omega)$ and $S_n^2(\omega)$ defined on $(\Omega, \mathcal{F}, P)$; $\bar{x}_n$ and s_n^2 are the values that these random variables take on when evaluated at a particular point $\omega \in \Omega$. Remember the paradigm: The random experiment is performed, $\omega \in \Omega$ is observed, and $\bar{x}_n = \bar{X}_n(\omega)$ and $s_n^2 = S_n^2(\omega)$ are recorded. However, we will usually follow the statistical convention of being sloppy with notation and will use $\bar{x}_n$ and s_n^2 to mean either as determined by context.

We shall now accumulate some facts regarding $\bar{X}_n$ and S_n^2 for use in the later sections. Let $X_1, \ldots, X_n$ be a random sample from a population with mean μ, variance σ^2, and moment generating function $M_X(t)$. Then

$$\mathscr{E}\bar{X}_n = \mathscr{E}\frac{1}{n}\sum_{i=1}^{n} X_i = \frac{1}{n}\sum_{i=1}^{n}\mathscr{E}X_i = \frac{1}{n}\sum_{i=1}^{n}\mu = \mu$$

$$\operatorname{Var}(\bar{X}_n) = \frac{1}{n^2}\sum_{i=1}^{n}\sum_{j=1}^{n}\operatorname{Cov}(X_i, X_j) = \frac{1}{n^2}\sum_{i=1}^{n}\operatorname{Cov}(X_i, X_i)$$

$$= \frac{1}{n^2}\sum_{i=1}^{n}\operatorname{Var}(X_i) = \frac{\sigma^2}{n}$$

$$\mathscr{E}S_n^2 = \mathscr{E}\left\{\frac{1}{n-1}\sum_{i=1}^{n}(X_i - \bar{X}_n)^2\right\}$$

$$= \mathscr{E}\left\{\frac{1}{n-1}\left[\sum_{i=1}^{n}X_i^2 - n(\bar{X}_n)^2\right]\right\}$$

$$= \frac{1}{n-1}\left[\sum_{i=1}^{n}\mathscr{E}X_i^2 - n\mathscr{E}(\bar{X}_n)^2\right]$$

$$= \frac{1}{n-1}\left[\sum_{i=1}^{n}(\operatorname{Var}X_i + \mu^2) - n(\operatorname{Var}\bar{X}_n + \mu^2)\right]$$

$$= \frac{1}{n-1}\left[n(\sigma^2 + \mu^2) - n\left(\frac{\sigma^2}{n} + \mu^2\right)\right] = \sigma^2$$

$$M_{\bar{X}}(t) = \mathscr{E}e^{t(X_1+\cdots+X_n)/n} = \mathscr{E}\prod_{i=1}^{n}e^{(t/n)X_i} = \prod_{i=1}^{n}\mathscr{E}e^{(t/n)X_i}$$

$$= \left[M_X\left(\frac{t}{n}\right)\right]^n$$

$$\mathscr{E}\left[\frac{\sqrt{n}(\bar{X}_n - \mu)}{\sigma}\right] = \frac{\sqrt{n}}{\sigma}\mathscr{E}(\bar{X}_n - \mu) = 0$$

$$\operatorname{Var}\left[\frac{\sqrt{n}(\bar{X}_n - \mu)}{\sigma}\right] = \frac{n}{\sigma^2}\operatorname{Var}(\bar{X}_n) = 1$$

$$M_{\sqrt{n}(\bar{X}-\mu)/\sigma}(t) = \mathscr{E}e^{\sqrt{n}t(X_1+\cdots+X_n)/(n\sigma) - \sqrt{n}t\mu/\sigma}$$

$$= e^{-\sqrt{n}t\mu/\sigma}\left[M_X\left(\frac{t}{\sqrt{n}\sigma}\right)\right]^n.$$

4.2 Almost Sure Convergence

Almost sure convergence is the standard notion of pointwise convergence that one studies in first-year calculus with one exception: Convergence is allowed to fail on an event that occurs with probability zero.

Definition 4.2. A sequence of random variables $X_1, X_2, \dots$ defined on a probability space $(\Omega, \mathcal{F}, P)$ *converges almost surely* to a random variable X if

$$\lim_{n\to\infty} X_n(\omega) = X(\omega)$$

for each $\omega \in \Omega$ except for $\omega \in E$ where $P(E) = 0$.

There are other ways of expressing the definition, such as

$$P(\lim_{n\to\infty} |X_n - X| > \epsilon) = 0 \quad \text{for every } \epsilon > 0$$

or

$$P\{\omega\colon \lim_{n\to\infty} X_n(\omega) = X(\omega)\} = 1.$$

This mode of convergence is also called *convergence almost everywhere* and *convergence with probability* 1. Abbreviations are a.s., a.e., and wp1. One sees $X_n \xrightarrow{a.s.} X$, $X_n \xrightarrow{wp1} X$, $\lim_{n\to\infty} X_n = X$ a.s., etc. If the random variable X is constant, that is, $X(\omega) = aI_\Omega(\omega)$ for some constant a, then one usually writes $X_n \xrightarrow{a.s.} a$, $X_n \xrightarrow{wp1} a$, or $\lim_{n\to\infty} X_n = a$ a.s.

A sequence of random vectors $X_n = (X_{1,n}, \dots, X_{d,n})$ converges almost surely to a random vector X if each component $X_{i,n}$ converges almost surely to the corresponding component X_i of X. It is sometimes easier to work with a norm such as $\|x\| = (x_1^2 + \cdots + x_d^2)^{1/2}$ or $\max_{1\le i\le d} |x_i|$ in which case X_n converges almost surely to X if $\lim_{n\to\infty} \|X_n(\omega) - X(\omega)\| = 0$ except for $\omega \in E$ where $P(E) = 0$. The component-wise and norm-based definitions of almost sure convergence are equivalent, which may be shown using $|X_{i,n}(\omega) - X_i(\omega)| \le \|X_n(\omega) - X(\omega)\| \le d \max_{1\le i\le d} |X_{i,n} - X(\omega)|$. Thus, for example, if $\|X_n(\omega) - X(\omega)\| \to 0$, then $|X_{i,n}(\omega) - X_i(\omega)| \to 0$ for each i, which implies $\max_{1\le i\le d} |X_{i,n}(\omega) - X(\omega)| \to 0$.

Because almost sure convergence is the same as the standard calculus notion of pointwise convergence, it obeys the same rules, the most important of which is the one for continuous functions: If (X_n, Y_n) converges almost surely to (X, Y), if $g(x, y)$ is a continuous function over some set $\mathcal{D}$, and if the images of Ω under $[X_n(\omega), Y_n(\omega)]$ and $[X(\omega), Y(\omega)]$ are in $\mathcal{D}$, then $g(X_n, Y_n)$ converges almost surely to $g(X, Y)$. For example, if $Y, Y_n > 0$ and (X_n, Y_n) converges almost surely to (X, Y), then X_n/Y_n converges almost surely to X/Y because the function $g(x, y) = x/y$ is continuous over $\mathcal{D} = \{(x, y)\colon -\infty < x < \infty, 0 < y < \infty\}$. The assumptions can be weakened. For instance, it is only necessary for the image under $[X_n(\omega), Y_n(\omega)]$ and $[X(\omega), Y(\omega)]$ of some set Ω^* with $P(\Omega^*) = 1$ to be in $\mathcal{D}$ and, as it applies to $[X_n(\omega), Y_n(\omega)]$, only for all n larger than some N.

One of the most remarkable results in probability is Kolmogorov's *strong law of large numbers*, often abreviated SLLN.

Theorem 4.1. *If $X_1, X_2, \ldots$ are independent and identically distributed random variables and $\mathcal{E}|X_1| < \infty$, then*

$$\lim_{n\to\infty} \frac{1}{n} \sum_{i=1}^{n} X_i = \mu \quad a.s.$$

where $\mu = \mathcal{E}X_1$ is the common mean.

That is, all that is required for the sample mean to converge almost surely to the population mean is that the population mean exist. Indeed this is an impressive result.

The proof is accomplished by means of an exponential inequality and the Borel-Cantelli lemma. An example of an exponential inequality is *Hoeffding's inequality*.

Lemma 4.1. *Let $Y_1, Y_2, \ldots, Y_n$ be independent random variables with zero means and bounded ranges $a_i \leq Y_i \leq b_i$. For each $\eta > 0$,*

$$P(|Y_1 + \cdots + Y_n| \geq \eta) \leq 2 \exp\left[\frac{-2\eta^2}{\sum_{i=1}^{n}(b_i - a_i)^2}\right].$$

The proof of Hoeffding's inequality is accomplished by using convexity and the bounds on Y_i to bound the moment generating function and then manipulating various inequalities and Taylor's expansions. The proof is not difficult, but it is not particularly enlightening and will therefore be omitted. It can be found in Pollard 1984, Appendix B. If you consult that reference, be aware that Pollard uses what he calls a linear functional notation: Pf means $\mathcal{E}f$ and $(Y \leq a)$ often means $I_{(-\infty, a]}(Y)$.

For any sequence of events $E_1, E_2, \ldots$, the *Borel-Cantelli lemma* states the following.

Lemma 4.2. *If $\sum_{n=1}^{\infty} P(E_i) < \infty$, then $P[E_i \, i.o.] = 0$.*

Proof. Recall from Section 1.3 that

$$[E_i \text{ i.o.}] = \bigcap_{I=1}^{\infty} \bigcup_{i=I}^{\infty} E_i.$$

Because $\bigcap_{I=1}^{\infty} \bigcup_{i=I}^{\infty} E_i \subset \bigcup_{i=I}^{\infty} E_i$ for every I,

$$0 \le P\left[\bigcap_{I=1}^{\infty} \bigcup_{i=I}^{\infty} E_i\right] \le P\left[\bigcup_{i=I}^{\infty} E_i\right] \tag{4.1}$$

for every I. By countable subadditivity (Section 1.5),

$$P\left[\bigcup_{i=I}^{\infty} E_i\right] \le \sum_{i=I}^{\infty} P(E_i).$$

Therefore Equation (4.1) becomes

$$0 \le P\left[\bigcap_{I=1}^{\infty} \bigcup_{i=I}^{\infty} E_i\right] \le \sum_{i=I}^{\infty} P(E_i). \tag{4.2}$$

If $\sum_{i=1}^{\infty} P(E_i) < \infty$, then $\lim_{I\to\infty} \sum_{i=I}^{\infty} P(E_i) = 0$ or else the sum would not converge. Taking limits of both sides of Equation (4.2), we have

$$0 \le P\left[\bigcap_{I=1}^{\infty} \bigcup_{i=I}^{\infty} E_i\right] \le \lim_{I\to\infty} \sum_{i=I}^{\infty} P(E_i) = 0,$$

which proves the result. □

We can now illustrate how a strong law of large numbers can be proved. Let $X_1, X_2, \ldots$ be a sequence of iid random variables from a density f_X. For convenience, assume that f_X is symmetric about zero, which implies $\mathscr{E}X_i = 0$, and assume that $P(|X| \ge B) \le k_0 e^{-k_1 B}$ for some constants k_0, $k_1 > 0$ and for every B (Problem 2). Let

$$Y_i = X_i I_{[-B,\,B]}(X_i).$$

Because f_X is symmetric, $\mathscr{E}Y_i = 0$ (Problem 3). Recall that $\bar{X}_n = (1/n)\sum_{t=1}^{n} X_i$; similarly for $\bar{Y}_n$. Now

$$\bar{X}_n = \bar{Y}_n + \bar{X}_n - \bar{Y}_n$$

so that, by the triangle inequality,

$$|\bar{X}_n| \le |\bar{Y}_n| + |\bar{X}_n - \bar{Y}_n|.$$

If $|\bar{X}_n| > \epsilon$, then either $|\bar{Y}_n| > \epsilon/2$ or $|\bar{X}_n - \bar{Y}_n| > \epsilon/2$, or both. Therefore,

$$\{w: |\bar{X}_n(\omega)| > \epsilon\} \subset \{w: |\bar{Y}_n(\omega)| > \epsilon/2\} \cup \{w: |\bar{X}_n(\omega) - \bar{Y}_n(\omega)| > \epsilon/2\}$$

and

$$\begin{aligned} P(|\bar{X}_n| > \epsilon) &\leq P(|\bar{Y}_n| > \epsilon/2) + P(|\bar{X}_n - \bar{Y}_n| > \epsilon/2) \\ &= P\left(\left|\sum_{i=1}^{n} Y_i\right| > n\epsilon/2\right) + P\left(\left|\sum_{i=1}^{n}(X_i - Y_i)\right| > n\epsilon/2\right). \end{aligned}$$

An argument similar to the above gives

$$\left|\sum_{i=1}^{n}(X_i - Y_i)\right| \leq \sum_{i=1}^{n} |X_i - Y_i|$$

and

$$\left\{w: \left|\sum_{i=1}^{n}[X_i(\omega) - Y_i(\omega)]\right| > n\epsilon/2\right\} \subset \bigcup_{i=1}^{n}\{\omega: |X_i - Y_i| > \epsilon/2\}$$

so that

$$\begin{aligned} P\left(\left|\sum_{i=1}^{n}(X_i - Y_i)\right| > n\epsilon/2\right) &\leq \sum_{i=1}^{n} P(|X_i - Y_i)| > \epsilon/2) \\ &= nP(|X_i - Y_i)| > \epsilon/2) \\ &= nP(|X_i - X_i I_{[-B, B]}(X_i)| > \epsilon/2) \\ &\leq nP(|X_i| > B) \\ &\leq nk_0 e^{-k_1 B}. \end{aligned}$$

Using Hoeffding's inequality, Lemma 4.1, and noting that $-B \leq Y_i \leq B$, we have

$$P\left(\left|\sum_{i=1}^{n} Y_i\right| > n\epsilon/2\right) \leq 2e^{(-2n^2 e^2/4)/4nB^2}.$$

Up to this point, we have shown that for any $\epsilon > 0$ and any $B > 0$

$$P(|\bar{X}_n| > \epsilon) \leq 2e^{(-n\epsilon^2)/8B^2} + nk_0 e^{-k_1 B}.$$

Put $\epsilon = n^{-1/2+\tau}$ for some $\tau > 0$ and put $B = 3\log n/k_1$. Then

$$P(|\bar{X}_n| > n^{-1/2+\tau}) \leq 2e^{-(n^\tau/8B^2)n^\tau} + k_0 n^{-2}.$$

For n larger than some N we will have $(n^\tau/8B^2) > 1$ so that

$$\sum_{n=1}^{\infty} e^{-(n^\tau/8B^2)n^\tau} < \infty \quad \text{and} \quad \sum_{n=1}^{\infty} k_0 n^{-2} < \infty.$$

We have shown that

$$\sum_{n=1}^{\infty} P(|\bar{X}_n| > n^{-1/2+\tau}) < \infty.$$

By the Borel-Cantelli lemma, Lemma 4.2,

$$P\big[|\bar{X}_n| > n^{-1/2+\tau} \text{ i.o.}\big] = 0.$$

This means that, except for $\omega \in E$ with $P(E) = 0$, $|\bar{X}_n(\omega)| < n^{-1/2+\tau}$ for all n larger than some N. Thus,

$$\lim_{n\to\infty} \bar{X}_n = 0 \quad \text{a.s.}$$

We assumed that $\mathscr{E}X_i = 0$ and that f_{X_i} was symmetric about zero. If $\mathscr{E}X_i = \mu$ and f_X were symmetric about μ, then $X_i^* = X_i - \mu$ would have $\mathscr{E}X_i^* = 0$ and $f_{X_i^*}$ symmetric about zero. The arguments above would give $\lim_{n\to\infty} \bar{X}_n^* = 0$ so that

$$\lim_{n\to\infty} \bar{X}_n = \lim_{n\to\infty} \bar{X}_n^* + \mu = \mu \quad \text{a.s.}$$

We have actually deduced a rate of convergence. Putting $\delta = 2\tau$, we have shown that

$$\lim_{n\to\infty} n^{1/2-\delta}|\bar{X}_n - \mu| = 0$$

for every $\delta > 0$. This is usually written

$$|\bar{X}_n - \mu| = o_s(n^{-1/2+\delta}).$$

Writing $Y_n = o_s(n^\alpha)$ means $\lim_{n\to\infty} Y_n/n^\alpha = 0$. Writing $Y_n = O_s(n^\alpha)$ means that there is a bound B such that $P(|\lim_{n\to\infty} Y_n/n^\alpha| > B) = 0$.

The *uniform strong law of large numbers*, abbreviated USLLN, has substantial application in econometrics.

Theorem 4.2. *If $X_1, X_2, \ldots$ are independent and identically distributed random variables, if $g(x, \theta)$ is continuous over $\mathscr{X} \times \Theta$ where $\mathscr{X}$ is the range of X_1 and Θ is a closed and bounded set, and if $\mathscr{E} \sup_{\theta \in \Theta} |g(X_1, \theta)| < \infty$, then*

$$\lim_{n\to\infty} \sup_{\theta \in \Theta} \left| \frac{1}{n} \sum_{i=1}^{n} g(X_i, \theta) - \mathscr{E} g(X_1, \theta) \right| = 0 \quad a.s.$$

Moreover, $\mathscr{E} g(X_1, \theta)$ is a continuous function of θ.

The result states that for each n the worst deviation of the sample average $(1/n) \sum_{i=1}^{n} g(X_i, \theta)$ from the population average $\mathscr{E} g(X_1, \theta)$ that one can find over all of Θ converges to zero almost surely. The proof is omitted; a reference is Gallant 1987, Chapter 3.

4.3 Convergence in Probability

Convergence in probability is somewhat bizarre. It is like almost sure convergence in that $|X_n(\omega) - X(\omega)|$ tends to zero, but the exceptional set E_n where convergence fails is indexed by n, which means that sometimes a given ω might be in E_n and sometimes not. Moreover, we do not have $P(E_n) = 0$, as with almost sure convergence, but rather $\lim_{n\to\infty} P(E_n) = 0$. The only merit to convergence in probability is that it is often easy to establish, as we shall see. The formal definition is as follows.

Definition 4.3. A sequence of random variables $X_1, X_2, \ldots$ *converges in probability* to a random variable X if, for every $\epsilon > 0$,

$$\lim_{n\to\infty} P(|X_n - X| > \epsilon) = 0.$$

There are other ways of expressing the definition, such as given $\epsilon > 0$ and $\delta > 0$ there exists an N, which depends on both δ and ϵ, such that $P(|X_n - X| > \epsilon) < \delta$ for all $n > N$. This mode of convergence is also called *convergence in measure*. Other notations for convergence in probability are $\text{plim}_{n\to\infty} X_n = X$ and $X_n \xrightarrow{P} X$. If the random variable X is a constant, that is, $X(\omega) = a I_\Omega(\omega)$ for some constant a, one usually writes $\text{plim}_{n\to\infty} X_n = a$ or $X_n \xrightarrow{P} a$.

As with almost sure convergence, a sequence of random vectors $X_n = (X_{1,n}, \ldots, X_{d,n})$ converges in probability to a random vector X if each component $X_{i,n}$ converges in probability to the corresponding component X_i of X. Equivalently, if $\|X_n - X\| \xrightarrow{P} 0$ for some norm $\|\cdot\|$.

Again, as with almost sure convergence, convergence in probability obeys the rule for continuous functions: If (X_n, Y_n) converges in probability to (X, Y), if $g(x, y)$ is a continuous function over some set $\mathscr{D}$, and if the images of Ω under $[X_n(\omega), Y_n(\omega)]$ and $[X(\omega), Y(\omega)]$ are in $\mathcal{D}$, then $g(X_n, Y_n)$ converges in probability to $g(X, Y)$.

Almost sure convergence is stronger than convergence in probability in that almost sure convergence of X_n to X implies X_n converges in probability to X but convergence in probability does not imply almost sure convergence (Problem 8).

The standard tool for proving convergence in probability is *Markov's inequality*.

Theorem 4.3. *If X is a random variable and if $\mathcal{E}|X|^r < \infty$ for $r > 0$ not necessarily an integer, then $P(|X| \geq \epsilon) < \mathcal{E}|X|^r/\epsilon^r$.*

Proof. We will assume that X is a continuous random variable:

$$\begin{aligned}
\mathcal{E}|X|^r &= \int_{-\infty}^{\infty} |x|^r f_X(x)\,dx \\
&= \int_{-\infty}^{-\epsilon} |x|^r f_X(x)\,dx + \int_{-\epsilon}^{\epsilon} |x|^r f_X(x)\,dx + \int_{\epsilon}^{\infty} |x|^r f_X(x)\,dx \\
&\geq \epsilon^r \int_{-\infty}^{-\epsilon} f_X(x)\,dx + \int_{-\epsilon}^{\epsilon} |x|^r f_X(x)\,dx + \epsilon^r \int_{\epsilon}^{\infty} f_X(x)\,dx \\
&\geq \epsilon^r \int_{-\infty}^{-\epsilon} f_X(x)\,dx + \epsilon^r \int_{\epsilon}^{\infty} f_X(x)\,dx \\
&= \epsilon^r P(|X| \geq \epsilon). \qquad \square
\end{aligned}$$

Markov's inequality implies *Chebishev's inequality*

$$P(|X - \mathcal{E}X| \geq \epsilon) \leq \mathrm{Var}(X)/\epsilon^2,$$

which is the form in which Markov's inequality is most often used. Chebishev's inequality can be used to establish the *weak law of large numbers*, often abbreviated WLLN.

Theorem 4.4. *If $X_1, X_2, \ldots$ are independent and identically distributed random variables with common mean μ and variance $\sigma^2 < \infty$, then*

$$\frac{1}{n}\sum_{i=1}^{n} X_i \xrightarrow{P} \mu$$

as $n \to \infty$.

Proof. The proof is a straightforward application of Chebishev's inequality:

$$\lim_{n\to\infty} P(|\bar{X}_n - \mu| \geq \epsilon) \leq \lim_{n\to\infty} \frac{\mathrm{Var}(\bar{X}_n)}{\epsilon^2} = \lim_{n\to\infty} \frac{\sigma^2}{n\epsilon^2} = 0. \qquad \square$$

Similarly to almost sure convergence, $Y_n = o_p(n^\alpha)$ means $Y_n/n^\alpha \xrightarrow{P} 0$ as $n \to \infty$. Writing $Y_n = O_p(n^\alpha)$ means that for given $\delta > 0$ there is a bound B and an N, both of which depend upon δ, such that $n > N$ implies $P(|Y_n/n^\alpha| > B) < \delta$ for all $n > N$. For instance, if $X_1, X_2, \ldots$ are independent and identically distributed random variables with common mean μ and variance $\sigma^2 < \infty$, then Chebishev's inequality implies

$$P(\sqrt{n}|\bar{X}_n - \mu| \geq B) \leq \sigma^2/B^2.$$

Thus

$$\bar{X}_n - \mu = O_p\left(\frac{1}{\sqrt{n}}\right),$$

because given $\delta > 0$, one can choose B large enough that $\sigma^2/B^2 < \delta$ for all $n > 1$.

4.4 Convergence in Distribution

Convergence in distribution is the tool that is used to obtain an asymptotic (or large sample) approximation to the exact (or small sample) distribution of a random variable.

Definition 4.4. A sequence of random variables X_1, X_2, ... *converges in distribution* to a random variable X if

$$\lim_{n\to\infty} F_{X_n}(x) = F_X(x)$$

at every x where $F(x)$ is continuous.

It is also called *convergence in law*. Common notations are $X_n \xrightarrow{d} X$, $X_n \xrightarrow{d} F_X$, $\mathcal{L}(X_n) \to \mathcal{L}(X)$, $\mathcal{L}(X_n) \to F_X$, and $X_n \xrightarrow{\mathcal{L}} F_X$. Although we say that X_n converges in distribution to X, it is actually the distribution functions that converge, not the random variables. For this reason, some authors prefer to say the law of X_n converges to the law of X, and restrict themselves to the notations $\mathcal{L}(X_n) \to \mathcal{L}(X)$ and $\mathcal{L}(X_n) \to F_X$. Most often, the limiting distribution function is the standard normal distribution function, which is usually denoted by $\Phi(x)$, $N(x\,|\,0, 1)$, or $N(x; 0, 1)$ so that one often sees $X_n \xrightarrow{d} \Phi$, $X_n \xrightarrow{d} N(0, 1)$, $\mathcal{L}(X_n) \to \Phi$, $X_n \xrightarrow{\mathcal{L}} N(0, 1)$, etc. Convergence in probability implies convergence in distribution.

A sequence of random vectors $X_n = (X_{1,n}, \ldots, X_{d,n})$ converges in distribution to a random vector X if

$$\lim_{n\to\infty} F_{X_n}(x_1, \ldots, x_d) = F_X(x_1, \ldots, x_d)$$

at every $x = (x_1, \ldots, x_d)$ where $F(x_1, \ldots, x_d)$ is continuous. Equivalently, letting $a'x = \sum_{i=1}^{d} a_i x_i$, a sequence of random vectors $X_n = (X_{1,n}, \ldots, X_{d,n})$ converges in distribution to a random vector X if the law of $a'X_n$ converges to the law of the random variable $a'X$ for every vector $a \neq 0$ (Problem 4). Most often, we are trying to show that a random vector converges to the multivariate normal distribution as described in Section 3.8. Therefore, to show $X_n \xrightarrow{\mathscr{L}} N(\mu, \Sigma)$ one would show that $a'X_n \xrightarrow{\mathscr{L}} N(a'\mu, a'\Sigma a)$ for every $a \neq 0$.

Establishing that a random variable converges in distribution is usually accomplished by means of a *central limit theorem*, often abbreviated CLT, an example of which is the following.

Theorem 4.5. *If $X_1, X_2, \ldots$ is a sequence of independent and identically distributed random variables, each with mean μ and variance σ^2, then*

$$\frac{1}{\sqrt{n}} \sum_{t=1}^{n} \left(\frac{X_i - \mu}{\sigma} \right) \xrightarrow{\mathscr{L}} N(0, 1)$$

provided $0 < \sigma^2 < \infty$.

Proof. We will prove the theorem under the additional assumption that the moment generating function $M_X(t)$ of X_i exists for all $|t| < h$ and that the third derivative of M_X is bounded by B for $|t| < h$. Put $Y_i = (X_i - \mu)/\sigma$ and note that the Y_i are independently and identically distributed because the X_i are. The plan is to show that the moment generating function $M_n(t)$ of the random variable

$$\sqrt{n}\bar{Y}_n = \frac{1}{\sqrt{n}} \sum_{i=1}^{n} Y_i = \frac{1}{\sqrt{n}} \sum_{t=1}^{n} \left(\frac{X_i - \mu}{\sigma} \right)$$

converges to $e^{t^2/2}$, which is the moment generating function of the $N(0, 1)$ distribution.

The moment generating function of Y_i is

$$M_Y(t) = \mathscr{E} e^{tY_i} = \mathscr{E} e^{t(X_i - \mu)/\sigma} = e^{-t\mu/\sigma} \mathscr{E} e^{tX_i/\sigma} = e^{-t\mu/\sigma} M_X(t/\sigma),$$

which exists and has bounded third derivative for $|t| < h\sigma$. Then

$$M_n(t) = \mathscr{E} e^{t(1/\sqrt{n}) \sum_{i=1}^{n} Y_i} = \prod_{i=1}^{n} \mathscr{E} e^{(t/\sqrt{n}) Y_i} = \left[M_Y\left(\frac{t}{\sqrt{n}} \right) \right]^n.$$

By Taylor's theorem, with mean value form (Lagrange form) of the remainder, (Bartle 1976, p. 206),

$$M_Y\left(\frac{t}{\sqrt{n}}\right) = M_Y(0) + \left[\left(\frac{d}{dt}\right)M_Y(0)\right]\left(\frac{t}{\sqrt{n}}\right)$$
$$+ \frac{1}{2}\left[\left(\frac{d^2}{dt^2}\right)M_Y(0)\right]\left(\frac{t}{\sqrt{n}}\right)^2$$
$$+ \frac{1}{6}\left[\left(\frac{d^3}{dt^3}\right)M_Y\left(\frac{\bar{t}}{\sqrt{n}}\right)\right]\left(\frac{t}{\sqrt{n}}\right)^3,$$

where $|\bar{t}| \leq |t|$. Let B_n denote $(d^3/dt^3)M_Y(\bar{t}/\sqrt{n})$. Note that B_n is bounded by B, $M_Y(0) = 1$ and, because Y_i has mean zero and variance 1, $(d/dt)M_Y(0) = 0$, and $(d^2/dt^2)M_Y(0) = 1$. Therefore we can rewrite the Taylor's expansion above as

$$M_Y\left(\frac{t}{\sqrt{n}}\right) = 1 + \frac{1}{2}\left(\frac{t}{\sqrt{n}}\right)^2 + \frac{B_n}{6}\left(\frac{t}{\sqrt{n}}\right)^3 = 1 + \frac{1}{n}\left[\frac{t^2}{2} + \frac{B_n}{6}\frac{t^3}{\sqrt{n}}\right]$$

and $M_n(t)$ becomes

$$M_n(t) = \left\{1 + \frac{1}{n}\left[\frac{t^2}{2} + \frac{B_n}{6}\frac{t^3}{\sqrt{n}}\right]\right\}^n.$$

A result from calculus (Bartle 1976, p. 209) is that if $\lim_{n\to\infty} a_n = a$, then $\lim_{n\to\infty}(1 + a_n/n)^n = e^a$. Therefore we have

$$\lim_{n\to\infty} M_n(t) = e^{t^2/2},$$

which proves the result. □

Let $\bar{X}_n = (1/n)\sum_{t=1}^{n} X_i$ where the X_i are iid with mean μ and variance σ^2. We can use the central limit theorem directly to get the approximation

$$P\left(\mu - \tfrac{a\sigma}{\sqrt{n}} < \bar{X}_n \leq \mu + \tfrac{b\sigma}{\sqrt{n}}\right) = P\left(a < \tfrac{\sqrt{n}(\bar{X}_n - \mu)}{\sigma} \leq b\right)$$
$$\doteq \Phi(b) - \Phi(a).$$

However, if we wish to approximate

$$P(a_n < \bar{X}_n \leq b_n) = P(\bar{X}_n \leq b_n) - P(\bar{X}_n \leq a_n)$$

for sequences $\{a_n\}$ and $\{b_n\}$ other than $\{\mu - a\sigma/\sqrt{n}\}$ and $\{\mu + b\sigma/\sqrt{n}\}$, we need to know more. We might, for instance, wish to consider the sequences $a_n \equiv a$ and $b_n \equiv b$. Due to the properties of distribution functions (Proposition 3.1), one can show (Problem 5) that if X_n converges in distribution to X and F_X is continuous, then

$$\lim_{n\to\infty} \sup_{-\infty<x<\infty} |F_{X_n}(x) - F_X(x)| = 0.$$

Using this fact and the central limit theorem, we have

$$\lim_{n\to\infty} \left|P[\sqrt{n}(\bar{X}_n - \mu)/\sigma \leq \sqrt{n}(b_n - \mu)/\sigma] - \Phi[\sqrt{n}(b_n - \mu)/\sigma]\right| = 0.$$

Thus, $P(\bar{X}_n \leq b_n)$ can be approximated by $\Phi[\sqrt{n}(b_n - \mu)/\sigma]$ for large n. Similarly, $P(\bar{X}_n \leq a_n)$ can be approximated by $\Phi[\sqrt{n}(a_n - \mu)/\sigma]$.

A very useful theorem in connection with convergence in distribution is *Slutsky's theorem*. The proof is difficult so we shall merely state the result.

Theorem 4.6. *If $\mathscr{L}(X_n) \to \mathscr{L}(X)$ and $Y_n \xrightarrow{P} a$ where a is a constant, then $\mathscr{L}(Y_n X_n) \to \mathscr{L}(aX)$ and $\mathscr{L}(X_n + Y_n) \to \mathscr{L}(X + a)$.*

A similar result holds for a random vector: If $\mathscr{L}(X_n) \to \mathscr{L}(X)$ and $Y_n \xrightarrow{P} A$, where A is a constant matrix, then $\mathscr{L}(Y_n X_n) \to \mathscr{L}(AX)$. If $\mathscr{L}(X_n) \to \mathscr{L}(X)$ and $Y_n \xrightarrow{P} a$, where a is a constant vector, then $\mathscr{L}(X_n + Y_n) \to \mathscr{L}(X + a)$. Of course, the dimensions of A and a must be such that matrix multiplication and vector addition make sense. To apply the theorem, the distributions $\mathscr{L}(aX)$, $\mathscr{L}(AX)$, or $\mathscr{L}(X + a)$, as the case may be, must be determined from $\mathscr{L}(X)$ using the methods for finding the distribution of a transformed random variable discussed in Sections 3.3 and 3.4.

An example is the following. Suppose that upon application of the central limit theorem we have $\mathscr{L}[\sqrt{n}(\bar{X}_n - \mu)/\sigma] \to N(0,1)$ which we could use to approximate $P(\sqrt{n}|\bar{X}_n - \mu| < a)$ if we knew σ. However, $S_n^2 = (n-1)^{-1}\sum_{i=1}^n (X_i - \bar{X}_n)^2$ converges in probability to σ^2, which implies that σ/S_n converges in probability to 1 where $S_n = \sqrt{S_n^2}$. Therefore, by Slutsky's theorem, $\sqrt{n}(\bar{X}_n - \mu)/S_n = (\sigma/S_n)[\sqrt{n}(\bar{X}_n - \mu)/\sigma]$ converges in distribution to $N(0,1)$ and we can approximate $P(\sqrt{n}|\bar{X}_n - \mu| < a)$ by $1 - 2\Phi(-a/S_n)$.

In this same vein, the following result is also true.

Theorem 4.7. *If X_n is a sequence of random vectors each with support $\mathscr{X}$, $g(x)$ is continuous on $\mathscr{X}$, and $\mathscr{L}(X_n) \to \mathscr{L}(X)$, then $\mathscr{L}[g(X_n)] \to \mathscr{L}[g(X)]$.*

If X_n is a scalar and $y = g(x)$ is an increasing function with continuous inverse $x = g^{-1}(y)$, then the result is easy to prove. The argument is as follows. The distribution of $Y_n = g(X_n)$ is

$$F_{Y_n}(y) = P[g(X_n) \leq y] = P[X_n \leq g^{-1}(y)] = F_{X_n}[g^{-1}(y)].$$

Similarly, the distribution of $Y = g(X)$ is $F_Y(y) = F_X[g^{-1}(y)]$. The points where $F_Y(y)$ is continuous will be the points where $F_X[g^{-1}(y)]$ is continuous. At those points the definition of convergence in distribution implies

$$\lim_{n\to\infty} F_{Y_n}(y) = \lim_{n\to\infty} F_{X_n}[g^{-1}(y)] = F_X[g^{-1}(y)] = F_Y(y),$$

which proves the result. As with Slutsky's theorem, to apply Theorem 4.7 the distributions $\mathscr{L}[g(X)]$ must be determined from $\mathscr{L}(X)$ using the methods for finding the distribution of a transformed random variable discussed in Sections 3.3 and 3.4.

An important application of Theorems 4.6 and 4.7 is the following. The proof is left as an exercise (Problem 6).

Corollary 4.1. *Let $\mathscr{L}(X_n) \to N(\mu, \Sigma)$ where X_n is a random vector with dimension m, μ has dimension m, and Σ is an $m \times m$ matrix with* $\det(\Sigma) > 0$. *If $A_n \xrightarrow{P} \Sigma$, then*

$$(X_n - \mu)'(A_n)^{-1}(X_n - \mu)$$

converges in distribution to the chi-squared distribution with m degrees of freedom.

4.5 L_p Convergence

We shall not use L_p convergence and therefore shall just define it for the sake of completeness. L_p convergence in used extensively in some subfields of statistics and econometrics, such as time series analysis and density estimation.

Definition 4.5. Let $0 < p < \infty$, let $X_1, X_2, \ldots$ be a sequence of random variables with $\mathscr{E}|X_n|^p < \infty$, and let X be a random variable with $\mathscr{E}|X|^p < \infty$. Then X_n *converges in* L_p to X if

$$\lim_{n\to\infty} \mathscr{E}|X_n - X|^p = 0.$$

A common notation is $\lim_{n\to\infty} \|X_n - X\|_p = 0$. L_p convergence does not imply almost sure convergence, nor does almost sure convergence imply L_p convergence. L_p convergence does imply convergence in probability.

In connection with L_p convergence, Hölder's inequality

$$\mathscr{E}|XY| \le (\mathscr{E}|X|^p)^{1/p}(\mathscr{E}|X|^q)^{1/q},$$

where $1/p + 1/q = 1$, and Minkowski's inequality

$$\mathscr{E}|X+Y|^p \le (\mathscr{E}|X|^p)^{1/p} + (\mathscr{E}|Y|^p)^{1/p}$$

are useful.

4.6 Problems

1. Plot the empirical distribution function of the numbers 0.7, 0.75, 1.57, 1.73, 0.02, 0.7, 0.67, 1.0, and 0.76.
2. Show that if f_X is a continuous density function that satisfies $f_X(x) < k_0 k_1 e^{-k_1|x|}$, then $P(|X| \ge B) \le k_0 e^{-k_1 B}$.
3. Let f_X be a density function, which may be either discrete or continuous, that is symmetric about zero and let $Y = XI_{[-B,B]}(X)$. Show that $\mathscr{E}Y = 0$.
4. Let $a'x = \sum_{i=1}^{d} a_i x_i$. Assume that the moment generating functions of X_n and X exist. Show that a sequence of random vectors $X_n = (X_{1,n}, \ldots, X_{d,n})$ converges in distribution to a random vector X if $a'X_n$ converges in distribution to the random variable $a'X$ for every $a \ne 0$. Hint: The moment generating function of $a'X_n$ must converge to the moment generating function of $a'X$. The moment generating function of X is $M_X(a) = \mathscr{E}\exp(a'x)$; similarly for X_n.
5. Assume that both $F_{X_n}(x)$ and $F_X(x)$ are continuous. Show that if $F_X(x)$ is continuous and $X_n \xrightarrow{\mathscr{L}} F_X$, then

   $$\lim_{n\to\infty} \sup_{-\infty<x<\infty} |F_{X_n}(x) - F_X(x)| = 0.$$

   Hint: Because $\lim_{x\to-\infty} F_X(x) = 0$ and both $F_{X_n}(x)$ and $F_X(x)$ are increasing functions, it is possible to choose a such that $F_X(x) < \epsilon$ for $x < a$ (Why?). It is possible to choose N such that $F_{X_n}(x) < 2\epsilon$ for $n > N$ and $x < a$ (Why?). Thus for $n > N$ and $x < a$, $F_{X_n}(x)$ and $F_X(x)$ differ by no more than 2ϵ. Also, one can choose N and b so that $F_{X_n}(x)$ and $F_X(x)$ differ by no more than 2ϵ for $x > b$ (Why?). Now for $a \le x \le b$, which is a closed and bounded interval, we have $\lim_{n\to\infty} F_{X_n}(x) = F_X(x)$. Pointwise convergence of continuous functions to a continuous function on a closed and bounded interval implies uniform convergence; that is,

$$\lim_{n\to\infty} \sup_{a\le x\le b} |F_{X_n}(x) - F_X(x)| = 0.$$

All the above, taken together, imply

$$\lim_{n\to\infty} \sup_{-\infty<x<\infty} |F_{X_n}(x) - F_X(x)| = 0$$

(Why?).

6. Prove Corollary 4.1. You may use without proof the fact that for large n, A_n can be factored as $A_n = P_n P_n'$ and that $P_n \xrightarrow{P} P$ and $(P_n)^{-1} \xrightarrow{P} P^{-1}$ where $\Sigma = PP'$. Hint: Note that

$$(X_n - \mu)'(A_n)^{-1}(X_n - \mu) = (X_n - \mu)'(P_n')^{-1}(P_n)^{-1}(X_n - \mu).$$

Use Theorem 4.6 to show that

$$(P_n)^{-1}(X_n - \mu) \xrightarrow{\mathcal{L}} N(0, I)$$

where I is the $m \times m$ identity matrix. Use Theorem 4.7 to conclude that

$$(X_n - \mu)'(P_n')^{-1}(P_n)^{-1}(X_n - \mu) \xrightarrow{\mathcal{L}} F_Y(y)$$

where $F_Y(y)$ is the distribution of $Y = \sum_{i=1}^m Z_i^2$ where the Z_i are iid $N(0, 1)$. Use the moment generating function approach to deduce that the distribution of Y is chi-squared with m degrees of freedom.

7. The moment generating function of the gamma(α, β) distribution is

$$M_X(t) = \left(\frac{1}{1-\beta t}\right)^\alpha.$$

Suppose that $X_1, X_2, \ldots$ are iid gamma(α, β). What is the moment generating function of $\sqrt{n}(\bar{x} - \alpha\beta)$? Derive the limit of $M_{\sqrt{n}(\bar{x}-\alpha\beta)}(t)$. From this limit, deduce the limiting distribution of $\sqrt{n}(\bar{x} - \alpha\beta)$.

8. Let the sample space Ω be the closed interval $[0, 1]$, let $P(\cdot)$ be the uniform distribution on Ω, and define a sequence of random variables $X_1, X_2, X_3, \ldots$ as follows:

$$\begin{array}{lll} X_1(\omega) = I_{[0,1]}(\omega) & X_2(\omega) = I_{[0,1/2]}(\omega) & X_4(\omega) = I_{[0,1/3]}(\omega) \\ & X_3(\omega) = I_{(1/2,1]}(\omega) & X_5(\omega) = I_{(1/3,2/3]}(\omega) \\ & & X_6(\omega) = I_{(2/3,1]}(\omega). \end{array}$$

Show that the sequence of random variables $\{X_i\}_{i=1}^{\infty}$ converges in probability to 0 but does not converge almost surely.

Define a sequence of random variables $Y_1, Y_2, Y_3, \ldots$ as follows:

$$
\begin{aligned}
Y_1(\omega) &= I_{[0,1]}(\omega) \quad & Y_2(\omega) &= I_{[0,1/2]}(\omega) \quad & Y_4(\omega) &= I_{[0,1/3]}(\omega) \\
& & Y_3(\omega) &= I_{(0,1/2]}(\omega) \quad & Y_5(\omega) &= I_{(0,1/3]}(\omega) \\
& & & & Y_6(\omega) &= I_{(0,1/3]}(\omega).
\end{aligned}
$$

Show that the sequence of random variables $\{Y_i\}_{i=1}^{\infty}$ converges in probability to 0 and converges almost surely to 0.

Derive the density function $f_{X_i}(x)$ of the random variable X_i. Derive the density function $f_{Y_i}(y)$ of the random variable Y_i. Notice that $f_{X_i}(t) = f_{Y_i}(t)$.

Usually all we know about random variables are their distributions. What sample space they are defined on is irrelevant. The Skorokhod representation theorem states that if a sequence of random variables $\{X_i\}_{i=1}^{\infty}$ converges in distribution to a random variable X, then it is always possible to find a (possibly different) probability space and random variables $\{Y_i\}_{i=1}^{\infty}$ and Y defined on it with $F_{Y_i}(t) = F_{X_i}(t)$ and $F_Y(t) = F_X(t)$ such that $\{Y_i\}_{i=1}^{\infty}$ converges almost surely to Y. In view of this, the statements such as "convergence in distribution does not imply convergence in probability" or "convergence in probability does not imply convergence almost surely" lose some of their force. The Skorokhod representation theorem says that you can change the rules of the game so that convergence in any one of the three modes implies convergence with respect to the other two.

9. Let X_i be independently and identically distributed with finite variance. Let $S_n^2 = (n-1)^{-1}\sum_{i=1}^{n}(X_i - \bar{X}_n)^2$ where $\bar{X}_n = n^{-1}\sum_{i=1}^{n} X_i$. Show that S_n^2 converges almost surely to $\operatorname{Var} X$.
10. Compute $P(|X - \mu_X| > \sigma_X)$ when X is $U(0,1)$ and $N(0,1)$ using Chebishev's inequality. Compare this value to the exact value.
11. Let X_i be independently and identically distributed with mean zero and variance 1. For $n = 25$, compute $P(\bar{X}_n > 1)$ where $\bar{X}_n = n^{-1}\sum_{i=1}^{n} X_i$ using both Chebishev's inequality and the central limit theorem.

5

Statistical Inference

5.1 Inference

This chapter introduces the basic ideas of statistical inference. The coverage is far from complete and is focused on methods specific to econometrics. For a more balanced and complete introduction, see Casella and Berger 1990 or Cox and Hinkley 1974. For the definitive treatment of statistical inference, see Lehmann 1983, 1986.

5.1.1 *Estimation*

Suppose we have data $x_1, \ldots, x_n$ that we presume to be generated by a random sample $X_1, \ldots, X_n$ from the density $f_X(x|\theta)$. Remember the paradigm: We have a probability space $(\Omega, \mathscr{F}, P)$ that describes a random experiment, the experiment is performed, $\omega \in \Omega$ is the outcome, and data $x_1 = X_1(\omega), \ldots, x_n = X_n(\omega)$ are observed. The probability $P(a_1 < X_1 \leq b_1, \ldots, a_n < X_n \leq b_n)$ that the data lie in the n-dimensional rectangle $(a_1, b_1] \times \cdots \times (a_n, b_n]$ may be computed as $\prod_{i=1}^n \int_{a_i}^{b_i} f_X(x_i|\theta)\, dx_i$.

We would like to determine the value of the parameter θ, which is unknown. For the most part, we shall consider the case when θ is a scalar rather than a vector. Because we shall be treating θ both as a variable and as a fixed unknown parameter to be estimated, let us write θ^o when we wish to emphasize that it is the true value of θ that is meant. Usually θ is presumed to be in some known set Θ called the parameter space. For example, let $f_X(x|\theta)$ be the normal density with unknown mean and variance 1, in which case $f_X(x|\theta) = (2\pi)^{-1/2} e^{-(x-\theta)^2/2}$ and the parameter space is $\Theta = (-\infty, \infty)$.

An *estimator* is some function of the data

$$\hat{\theta}_n = W(x_1, \ldots, x_n)$$

that has desirable properties when considered as the random variable $W(X_1, \ldots, X_n)$. More precisely, an estimator is a statistic, which is to say that W cannot depend on θ or any other unknown parameters, that has desirable properties when considered as a random variable. Some properties that might be viewed as desirable are strong consistency, weak consistency, minimum mean squared error, unbiasedness, and uniform minimum variance unbiasedness.

An estimator $\hat{\theta}_n$ is *strongly consistent* if $\hat{\theta}_n$ converges almost surely to θ^o. An estimator $\hat{\theta}_n$ is *weakly consistent* if $\hat{\theta}_n$ converges in probability to θ^o. The true value θ^o might be any value in Θ so consistency should hold for every $\theta \in \Theta$.

For the normal example, $\hat{\theta}_n = (1/n)\sum_{i=1}^n x_i$ is strongly consistent by the strong law of large numbers (Theorem 4.1) and is weakly consistent by the weak law of large numbers (Theorem 4.4).

An estimator $\hat{\theta}_n$ is *minimum mean squared error* if $\hat{\theta}_n = W(x_1, \ldots, x_n)$ and W is the function that minimizes

$$\text{MSE}(W) = \int \cdots \int \left[W(x_1, \ldots, x_n) - \theta\right]^2 \prod_{i=1}^n f_X(x_i|\theta)\, dx_1 \cdots dx_n$$

for every $\theta \in \Theta$.

An estimator $\hat{\theta}_n = W(x_1, \ldots, x_n)$ is *unbiased* if

$$\theta = \int \cdots \int W(x_1, \ldots, x_n) \prod_{i=1}^n f_X(x_i|\theta)\, dx_1 \cdots dx_n$$

holds for every θ in the parameter space Θ. An estimator is *uniformly minimum variance unbiased* if it is minimum mean square error among those estimators that are unbiased. For the normal example, $\hat{\theta}_n = (1/n)\sum_{i=1}^n x_i$ is uniform minimum variance unbiased.

This list of desirable properties is far from exhaustive. Moreover, it is often quite difficult and tedious to verify that an estimator has such properties. In fact, it is often so difficult and tedious that by the time the best estimator is found for an estimation problem of scientific interest, science is no longer interested in the question. Thus, it makes more sense for the practicing scientist to know a few general-purpose methods for constructing estimators that usually have desirable properties and apply them rather than to seek the best estimator according to some criterion such as uniform minimum variance unbiased. Three such methods are the method of maximum likelihood, the method of moments, and estimators constructed through use of Bayes theorem. We discuss each of these later.

5.1.2 *Hypothesis Testing*

As with estimation, we have data $x_1, \ldots, x_n$ that we presume to be generated by a random sample $X_1, \ldots, X_n$ from a density $f_X(x|\theta)$ and we presume that the unknown parameter θ is in a known parameter space Θ. In hypothesis testing, the parameter space is divided into two sets Θ_H and Θ_A that are mutually exclusive, $\Theta_H \cap \Theta_A = \emptyset$, and exhaustive, $\Theta_H \cup \Theta_A = \Theta$. The problem is to determine to which of these two sets the true value θ^o of the parameter belongs. That is, based upon observing $x_1, \ldots, x_n$, one is trying to choose between the two hypotheses

$$H: \theta \in \Theta_H \quad \text{and} \quad A: \theta \in \Theta_A.$$

For example, let $f_X(x|\theta)$ be the normal density $f_X(x|\theta) = (2\pi)^{-1/2} \cdot e^{-(x-\theta)^2/2}$ and let the parameter space be $\Theta = (-\infty, \infty)$. One might test

$$H: \theta = 0 \quad \text{against} \quad A: \theta \neq 0,$$

in which case $\Theta_H = \{0\}$ and $\Theta_A = (-\infty, 0) \cup (0, \infty)$. The first hypothesis, $\theta \in \Theta_H$, is called the *null hypothesis* and the second, $\theta \in \Theta_A$, is called the *alternative hypothesis*. They have labels because, as we shall see, they are treated asymmetrically in the theory of hypothesis testing.

A standard approach to hypothesis testing is to choose some statistic $W(x_1, \ldots, x_n)$ and use it to divide the sample space $\mathscr{X}$ into two mutually exclusive and exhaustive regions

$$\mathscr{X}_H = \{(x_1, \ldots, x_n): W(x_1, \ldots, x_n) \leq c\}$$

and

$$\mathscr{X}_R = \{(x_1, \ldots, x_n): W(x_1, \ldots, x_n) > c\}.$$

The first region, $\mathscr{X}_H$, is called the *acceptance region* and the second, $\mathscr{X}_R$, is called the *rejection region*. The cut-off point c is called the *critical point* and W is called a *test statistic*.

For example, if we are testing

$$H: \theta = 0 \quad \text{against} \quad A: \theta \neq 0$$

for the normal example, we might put

$$\mathscr{X}_{R_1} = \left\{(x_1, \ldots, x_n): \left|\frac{1}{\sqrt{n}} \sum_{i=1}^{n} x_i\right| > 1.96\right\}.$$

If we were testing

$$H: \theta \le 0 \quad \text{against} \quad A: \theta > 0,$$

we might put

$$\mathscr{X}_{R_2} = \left\{ (x_1, \ldots, x_n): \frac{1}{\sqrt{n}} \sum_{i=1}^{n} x_i > 1.65 \right\}.$$

As suggested by the examples, it is customary to describe only $\mathscr{X}_R$ and use the formula $\mathscr{X}_H = \mathscr{X} \cap \tilde{\mathscr{X}}_R$ to define the acceptance region. On the other hand, it is customary to describe both Θ_H and Θ_A and use the formula $\Theta = \Theta_H \cup \Theta_A$ to define the parameter space.

The relevant properties of the rejection region

$$\mathscr{X}_R = \{(x_1, \ldots, x_n): W(x_1, \ldots, x_n) > c\}$$

are described by the *power function*

$$\beta_W(\theta) = \int \cdots \int I_{\mathscr{X}_R}(x_1, \ldots, x_n) \prod_{i=1}^{n} f_X(x_i|\theta)\, dx_1 \cdots dx_n,$$

which gives the probability that the null hypothesis H is rejected when θ is the true value of the parameter. For the first example, where

$$\mathscr{X}_{R_1} = \{(x_1, \ldots, x_n): W_1 > 1.96\}, \qquad W_1(x_1, \ldots, x_n) = \left| \frac{1}{\sqrt{n}} \sum_{i=1}^{n} x_i \right|,$$

the power function is

$$\begin{aligned}
\beta_{W_1}(\theta) &= P\left(\left| \frac{1}{\sqrt{n}} \sum_{i=1}^{n} x_i \right| > 1.96 \right) \\
&= 1 - P\left(\left| \frac{1}{\sqrt{n}} \sum_{i=1}^{n} x_i \right| \le 1.96 \right) \\
&= 1 - P\left(-1.96 \le \frac{1}{\sqrt{n}} \sum_{i=1}^{n} x_i \le 1.96 \right) \\
&= 1 - P\left(-1.96 - \sqrt{n}\theta \le \frac{1}{\sqrt{n}} \sum_{i=1}^{n} (x_i - \theta) \le 1.96 - \sqrt{n}\theta \right) \\
&= 1 - [\Phi(1.96 - \sqrt{n}\theta) - \Phi(-1.96 - \sqrt{n}\theta)] \\
&= 1 - \Phi(1.96 - \sqrt{n}\theta) + \Phi(-1.96 - \sqrt{n}\theta).
\end{aligned}$$

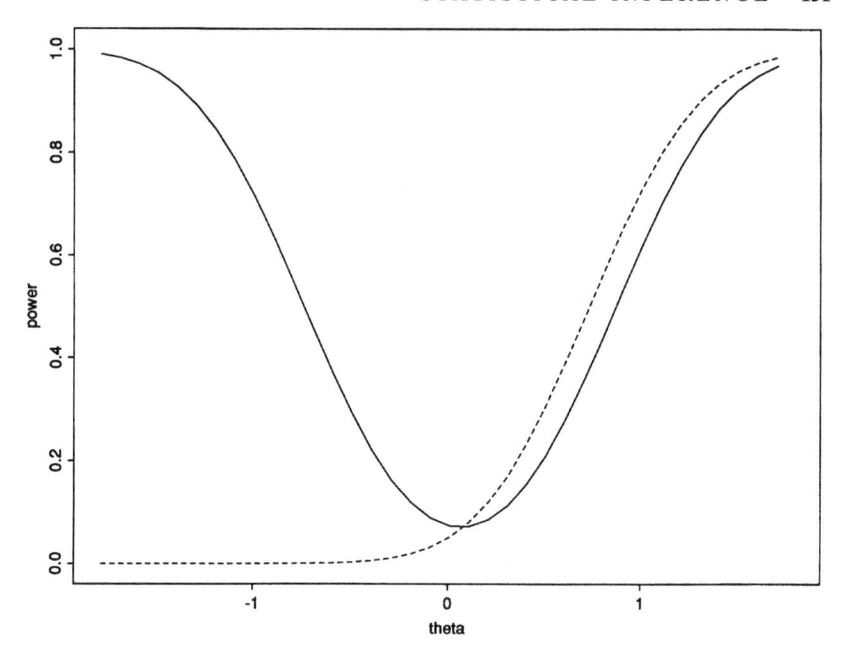

Figure 5.1. The solid line shows the power function for the test that rejects when $|(1/\sqrt{n})\sum_{i=1}^{n} X_i| > 1.96$. The dashed line shows the power function for the test that rejects when $(1/\sqrt{n})\sum_{i=1}^{n} X_i > 1.65$. In both cases $n = 5$ and X_i is normally distributed with mean θ and variance 1.

Similarly, $\beta_{W_2}(\theta) = 1 - \Phi(1.65 - \sqrt{n}\theta)$. The power functions of the tests W_1 and W_2 are plotted in Figure 5.1. If θ is in Θ_H, then rejecting H is an error and $\beta(\theta)$ gives the probability of that error. Rejecting H when θ is in Θ_H is called a *type I* error. Similarly, if θ is in Θ_A, then accepting H is an error and $1 - \beta(\theta)$ gives the probability of that error. Accepting H when θ is in Θ_A is called a *type II* error.

The classical (Neyman-Pearson) approach to testing statistical hypotheses is to bound the probability of a type I error by some value α such as .05 or .01 over all of Θ_H and to try to find a test that minimizes the probability of a type II error over all of Θ_A. Equivalently, one is trying to find the test statistic $W(x_1, \ldots, x_n)$ that satisfies $\beta_W(\theta) \leq \alpha$ for all $\theta \in \Theta_H$ and has the property that if W^* is any other test statistic that satisfies $\beta_{W^*}(\theta) \leq \alpha$ for all $\theta \in \Theta_H$, then $\beta_{W^*}(\theta) \leq \beta_W(\theta)$ for all $\theta \in \Theta_A$. A test W that does this is called *uniformly most powerful*. The value of α is called the *level* of the test. If W is level α and $\beta_W(\theta) = \alpha$ for some $\theta \in \Theta_H$, then the test is called a *size* α test. As seen from Figure 5.1, both W_1 and W_2 are size .05 tests.

Finding a uniformly most powerful test is a calculus of variations problem that has no solution for most statistical hypothesis testing problems. To obtain a problem that has a solution, it is customary to restrict the class of test statistics that one is willing to consider, which gives rise to tests called uniformly most powerful unbiased or uniformly most powerful invariant. There is a huge literature on constructing tests of this sort, but, as with estimation, a serious scientist would be better advised to learn some general methods of test construction that usually lead to reasonable tests and apply them. Four such methods are the Wald test, the likelihood ratio test, the Lagrange multiplier test, and Bayesian tests. We shall discuss each of these later.

5.1.3 *Confidence Intervals*

As with estimation and hypothesis testing, we have data $x_1, \ldots, x_n$ that we presume to be generated by a random sample $X_1, \ldots, X_n$ from a density $f_X(x|\theta)$ and we presume that the unknown parameter θ is in a known parameter space Θ. A *confidence interval* is a random interval

$$S(x_1, \ldots, x_n) = [L(x_1, \ldots, x_n),\ U(x_1, \ldots, x_n)]$$

where U and L are statistics. The random interval is expected to contain the true parameter θ with preassigned probability $1 - \alpha$. That is,

$$\int \cdots \int I_{S(x_1,\ldots,x_n)}(\theta) \prod_{i=1}^{n} f_X(x_i|\theta)\, dx_1 \cdots dx_n \geq 1 - \alpha$$

for all θ in Θ. The value $1 - \alpha$ is called the *confidence level*. As an example, for the normal density $f_X(x|\theta) = (2\pi)^{-1/2} e^{-(x-\theta)^2/2}$ we might choose

$$L(x_1, \ldots, x_n) = \frac{1}{n} \sum_{i=1}^{n} x_i - \frac{1.96}{\sqrt{n}}$$

$$U(x_1, \ldots, x_n) = \frac{1}{n} \sum_{i=1}^{n} x_i + \frac{1.96}{\sqrt{n}},$$

which will have confidence level $1 - \alpha = .95$. Of confidence procedures that have confidence level $1 - \alpha$, one seeks to find that procedure that has shortest expected length

$$\int \cdots \int [U(x_1, \ldots, x_n) - L(x_1, \ldots, x_n)] \prod_{i=1}^{n} f_X(x_i|\theta)\, dx_1 \cdots dx_n$$

for all θ in Θ. For the normal example, the expected length is

$$\int \cdots \int \left[\frac{1}{n} \sum_{i=1}^{n} x_i + \frac{1.96}{\sqrt{n}} - \frac{1}{n} \sum_{i=1}^{n} x_i + \frac{1.96}{\sqrt{n}} \right] \prod_{i=1}^{n} f_X(x_i|\theta)\, dx_1 \cdots dx_n = \frac{3.82}{\sqrt{n}}.$$

One can construct a $1-\alpha$ level confidence interval from a level α test $W_\gamma(x_1, \ldots, x_n)$ of the hypothesis

$$H\colon \theta = \gamma \quad \text{against} \quad A\colon \theta \neq \gamma \in \Theta$$

by putting

$$S(x_1, \ldots, x_n) = \{\gamma\colon W_\gamma(x_1, \ldots, x_n) \le c\}.$$

For the normal example, consider the test statistic

$$W_\gamma(x_1, \ldots, x_n) = \left| \frac{1}{\sqrt{n}} \sum_{i=1}^{n} (x_i - \gamma) \right|.$$

If we invert the test that rejects H when $W_\gamma > 1.96$, we get the confidence interval

$$\begin{aligned} S(x_1, \ldots, x_n) &= \{\gamma\colon W_\gamma(x_1, \ldots, x_n) \le 1.96\} \\ &= \left\{ \gamma\colon \left| \frac{1}{\sqrt{n}} \sum_{i=1}^{n} (x_i - \gamma) \right| \le 1.96 \right\} \\ &= \left\{ \gamma\colon \frac{1}{n} \sum_{i=1}^{n} x_i - \frac{1.96}{\sqrt{n}} \le \gamma \le \frac{1}{n} \sum_{i=1}^{n} x_i + \frac{1.96}{\sqrt{n}} \right\}. \end{aligned}$$

To see that the rule

$$S(x_1, \ldots, x_n) = \{\gamma\colon W_\gamma(x_1, \ldots, x_n) \le c\}$$

produces a $1-\alpha$ level confidence interval, note that

$$\begin{aligned} &\int \cdots \int I_{S(x_1, \ldots, x_n)}(\theta) \prod_{i=1}^{n} f_X(x_i|\theta)\, dx_1 \cdots dx_n \\ &= \int \cdots \int I_{(-\infty, c]}[W_\theta(x_1, \ldots, x_n)] \prod_{i=1}^{n} f_X(x_i|\theta)\, dx_1 \cdots dx_n \\ &= 1 - \int \cdots \int I_{(c, \infty)}[W_\theta(x_1, \ldots, x_n)] \prod_{i=1}^{n} f_X(x_i|\theta)\, dx_1 \cdots dx_n \\ &\le 1 - \alpha. \end{aligned}$$

If one family of level α tests W_γ for $H: \theta = \gamma$ against $A: \theta \neq \gamma \in \Theta$ has better power than some other family of level α tests W_γ^* in the sense that $\beta_{W_\gamma}(\theta) \geq \beta_{W_\gamma^*}(\theta)$ for every $\theta, \gamma \in \Theta$, then the confidence procedure

$$S(x_1, \ldots, x_n) = \{\gamma: W_\gamma(x_1, \ldots, x_n) \leq c\}$$

will have shorter expected length than the confidence procedure

$$S^*(x_1, \ldots, x_n) = \{\gamma: W_\gamma^*(x_1, \ldots, x_n) \leq c^*\}$$

(Pratt 1961). Therefore, if we can find a good test, we automatically have a good confidence procedure. A separate study of confidence procedures is unnecessary; it suffices to study hypothesis testing.

5.2 Maximum Likelihood Estimation

5.2.1 *The Method of Maximum Likelihood*

We shall introduce the method of maximum likelihood with an example. Suppose that $X_1, \ldots, X_n$ is a random sample from the binomial density $f(x|p) = p^x(1-p)^{(1-x)}$. Suppose that $n = 5$ and that the sequence

$$(x_1, x_2, x_3, x_4, x_5) = (0, 1, 1, 0, 0)$$

is observed. The probability of observing this sequence is

$$\prod_{i=1}^{5} f(x_i|p) = p^2(1-p)^3.$$

What value of p would make the observed sequence most probable? The first-order condition for this maximization problem is

$$0 = \frac{d}{dp} p^2(1-p)^3 = 2p(1-p)^3 - 3p^2(1-p)^2.$$

The solution of the first-order condition is

$$\hat{p} = \frac{2}{5} = \frac{\#\text{heads}}{\#\text{tosses}}.$$

If there are n tosses and r heads are observed, we obtain the same results:

$$\prod_{i=1}^{n} f(x_i|p) = p^r(1-p)^{n-r}$$

$$0 = \frac{d}{dp}p^r(1-p)^{n-r} = rp^{r-1}(1-p)^{n-r} - (n-r)p^r(1-p)^{n-r-1}$$

$$\hat{p} = \frac{r}{n} = \frac{\#\text{heads}}{\#\text{tosses}}.$$

To generalize these ideas, let $X_1, \ldots, X_n$ be a random sample from the density $f(x|\theta)$ where θ is the unknown parameter to be estimated, which is in the known parameter space Θ. The *likelihood function* is defined to be

$$L(\theta) = \prod_{i=1}^{n} f(x_i|\theta).$$

It is regarded as a function of θ with the data $x_1, \ldots, x_n$ regarded as fixed. The *maximum likelihood estimator* is defined as

$$\hat{\theta}_n = \underset{\theta \in \Theta}{\text{argmax}}\ L(\theta),$$

which is usually obtained by solving first-order conditions of the form $(\partial/\partial\theta)L(\theta) = 0$ for θ.

For the normal density, letting the unknown parameters be μ and $\tau = \sigma^2$ and the parameter space be $\Theta = (-\infty, \infty) \times (0, \infty)$, the likelihood is

$$L(\mu, \tau) = (2\pi\tau)^{-n/2} \exp\left[-\frac{1}{2}\tau^{-1}\sum_{t=1}^{n}(x_i - \mu)^2\right].$$

The maximum of $L(\mu, \tau)$ is the same as the maximum of

$$\log L(\mu, \tau) = \frac{1}{2}\left[-n\log(2\pi) - n\log\tau - \tau^{-1}\sum_{t=1}^{n}(x_i - \mu)^2\right].$$

The first-order conditions are

$$0 = \frac{\partial}{\partial\mu}\log L(\mu, \tau) = \tau^{-1}\sum_{t=1}^{n}(x_i - \mu)$$

$$0 = \frac{\partial}{\partial\tau}\log L(\mu, \tau) = \frac{1}{2}\left[-n\tau^{-1} + \tau^{-2}\sum_{t=1}^{n}(x_i - \mu)^2\right].$$

The solution is

$$\hat{\mu} = \bar{x} = \frac{1}{n}\sum_{i=1}^{n} x_i$$

$$\hat{\tau} = \hat{\sigma}^2 = \frac{1}{n}\sum_{t=1}^{n}(x_i - \bar{x})^2.$$

5.2.2 *Asymptotics of Maximum Likelihood Estimators*

In this subsection we shall sketch the main ideas of an asymptotic analysis of maximum likelihood estimators. For a more thorough development see Lehmann 1983.

5.2.2.1 *Strong Consistency*

We shall assume that θ is a scalar, not a vector, that the parameter space Θ is a closed and bounded interval, and that $\log f(x|\theta)$ is continuous in (x, θ) and bounded by an integrable function $b(x)$ in the sense that $\sup_{\theta\in\Theta} |\log f(x|\theta)| < b(x)$ and $\int b(x) f(x|\theta^o)\,dx < \infty$.

The normalized log likelihood is

$$s_n(\theta) = \frac{1}{n}\log L(\theta) = \frac{1}{n}\sum_{i=1}^{n}\log f(x_i|\theta).$$

The uniform strong law of large numbers (Theorem 4.2) implies that

$$\lim_{n\to\infty} \sup_{\theta\in\Theta} \left| s_n(\theta) - \int \log f(x|\theta) f(x|\theta^o)\,dx \right| = 0 \quad \text{a.s.}$$

What can one say about $\int \log f(x|\theta) f(x|\theta^o)\,dx$?

The function $y = \log u$ is a concave function. The tangent line at the point $u = 1$ is $y = -1 + u$. Because a concave function plots below any tangent line, we have the inequality

$$\log u \leq -1 + u.$$

Therefore,

$$\log\frac{f(x|\theta)}{f(x|\theta^o)} \leq -1 + \frac{f(x|\theta)}{f(x|\theta^o)},$$

which, upon multiplication of both sides by $f(x|\theta^o)$, implies

$$[\log f(x|\theta) - \log f(x|\theta^o)]f(x|\theta^o) \leq -f(x|\theta^o) + f(x|\theta).$$

Upon integrating both sides we have

$$\int [\log f(x|\theta) - \log f(x|\theta^o)]f(x|\theta^o)\, dx \leq -1 + 1 = 0,$$

which implies the *information inequality*

$$\int \log f(x|\theta) f(x|\theta^o)\, dx \leq \int \log f(x|\theta^o) f(x|\theta^o)\, dx.$$

The information inequality implies that

$$\theta^o = \operatorname*{argmax}_{\theta \in \Theta} \int \log f(x|\theta) f(x|\theta^o)\, dx.$$

Assume that this maximum is unique over the interval Θ.

Consider what happens as data are acquired. Recall the paradigm: There is a random experiment $(\Omega, \mathcal{F}, P)$ that is rich enough to support the infinite sequence of random variables $X_1(\omega)$, $X_2(\omega)$, ..., ω is the outcome, data $x_1 = X_1(\omega)$, $x_2 = X_2(\omega)$, ..., are observed, and for each n we construct

$$\hat{\theta}_n(\omega) = \operatorname*{argmax}_{\theta \in \Theta} \frac{1}{n} \sum_{i=1}^{n} \log f[X_i(\omega)|\theta].$$

Therefore, for each $\omega \in \Omega$, $\hat{\theta}_n = \hat{\theta}_n(\omega)$ can be regarded as a sequence of numbers in the closed and bounded interval Θ. A sequence of points in a closed and bounded set has the Bolzano-Weierstrass property (Bartle 1976, p. 70), which is that there must exist at least one point θ^* and a subsequence $\hat{\theta}_{n_j} = \hat{\theta}_{n_j}(\omega)$ such that

$$\lim_{j \to \infty} \hat{\theta}_{n_j} = \theta^*.$$

The consequence of uniform convergence and continuity is that a joint limit can be computed as an iterated limit (Problem 1),

$$\lim_{j \to \infty} s_{n_j}(\hat{\theta}_{n_j}) = \lim_{j \to \infty} s_{n_j}\Big(\lim_{k \to \infty} \hat{\theta}_{n_k}\Big).$$

Therefore, we have that

$$\lim_{j\to\infty} s_{n_j}(\hat{\theta}_{n_j}) = \int \log f(x|\theta^*) f(x|\theta^o)\, dx$$

$$\lim_{j\to\infty} s_{n_j}(\theta^o) = \int \log f(x|\theta^o) f(x|\theta^o)\, dx.$$

Now $\hat{\theta}_{n_j}$ maximizes $s_{n_j}(\theta)$ and θ^o might not. Therefore we have

$$s_{n_j}(\hat{\theta}_{n_j}) \geq s_{n_j}(\theta^o).$$

This inequality is preserved in the limit so we have

$$\int \log f(x|\theta^*) f(x|\theta^o)\, dx \geq \int \log f(x|\theta^o) f(x|\theta^o)\, dx.$$

We assumed that θ^o is the unique maximum of $\int \log f(x|\theta) f(x|\theta^o)\, dx$, which implies $\theta^* = \theta^o$. Therefore, the sequence $\hat{\theta}_n = \hat{\theta}_n(\omega)$ has only one limit point, which is θ^o.

We have reached this point in our argument: Except for outcomes ω in the event E where the uniform strong law of large numbers fails, $\lim_{n\to\infty} \hat{\theta}_n(\omega) = \theta^o$. However, $P(E) = 0$ and we conclude that

$$\lim_{n\to\infty} \hat{\theta}_n = \theta^o \quad \text{a.s.}$$

That is, the maximum likelihood estimator is strongly consistent.

The same proof will work if θ is a vector. In that case, Θ must be closed and bounded. This restriction can be removed by imposing restrictions on the tails of $f(x|\theta)$ and then proving that these restrictions imply that for some N large enough it must be true that $\hat{\theta}_n$ is in a closed and bounded set for all $n > N$. See Wald 1949 for this argument and for one of the nicest general proofs of the consistency of maximum likelihood estimators.

Asymptotic Normality

We shall assume that θ is a scalar, not a vector, that the parameter space Θ is a closed and bounded interval, that θ^o is not one of the endpoints of the interval, that $\log f(x|\theta)$, $(d/d\theta)\log f(x|\theta)$, and $(d^2/d\theta^2)\log f(x|\theta)$ are continuous in (x, θ) and are bounded by an integrable function $b(x)$ in the sense that, e.g., $\sup_{\theta\in\Theta} |(d/d\theta)\log f(x|\theta)| < b(x)$ and $\int b(x) f(x|\theta^o)\, dx < \infty$. We shall also assume that $0 < \int [(d/d\theta)\log f(x|\theta^o)]^2 f(x|\theta^o)\, dx < \infty$ and that $\lim_{n\to\infty} \hat{\theta}_n = \theta^o$ a.s.

The first-order condition $0 = (d/d\theta)s_n(\theta)$ for maximizing

$$s_n(\theta) = \frac{1}{n}\log L(\theta) = \frac{1}{n}\sum_{i=1}^{n}\log f(x_i|\theta) \tag{5.1}$$

is solved by $\hat{\theta}_n$ and can be expanded using Taylor's theorem (Bartle 1976, p. 206) as follows:

$$0 = \frac{d}{d\theta}s_n(\hat{\theta}_n) = \frac{d}{d\theta}s_n(\theta^o) + \frac{d^2}{d\theta^2}s_n(\bar{\theta}_n)(\hat{\theta}_n - \theta^o), \tag{5.2}$$

where either $\hat{\theta}_n \le \bar{\theta}_n \le \theta^o$ or $\theta^o \le \bar{\theta}_n \le \hat{\theta}_n$. Whichever, $\bar{\theta}_n$ is trapped in the middle so that $\lim_{n\to\infty}\hat{\theta}_n = \theta^o$ a.s. implies $\lim_{n\to\infty}\bar{\theta}_n = \theta^o$ a.s. Upon substituting Equation (5.1) in Equation (5.2), multiplying through by $\sqrt{n}$, and rearranging terms, we have

$$\left[\frac{1}{n}\sum_{i=1}^{n}\frac{d^2}{d\theta^2}\log f(x_i|\bar{\theta}_n)\right]\sqrt{n}(\hat{\theta}_n - \theta^o) = -\frac{1}{\sqrt{n}}\sum_{i=1}^{n}\frac{d}{d\theta}\log f(x_i|\theta^o).$$

As shown above, θ^o maximizes $\int \log f(x|\theta)f(x|\theta^o)\,dx$ and therefore satisfies the first-order condition $0 = (d/d\theta)\int \log f(x|\theta)f(x|\theta^o)\,dx$. The assumptions in place are adequate to imply that differentiation and integration interchange (Problem 11) so that

$$0 = \frac{d}{d\theta}\int \log f(x|\theta)f(x|\theta^o)\,dx\,\bigg|_{\theta=\theta^o} = \int \frac{d}{d\theta}\log f(x|\theta)f(x|\theta^o)\,dx\,\bigg|_{\theta=\theta^o}.$$

This implies that the random variable $(d/d\theta)\log f(X_i|\theta^o)$ has mean zero. We assumed that $0 < \int[(d/d\theta)\log f(x|\theta^o)]^2 f(x|\theta^o)\,dx < \infty$, which implies it has finite variance as well. Therefore, the sequence of random variables $(d/d\theta)\log f(X_i|\theta^o)$, $i = 1, \ldots, n$, is iid with mean zero and finite variance and we can apply the central limit theorem (Theorem 4.5) to conclude that

$$-\frac{1}{\sqrt{n}}\sum_{i=1}^{n}\frac{d}{d\theta}\log f(X_i|\theta^o) \xrightarrow{\mathscr{L}} N(0, \mathscr{I})$$

where

$$\mathscr{I} = \int\left[\frac{d}{d\theta}\log f(x|\theta^o)\right]^2 f(x|\theta^o)\,dx.$$

The uniform strong law of large numbers (Theorem 4.2) implies that

$$\lim_{n\to\infty} \sup_{\theta\in\Theta} \left[\frac{1}{n} \sum_{i=1}^{n} \frac{d^2}{d\theta^2} \log f(x_i|\theta) - \int \frac{d^2}{d\theta^2} \log f(x|\theta) f(x|\theta^o)\, dx \right] = 0 \quad \text{a.s.}$$

Because $\lim_{n\to\infty} \bar{\theta}_n = \theta^o$ a.s., this implies (Problem 1)

$$\lim_{n\to\infty} \frac{1}{n} \sum_{i=1}^{n} \frac{d^2}{d\theta^2} \log f(x_i|\bar{\theta}_n) = \mathcal{J}$$

where

$$\mathcal{J} = \int \left[\frac{d^2}{d\theta^2} \log f(x|\theta^o) \right] f(x|\theta^o)\, dx.$$

We now have that

$$\begin{aligned} &\left[\frac{1}{n} \sum_{i=1}^{n} \frac{d^2}{d\theta^2} \log f(x_i|\bar{\theta}_n) \right] \sqrt{n}(\hat{\theta}_n - \theta^o) \\ &\quad = -\frac{1}{\sqrt{n}} \sum_{i=1}^{n} \frac{d}{d\theta} \log f(x_i|\theta^o) - \frac{1}{\sqrt{n}} \sum_{i=1}^{n} \frac{d}{d\theta} \log f(x_i|\theta^o) \\ &\quad \xrightarrow{\mathcal{L}} N(0, \mathcal{I}) \end{aligned}$$

and

$$\lim_{n\to\infty} \frac{1}{n} \sum_{i=1}^{n} \frac{d^2}{d\theta^2} \log f(x_i|\bar{\theta}_n) = \mathcal{J} \quad \text{a.s.}$$

Slutsky's theorem (Theorem 4.6) implies

$$\sqrt{n}(\hat{\theta}_n - \theta^o) \xrightarrow{\mathcal{L}} N\left(0, \frac{\mathcal{I}}{\mathcal{J}^2}\right).$$

From Problem 2 we have $\mathcal{I} = -\mathcal{J}$ so that

$$\sqrt{n}(\hat{\theta}_n - \theta^o) \xrightarrow{\mathcal{L}} N(0, \mathcal{I}^{-1}),$$

which is our main result. $\mathcal{I}$ can be estimated using

$$\hat{\mathcal{I}}_n = \frac{1}{n} \sum_{i=1}^{n} \left[\frac{d}{d\theta} \log f(x_i|\hat{\theta}_n) \right]^2$$

(Problem 3). The principal application of these results is that the confidence interval

$$\hat{\theta}_n - \frac{1.96}{\sqrt{n\hat{\mathcal{I}}_n}} \leq \theta \leq \hat{\theta}_n + \frac{1.96}{\sqrt{n\hat{\mathcal{I}}_n}}$$

is approximately 95% for large n (Problem 4).

The argument when θ is a vector is similar, and we shall see how the details are dealt with in the next few sections. The relevant equations are

$$\left[\frac{1}{n}\sum_{i=1}^{n}\frac{\partial^2}{\partial\theta\,\partial\theta'}\log f(x_i|\bar{\theta}_n)\right]\sqrt{n}(\hat{\theta}_n - \theta^o) = -\frac{1}{\sqrt{n}}\sum_{i=1}^{n}\frac{\partial}{\partial\theta}\log f(x_i|\theta^o)$$

$$\mathcal{I} = \int\left[\frac{\partial}{\partial\theta}\log f(x|\theta^o)\right]\left[\frac{\partial}{\partial\theta}\log f(x|\theta^o)\right]' f(x|\theta^o)\,dx$$

$$\mathcal{J} = \int\left[\frac{\partial^2}{\partial\theta\,\partial\theta'}\log f(x|\theta^o)\right] f(x|\theta^o)\,dx$$

$$-\frac{1}{\sqrt{n}}\sum_{i=1}^{n}\frac{\partial}{\partial\theta}\log f(x_i|\theta^o) \xrightarrow{\mathcal{L}} N(0, \mathcal{I})$$

$$\sqrt{n}(\hat{\theta}_n - \theta^o) \xrightarrow{\mathcal{L}} N(0, \mathcal{J}^{-1}\mathcal{I}\mathcal{J}^{-1}) = N(0, \mathcal{I}^{-1})$$

$$\hat{\mathcal{I}}_n = \frac{1}{n}\sum_{i=1}^{n}\left[\frac{\partial}{\partial\theta}\log f(x_i|\hat{\theta}_n)\right]\left[\frac{\partial}{\partial\theta}\log f(x_i|\hat{\theta}_n)\right]' \to \mathcal{I} \quad \text{a.s.}$$

and $\mathcal{I} = -\mathcal{J}$. Recall from Section 3.7 that one computes the integral of a matrix by integrating each element of the matrix individually.

5.2.3 *Quasi Maximum Likelihood*

Suppose that we use the estimator

$$\tilde{\theta}_n = \underset{\theta\in\Theta}{\operatorname{argmax}}\, s_n(\theta)$$

where

$$s_n(\theta) = \frac{1}{n}\sum_{i=1}^{n} \log f(x_i|\theta)$$

when the true density of the data is actually

$$p(x|\rho), \qquad \rho \in R.$$

What changes? The answer is not much.

Almost Sure Convergence

Assume that θ is a vector and that Θ is closed and bounded. Also assume that $\log f(x|\theta)$ is continuous in (x, θ) and bounded by an integrable function $b(x)$ in the sense that $\sup_{\theta\in\Theta} |\log f(x|\theta)| < b(x)$ and $\int b(x)p(x|\rho^o)\,dx < \infty$, where ρ^o denotes the true value of ρ.

The uniform strong law of large numbers (Theorem 4.2) implies that

$$\lim_{n\to\infty} \sup_{\theta\in\Theta} |s_n(\theta) - \bar{s}(\theta, \rho^o)| = 0 \quad \text{a.s.}$$

where

$$\bar{s}(\theta, \rho) = \int \log f(x|\theta)\, p(x|\rho)\, dx.$$

If $\bar{s}(\theta, \rho^o)$ has a unique maximum θ^o over Θ, then the analysis of Section 5.2.2 can be repeated to conclude that

$$\lim_{n\to\infty} \tilde{\theta}_n = \theta^o \quad \text{a.s.}$$

The quantity

$$\int [\log p(x|\rho^o) - \log f(x|\theta)]\, p(x|\rho^o)\, dx$$

is called the *Kullback-Liebler discrepancy*. Provided $p(x|\rho^o)$ and $f(x|\theta)$ are both continuous in x, the analysis of Section 5.2.2 shows that the Kullback-Liebler discrepancy is positive when $p(x|\rho^o) \neq f(x|\theta)$ for some x and is zero when $p(x|\rho^o) = f(x|\theta)$ for all x. Therefore, what we have shown here is that quasi maximum likelihood finds that density $f(x|\theta^o)$ in the family of densities $\{f(x|\theta) : \theta \in \Theta\}$ that minimizes the Kullback-Liebler discrepancy. This may or may not be a sensible thing to do, depending on the choice of $f(x|\theta)$. If, for example, one puts $f(x|\theta)$ to the *SNP density*

$$f_K(x|\theta) = \frac{[\sum_{j=0}^{K} \theta_j x^j]^2 \phi(x)}{\int [\sum_{j=0}^{K} \theta_j u^j]^2 \phi(u)\, du},$$

where $\phi(x)$ is the standard normal density function and $\theta_0 \equiv 1$, the approximation of $p(x|\rho^o)$ by $f(x|\theta^o)$ can be very accurate (Gallant and Nychka 1987).

Asymptotic Normality

In addition to the assumptions above, assume that θ^o is an interior point of Θ and that the elements of $(\partial/\partial\theta)\log f(x|\theta)$ and $(\partial^2/\partial\theta\,\partial\theta')\log f(x|\theta)$ are continuous in (x, θ) and are bounded by an integrable function. For every nonzero vector a, assume that

$$0 < \int \left[a' \frac{\partial}{\partial\theta} \log f(x|\theta^o) \right]^2 p(x|\rho^o)\, dx < \infty.$$

Because θ^o maximizes $\int \log f(x|\theta) p(x|\rho^o)\, dx$, θ^o satisfies the first-order conditions

$$0 = \frac{\partial}{\partial\theta} \int \log f(x|\theta^o) p(x|\rho^o)\, dx = \int \frac{\partial}{\partial\theta} \log f(x|\theta^o) p(x|\rho^o)\, dx. \quad (5.3)$$

This implies that the random variable $a'(\partial/\partial\theta)\log f(X_i|\theta^o)$ has mean zero. We assumed that $0 < \int [a'(\partial/\partial\theta)\log f(x|\theta^o)]^2 p(x|\rho^o)\, dx < \infty$ which implies it has finite variance as well. Therefore, the sequence of random variables $a'(\partial/\partial\theta)\log f(X_i|\theta^o)$, $i = 1, \ldots, n$, is iid with mean zero and finite variance and we can apply the central limit theorem (Theorem 4.5) to conclude that

$$\frac{1}{\sqrt{n}} \sum_{i=1}^{n} a' \frac{\partial}{\partial\theta} \log f(X_i|\theta^o) \xrightarrow{\mathscr{L}} N(0, a'\mathscr{I}a) \quad (5.4)$$

for every nonzero a, where

$$\mathscr{I} = \int \left[\frac{\partial}{\partial\theta} \log f(x|\theta^o) \right] \left[\frac{\partial}{\partial\theta} \log f(x|\theta^o) \right]' p(x|\rho^o)\, dx.$$

As mentioned in Section 4.4, if Y_n is a random vector and $a'Y_n \xrightarrow{\mathcal{L}} N(0, a'\mathcal{I}a)$ for every $a \neq 0$, then $Y_n \xrightarrow{\mathcal{L}} N(0, \mathcal{I})$. Therefore, Equation (5.4) implies that

$$\frac{1}{\sqrt{n}} \sum_{i=1}^{n} \frac{\partial}{\partial \theta} \log f(X_i|\theta^o) \xrightarrow{\mathcal{L}} N(0, \mathcal{I}). \tag{5.5}$$

With asymptotic normality of the *score vector* $(\partial/\partial\theta) \log f(X_i|\theta^o)$ established, the remainder of the argument to establish the asymptotic normality of $\sqrt{n}(\tilde{\theta}_n - \theta^o)$ is the same as in Section 5.2.2. There are some slight differences in details necessary to handle the difference between the scalar and the vector case. An example of how these details are handled is in Section 5.3.3. Because the argument is so similar to Section 5.2.2 and an example of how differences in the details are handled is available, we shall merely display the key equations and sketch the main points of the remainder of the argument.

Taylor's theorem and some algebra allow one to put the first-order conditions

$$0 = \sqrt{n} \frac{\partial}{\partial \theta} s_n(\tilde{\theta}_n) = \frac{1}{\sqrt{n}} \sum_{i=1}^{n} \frac{\partial}{\partial \theta} \log f(x_i|\tilde{\theta}_n)$$

in the form

$$\left[\frac{1}{n} \sum_{i=1}^{n} \frac{\partial^2}{\partial \theta \, \partial \theta'} \log f(x_i|\bar{\theta}_n)\right] \sqrt{n}(\tilde{\theta}_n - \theta^o) = -\frac{1}{\sqrt{n}} \sum_{i=1}^{n} \frac{\partial}{\partial \theta} \log f(x_i|\theta^o),$$

where $(\partial^2/\partial\theta\,\partial\theta') \log f(x|\bar{\theta}_n)$ has typical row $(\partial/\partial\theta')(\partial/\partial\theta_i) \log f(x|\bar{\theta}_n)$ and $\bar{\theta}_n$ lies on the line segment that joins $\tilde{\theta}_n$ to θ^o; the vector $\bar{\theta}_n$ will differ from row to row. The almost sure convergence of $\tilde{\theta}_n$ to θ^o and the uniform strong law of large numbers (Theorem 4.2) imply that the elements of $(1/n)\sum_{i=1}^{n}(\partial^2/\partial\theta\,\partial\theta') \log f(x_i|\bar{\theta}_n)$ converge almost surely to the elements of

$$\mathcal{J} = \int \left[\frac{\partial^2}{\partial \theta \, \partial \theta'} \log f(x|\theta^o)\right] p(x|\rho^o) \, dx.$$

Slutsky's theorem (Theorem 4.6 with following remarks) and Equation (5.5) imply

$$\sqrt{n}(\tilde{\theta}_n - \theta^o) \xrightarrow{\mathcal{L}} N(0, \mathcal{J}^{-1}\mathcal{I}\mathcal{J}^{-1}).$$

The matrix $\mathcal{I}$ can be estimated consistently by

$$\tilde{\mathcal{I}}_n = \frac{1}{n} \sum_{i=1}^{n} \left[\frac{\partial}{\partial \theta} \log f(x_i | \tilde{\theta}_n) \right] \left[\frac{\partial}{\partial \theta} \log f(x_i | \tilde{\theta}_n) \right]'$$

and the matrix $\mathcal{J}$ by

$$\mathcal{J} = \frac{1}{n} \sum_{i=1}^{n} \frac{\partial^2}{\partial \theta \, \partial \theta'} \log f(x_i | \theta^o).$$

5.3 Method of Moments Estimation

5.3.1 *The Method of Moments*

The method of moments is one of the oldest and most straightforward methods of constructing an estimator. One defines a statistic $\bar{W}_n = W(x_1, \ldots, x_n)$, computes its expectation

$$\mathcal{M}(\theta) = \int \cdots \int W(x_1, \ldots, x_n) \prod_{i=1}^{n} f(x_i | \theta) \, dx_1 \cdots dx_n,$$

and solves the equations

$$\bar{W}_n = \mathcal{M}(\theta).$$

The solution $\hat{\theta}_n$ is the method of moments estimator.

As an example, let

$$\bar{W}_n = \begin{pmatrix} \bar{x} \\ s^2 \end{pmatrix}$$

where

$$\bar{x} = \frac{1}{n} \sum_{i=1}^{n} x_i, \qquad s^2 = \frac{1}{n-1} \sum_{i=1}^{n} (x_i - \bar{x})^2.$$

If $f(x|\theta)$ is the normal distribution with parameter

$$\theta = \begin{pmatrix} \mu \\ \sigma^2 \end{pmatrix},$$

then $\mathcal{M}(\theta) = \theta$ and the solution of the equations $\bar{W}_n = \mathcal{M}(\theta)$ is

$$\hat{\theta}_n = \begin{pmatrix} \bar{x} \\ s^2 \end{pmatrix},$$

which is the estimator.

To provide intuition for the next subsection, note that if we put $m_n(\theta) = W(x_1, \ldots, x_n) - \mathcal{M}(\theta)$, then the method of moments estimator is the solution of the equations $m_n(\theta) = 0$.

5.3.2 *Generalized Method of Moments*

Often in econometrics, $\mathcal{M}(\theta)$ cannot be computed, but for some function of parameters and data

$$m_n(\theta) = m_n(\theta, x_1, \ldots, x_n)$$

the following results are available:

$$\lim_{n\to\infty} m_n(\theta^o) = 0 \quad \text{a.s.}$$

$$\sqrt{n}\, m_n(\theta^o) \xrightarrow{\mathcal{L}} N(0, V),$$

and there is an estimator $\tilde{V}_n$ of V for which

$$\lim_{n\to\infty} \tilde{V}_n = V \quad \text{a.s.}$$

In this case one solves $m_n(\theta) = 0$ to obtain an estimator. If the dimension of $m_n(\theta)$ is larger than the dimension of θ, which is usually the case, one uses

$$\hat{\theta}_n = \underset{\theta\in\Theta}{\operatorname{argmin}}\, m_n'(\theta)\tilde{V}_n^{-1} m_n(\theta)$$

instead.

The estimator in the latter form is usually called *minimum chi-square* in the statistics literature. In the econometrics literature it is called *generalized method of moments*, *two stage least squares*, or *three stage least squares*. Most often, the method is used in connection with instrumental variables, as in the example immediately below. The classic references are Theil 1961, Zellner and Theil 1962, and Hansen 1982. Optimal choice of instruments is discussed in Newey 1990.

We illustrate with the asset pricing application of Hansen and Singleton 1982. Suppose that a representative agent has constant relative risk aversion utility

$$U = \sum_{t=0}^{n} \beta^t \frac{c_t^\gamma - 1}{\gamma},$$

where $\beta > 0$ is the agent's discount factor, $\gamma \geq 0$ is the risk aversion parameter, and c_t is consumption during period t. Let the information available to the agent at time t be represented by the σ-algebra $\mathcal{F}_t$—in the sense that any variable whose value is known at time t is presumed to be $\mathcal{F}_t$-measurable—and let $r_t = p_t/p_{t-1}$ be the gross return to an asset acquired at time $t-1$ at a price of p_{t-1}. The agent's optimization problem is to maximize $\mathscr{E}(U|\mathcal{F}_0)$ subject to $c_t + p_t q_t \leq w_t + p_t q_{t-1}$, where q_t is the quantity of the asset purchased at time t and w_t is the agent's period t income. The marginal rate of intertemporal substitution is

$$\mathrm{MRS}_{t+1}(\beta, \gamma) = \frac{(\partial/\partial c_{t+1})U}{(\partial/\partial c_t)U} = \beta \left(\frac{c_{t+1}}{c_t} \right)^{\gamma - 1}.$$

The first-order conditions of the agent's optimization problem are

$$\mathscr{E}[\mathrm{MRS}_{t+1}(\beta, \gamma) r_{t+1} | \mathcal{F}_t] = 1;$$

that is, the marginal rate of intertemporal substitution discounts gross returns to unity.

Upon application of Theorem 2.6, which states that variables that are measurable $\mathcal{F}_t$ may be moved outside the conditional expectation operator, we can deduce the following conditional moment restrictions:

$$\mathscr{E}\left\{[\mathrm{MRS}_{t+1}(\beta, \gamma) r_{t+1} - 1] \middle| \mathcal{F}_t\right\} = 0$$

$$\mathscr{E}\left\{\frac{c_t}{c_{t-1}}[\mathrm{MRS}_{t+1}(\beta, \gamma) r_{t+1} - 1] \middle| \mathcal{F}_t\right\} = 0$$

$$\mathscr{E}\left\{r_t[\mathrm{MRS}_{t+1}(\beta, \gamma) r_{t+1} - 1] \middle| \mathcal{F}_t\right\} = 0.$$

Upon application of Theorem 2.5, which is the law of iterated expectations, we can deduce the following unconditional moment restrictions:

$$\mathscr{E}\{[\mathrm{MRS}_{t+1}(\beta, \gamma) r_{t+1} - 1]\} = 0$$

$$\mathscr{E}\left\{\frac{c_t}{c_{t-1}}[\mathrm{MRS}_{t+1}(\beta, \gamma) r_{t+1} - 1]\right\} = 0$$

$$\mathscr{E}\{r_t[\mathrm{MRS}_{t+1}(\beta, \gamma) r_{t+1} - 1]\} = 0.$$

Therefore, the sample moments

$$m_n(\beta, \gamma) = \frac{1}{n} \sum_{t=1}^{n} m_t(\beta, \gamma)$$

where

$$m_t(\beta, \gamma) = [\text{MRS}(\beta, \gamma) r_{t+1} - 1] \begin{pmatrix} 1 \\ \dfrac{c_t}{c_{t-1}} \\ r_t \end{pmatrix}$$

can serve as the basis for estimation. The elements of the vector

$$z_t = \begin{pmatrix} 1 \\ \dfrac{c_t}{c_{t-1}} \\ r_t \end{pmatrix}$$

are called instrumental variables. We shall presume that

$$\lim_{n \to \infty} m_n(\beta^o, \gamma^o) = 0 \quad \text{a.s.}$$

$$\sqrt{n}\, m_n(\beta^o, \gamma^o) \xrightarrow{\mathscr{L}} N(0, V),$$

where V is unknown. We can estimate V by

$$\tilde{V}_n = \frac{1}{n} \sum_{t=1}^{n} m_t(\bar{\beta}_n, \bar{\gamma}_n) m_t'(\bar{\beta}_n, \bar{\gamma}_n)$$

where

$$(\bar{\beta}_n, \bar{\gamma}_n) = \underset{\beta>0,\, \gamma\geq 0}{\operatorname{argmin}}\, m_n'(\beta, \gamma) \left(\frac{1}{n} \sum_{t=1}^{n} z_t z_t' \right)^{-1} m_n(\beta, \gamma).$$

The generalized method of moments estimator is

$$(\hat{\beta}_n, \hat{\gamma}_n) = \underset{\beta>0,\, \gamma\geq 0}{\operatorname{argmin}}\, m_n'(\beta, \gamma) \tilde{V}_n^{-1} m_n(\beta, \gamma).$$

5.3.3 *Asymptotics of Method of Moments*

In this subsection we shall sketch the main ideas of an asymptotic analysis of method of moments estimators. For a more thorough development see Gallant 1987, Chapter 3.

Strong Consistency

The proof of consistency is basically the same as the proof of consistency for maximum likelihood estimators (Section 5.2.2). Put

$$s_n(\theta) = m_n'(\theta)\tilde{V}_n^{-1}m_n(\theta).$$

What is needed are plausible conditions such that $s_n(\theta)$ converges uniformly over Θ to some function $s(\theta)$ that has a unique minimum at θ^o. Thereafter the argument is the same as used in Section 5.2.2.

Suppose that the parameter space Θ is closed and bounded, that $m_n(\theta)$ is continuous, and that $m_n(\theta)$ converges uniformly over Θ to some function $m(\theta)$ almost surely. Then $s_n(\theta)$ converges uniformly over Θ to $s(\theta) = m'(\theta)V^{-1}m(\theta)$ almost surely. We have assumed that $\lim_{n\to\infty} m_n(\theta^o) = 0$ almost surely, which implies $m(\theta^o) = 0$. If θ^o is the only solution of $m(\theta) = 0$ over Θ, then $s(\theta)$ has a unique minimum at θ^o.

In summary, if Θ is closed and bounded, if $m_n(\theta)$ is continuous, if $m_n(\theta)$ converges uniformly to $m(\theta)$ almost surely, and if θ^o is the only solution of $m(\theta) = 0$, then $\lim_{n\to\infty} \hat{\theta}_n = \theta^o$.

Asymptotic Normality

In addition to the assumptions above, assume that θ^o is an interior point of Θ. Let $M_n(\theta) = (\partial/\partial\theta')m_n(\theta)$, which we shall presume is continuous and converges uniformly over Θ to $M(\theta) = (\partial/\partial\theta')m(\theta)$. The first-order conditions for the minimization of $s_n(\theta)$ are

$$0 = \frac{\partial}{\partial\theta}s_n(\hat{\theta}_n) = 2M'(\hat{\theta}_n)\tilde{V}_n^{-1}m_n(\hat{\theta}_n).$$

Using Taylor's theorem (Bartle 1976, p. 206) to expand a typical row of $m_n(\hat{\theta}_n)$, we have

$$\sqrt{n}\, m_{i,n}(\hat{\theta}_n) = \sqrt{n}\, m_{i,n}(\theta^o) + \frac{\partial}{\partial\theta'}m_{i,n}(\bar{\theta}_n)\sqrt{n}(\hat{\theta}_n - \theta^o),$$

where $\bar{\theta}_n$ is on the line segment joining θ^o to $\hat{\theta}_n$. Because $\bar{\theta}_n$ is thereby trapped between θ^o and $\hat{\theta}_n$, $\bar{\theta}_n$ converges almost surely to θ^o. Moreover, $(\partial/\partial\theta')m_{i,n}(\theta)$ is a typical row of $M_n(\theta)$, which converges uniformly over Θ to $M(\theta)$ almost surely. Therefore,

$$\lim_{n\to\infty} \frac{\partial}{\partial\theta}m_{i,n}(\bar{\theta}_n) = \frac{\partial}{\partial\theta}m_i(\theta^o) \quad \text{a.s.},$$

which we write as

$$\frac{\partial}{\partial \theta} m_{i,n}(\bar{\theta}_n) = \frac{\partial}{\partial \theta} m_i(\theta^o) + o_s(1).$$

Applying this argument to each row of $m_n(\theta)$, we have

$$\sqrt{n}\, m_n(\hat{\theta}_n) = \sqrt{n}\, m_n(\theta^o) + [M(\theta^o) + o_s(1)]\sqrt{n}(\hat{\theta}_n - \theta^o). \qquad (5.6)$$

Substituting Equation (5.6) into the first-order conditions, we have

$$\begin{aligned} 0 &= M'(\hat{\theta}_n)\tilde{V}_n^{-1}\sqrt{n}\, m_n(\theta^o) \\ &\quad + M'(\hat{\theta}_n)\tilde{V}_n^{-1}[M(\theta^o) + o_s(1)]\sqrt{n}(\hat{\theta}_n - \theta^o). \end{aligned} \qquad (5.7)$$

Because the sequence $M'(\hat{\theta}_n)\tilde{V}_n^{-1}$ converges almost surely to $M'(\theta^o)V^{-1}$ and $\sqrt{n}\, m_n(\theta^o) \xrightarrow{\mathscr{L}} N(0, V)$, Slutsky's theorem (Theorem 4.6 with following remarks) implies

$$M'(\hat{\theta}_n)\tilde{V}_n^{-1}\sqrt{n}\, m_n(\theta^o) \xrightarrow{\mathscr{L}} N[0, M'(\theta^o)V^{-1}VV^{-1}M(\theta^o)]. \qquad (5.8)$$

The matrix $M'(\hat{\theta}_n)\tilde{V}_n^{-1}[(M(\theta^o) + o_s(1)]$ converges to $M'(\theta^o)V^{-1}M(\theta^o)$ almost surely. This, Equations (5.7) and (5.8), and Slutsky's theorem imply $\sqrt{n}(\hat{\theta}_n - \theta^o) \xrightarrow{\mathscr{L}} N(0, \Sigma)$, where

$$\Sigma = [M'(\theta^o)V^{-1}M(\theta^o)]^{-1}M'(\theta^o)V^{-1}VV^{-1}M(\theta^o)[M'(\theta^o)V^{-1}M(\theta^o)]^{-1},$$

which simplifies to

$$\sqrt{n}(\hat{\theta}_n - \theta^o) \xrightarrow{\mathscr{L}} N\{0, [M'(\theta^o)V^{-1}M(\theta^o)]^{-1}\}.$$

5.3.4 *Efficient Method of Moments*

Often in economics, and throughout the sciences for that matter, one has a model for which one cannot find an analytic expression for the density $p(x|\rho)$ but from which one can generate a simulation $\{\hat{x}_j\}_{j=1}^N$ on a computer. Examples are general equilibrium models, auction models, and stochastic differential equations. However, if one can simulate, then one can compute the expectation

$$\mathscr{E}_\rho g = \int g(x)p(x|\rho)\, dx$$

of a function g using the formula

$$\mathscr{E}_\rho g \doteq \frac{1}{N}\sum_{j=1}^{N} g(\hat{x}_j).$$

This is the conclusion of the strong law of large numbers (Theorem 4.1), which states that $\mathscr{E}_\rho g$ can be computed to any desired accuracy in this fashion by taking N sufficiently large.

We are in a situation where we cannot apply the method of maximum likelihood, because we cannot obtain $p(x|\rho)$, but we can apply the method of moments, because we can compute expectations. As a general rule, maximum likelihood estimators are consistent, asymptotically normally distributed, and have the smallest asymptotic variance of all estimators that are both consistent and asymptotically normally distributed. The challenge is to come up with a method of moments estimator that does as well as maximum likelihood. Here we describe an estimator proposed by Bansal, Gallant, Hussey, and Tauchen 1993 that accomplishes this objective and is computationally feasible. We shall derive the asymptotics of the estimator for the iid case; more generally applicable asymptotics are in Gallant and Tauchen 1996. See Gourieroux, Monfort, and Renault 1993 for extensions and the similar notion of indirect inference.

To define a method of moments estimator, one's task is to produce a function $m_n(\rho)$ of parameters and data for which the following results are available:

$$\lim_{n\to\infty} m_n(\rho^o) = 0 \quad \text{a.s.}$$

$$\sqrt{n}\, m_n(\rho^o) \xrightarrow{\mathscr{L}} N(0, \mathscr{I}),$$

where ρ^o denotes the true value of the parameter vector ρ. One must also produce an estimator $\tilde{\mathscr{I}}_n$ of $\mathscr{I}$ for which

$$\lim_{n\to\infty} \tilde{\mathscr{I}}_n^{-1} = \mathscr{I}^{-1} \quad \text{a.s.}$$

Consider the density $f(x|\theta)$ and its quasi maximum likelihood estimator

$$\tilde{\theta}_n = \underset{\theta\in\Theta}{\operatorname{argmax}}\, \frac{1}{n}\sum_{i=1}^{n} \log f(x_i|\theta).$$

The density $f(x|\theta)$ is called the *auxiliary model* in this literature. The dimension of θ must be larger than the dimension of ρ. Let

$$m_n(\rho) = \mathscr{E}_\rho \frac{\partial}{\partial \theta} \log f(x|\tilde{\theta}_n).$$

We shall assume that the assumptions stated in Subsection 5.2.3 are in force for $f(x|\theta)$, $\theta \in \Theta$, and those of Subsection 5.2.2 for $p(x|\rho)$, $\rho \in R$. Among these assumptions is that the elements of $(\partial/\partial\theta)\log f(x|\theta)$ are dominated by an integrable function. From our analysis of quasi maximum likelihood estimators in Subsection 5.2.3 we have that there is a value θ^o for which $\lim_{n\to\infty} \tilde{\theta}_n = \theta^o$ almost surely, so that upon application of the dominated convergence theorem (Theorem 2.3), we have

$$\begin{aligned}\lim_{n\to\infty} m_n(\rho) &= \lim_{n\to\infty} \mathscr{E}_\rho \frac{\partial}{\partial \theta} \log f(x|\tilde{\theta}_n) \\ &= \mathscr{E}_\rho \lim_{n\to\infty} \frac{\partial}{\partial \theta} \log f(x|\tilde{\theta}_n) = m(\rho) \quad \text{a.s.,}\end{aligned}$$

where

$$m(\rho) = \mathscr{E}_\rho \frac{\partial}{\partial \theta} \log f(x|\theta^o) = \int \frac{\partial}{\partial \theta} \log f(x|\theta^o) p(x|\rho)\, dx.$$

The first-order conditions of quasi maximum likelihood (Equation (5.3)) imply $m(\rho^o) = 0$. We have therefore verified the first requirement, which is that $\lim_{n\to\infty} m_n(\rho^o) = 0$ almost surely. By Taylor's theorem and the same type of argument used in Subsection 5.3.3 we have

$$\begin{aligned}\sqrt{n}\, m_n(\rho^o) &= \left[\int \frac{\partial^2}{\partial\theta\,\partial\theta'} \log f(x|\bar{\theta}_n) p(y|\rho^o)\, dx\right] \sqrt{n}(\tilde{\theta} - \theta^o) \\ &= [\mathscr{J} + o_s(1)]\sqrt{n}(\tilde{\theta} - \theta^o)\end{aligned}$$

where $\mathscr{J}$ is as in Subsection 5.2.3. Because $\sqrt{n}(\tilde{\theta} - \theta^o) \xrightarrow{\mathscr{L}} N(0, \mathscr{J}^{-1}\mathscr{I}\mathscr{J}^{-1})$, where $\mathscr{I}$ is as in Subsection 5.2.3, Slutsky's theorem (Theorem 4.6 with following remarks) implies $[\mathscr{J} + o_s(1)]\sqrt{n}(\tilde{\theta} - \theta^o) \xrightarrow{\mathscr{L}} N(0, \mathscr{I})$. This establishes the second requirement, which is that $\sqrt{n}\, m_n(\rho^o) \xrightarrow{\mathscr{L}} N(0, \mathscr{I})$. Lastly, as verified in Subsection 5.2.3, $\lim_{n\to\infty} \tilde{\mathscr{I}}_n = \mathscr{I}$ almost surely, where

$$\tilde{\mathscr{I}}_n = \frac{1}{n}\sum_{i=1}^{n}\left[\frac{\partial}{\partial\theta}\log f(x_i|\tilde{\theta}_n)\right]\left[\frac{\partial}{\partial\theta}\log f(x_i|\tilde{\theta}_n)\right]'.$$

The requisite conditions for method of moments estimation are in place, and

$$\hat{\rho}_n = \underset{\rho \in R}{\operatorname{argmin}}\, m_n'(\rho)\tilde{\mathcal{I}}_n^{-1} m_n(\rho)$$

is a method of moments estimator for the parameters of the economic model. From Subsection 5.3.3 we have

$$\sqrt{n}(\hat{\rho}_n - \rho^o) \xrightarrow{\mathcal{L}} N\{0, [M'(\rho^o)\mathcal{I}^{-1}M(\rho^o)]^{-1}\},$$

where $M(\rho) = (\partial/\partial\rho')m(\rho)$.

The next question is how best to choose $f(x|\theta)$. It would seem that the better that the density $f(x|\theta^o)$ approximates the true density $p(x|\rho^o)$, the better we ought to do. This is indeed correct, which is most easily seen by examining the extreme case where the family $\{f(x|\theta)\colon \theta \in \Theta\}$ contains the family $\{p(x|\rho)\colon \rho \in R\}$. Specifically, assume that there is a differentiable function $\theta = g(\rho)$ mapping R into Θ such that $f[x|g(\rho)] = p(x|\rho)$ for all x. Let $G(\rho) = (\partial/\partial\rho')g(\rho)$. Observe that

$$\begin{aligned}
M(\rho^o) &= \frac{\partial}{\partial\rho'}\int \frac{\partial}{\partial\theta}\log f(x|\theta^o)\, p(x|\rho^o)\, dx \\
&= \int \frac{\partial}{\partial\theta}\log f(x|\theta^o)\left[\frac{\partial}{\partial\rho'}p(x|\rho^o)\right] dx \\
&= \int \frac{\partial}{\partial\theta}\log f(x|\theta^o)\left[\frac{\partial}{\partial\rho'}p(x|\rho^o)\right]\frac{p(x|\rho^o)}{p(x|\rho^o)}\, dx \\
&= \int \frac{\partial}{\partial\theta}\log f(x|\theta^o)\left[\frac{\partial}{\partial\rho'}\log p(x|\rho^o)\right] p(x|\rho^o)\, dx \\
&= \int \frac{\partial}{\partial\theta}\log f(x|\theta^o)\left\{\frac{\partial}{\partial\rho'}\log f[x|g(\rho^o)]\right\} p(x|\rho^o)\, dx \\
&= \int \frac{\partial}{\partial\theta}\log f(x|\theta^o)\left[\frac{\partial}{\partial\theta'}\log f(x|\theta^o)\, G(\rho^o)\right] p(x|\rho^o)\, dx \\
&= \int \frac{\partial}{\partial\theta}\log f(x|\theta^o)\left[\frac{\partial}{\partial\theta'}\log f(x|\theta^o)\right] p(x|\rho^o)\, dx\, G(\rho^o) \\
&= \mathcal{I}\, G(\rho^o).
\end{aligned}$$

Maximum likelihood applied to $f[x|g(\rho)]$ will give the same results as maximum likelihood applied to $p(x|\rho)$, because the two densities are exactly the same. From Subsection 5.2.2 we have that the inverse of the asymptotic variance of the maximum likelihood estimator based on $f[x|g(\rho)]$ is

$$\begin{aligned}
&\int\left\{\frac{\partial}{\partial\rho}\log f[x|g(\rho^o)]\right\}\left\{\frac{\partial}{\partial\rho}\log f[x|g(\rho^o)]\right\}' p(x|\rho^o)\,dx \\
&\quad=\int\left[G'(\rho^o)\frac{\partial}{\partial\theta}\log f(x|\theta^o)\right]\left[G'(\rho^o)\frac{\partial}{\partial\theta}\log f(x|\theta^o)\right]' p(x|\rho^o)\,dx \\
&\quad= G'(\rho^o)\,\mathcal{I}\,G(\rho^o) = G'(\rho^o)\,\mathcal{I}\,\mathcal{I}^{-1}\mathcal{I}\,G(\rho^o) \\
&\quad= M'(\rho^o)\,\mathcal{I}^{-1}M(\rho^o).
\end{aligned}$$

Therefore, when the family $\{f(x|\theta)\colon \theta\in\Theta\}$ contains the family $\{p(x|\rho)\colon \rho\in R\}$, the asymptotic variance of the efficient method of moments estimator is the same as the asymptotic variance of the maximum likelihood estimator.

If one uses an auxiliary model from a family that is capable of close approximation, such as the family of SNP densities

$$f_K(x|\theta)=\frac{[\sum_{j=0}^{K}\theta_j x^j]^2\phi(x)}{\int[\sum_{j=0}^{K}\theta_j u^j]^2\phi(u)\,du},\qquad \theta_0=1,\quad K=0,1,\ldots$$

introduced in Subsection 5.2.3, then the asymptotic variance of the efficient method of moments estimator converges to the asymptotic variance of the maximum likelihood estimator as K tends to infinity (Gallant and Long 1997).

5.4 Bayesian Estimation

As in Section 5.2, let $X_1,\ldots,X_n$ be a random sample from a density $f(x|\theta)$ and let θ be an unknown parameter known to be in a parameter space Θ. Write the likelihood as

$$\ell(x_1,\ldots,x_n|\theta)=\prod_{i=1}^{n} f(x_i|\theta).$$

In Bayesian inference, parameter θ is viewed as a random variable and $\ell(x_1,\ldots,x_n|\theta)$ is viewed as the conditional density of the data given θ, which calls for the notation $\ell(x_1,\ldots,x_n|\theta)$ to denote the likelihood rather than $L(\theta)$ as in Section 5.2.

One has a *prior density* $\pi(\theta)$ that gives the subjective probability that θ is an interval $(a,b]$; that is, the prior probability of $\theta\in(a,b]$ is

$\int_a^b \pi(\theta)\,d\theta$ if θ is a continuous random variable or $\sum_{a<\theta_i\leq b} \pi(\theta_i)$ if θ is discrete. Of course, θ could be a parameter vector of length p, making $\pi(\theta)$ a joint density and events rectangles $\times_{i=1}^{p}(a_i, b_i]$, but the ideas are the same. The density $\pi(\theta)$ is called the prior density because it is an opinion regarding θ that is formed prior to the analysis of the data. Multiplication of the likelihood by the prior gives the joint density of the data and parameters

$$f(x_1, \ldots, x_n, \theta) = \ell(x_1, \ldots, x_n|\theta)\pi(\theta).$$

The idea is to use the likelihood to update the prior and thereby refine it using the information contained in the data. The updated density is called the *posterior density* and is denoted by $f(\theta|x_1, \ldots, x_n)$, which indicates that it is viewed as the conditional density of θ given the data. Updating is accomplished by means of Bayes rule, which is

$$\begin{aligned} f(\theta|x_1, \ldots, x_n) &= \frac{f(x_1, \ldots, x_n, \theta)}{\int f(x_1, \ldots, x_n, \theta)\,d\theta} \\ &= \frac{\ell(x_1, \ldots, x_n|\theta)\pi(\theta)}{\int \ell(x_1, \ldots, x_n|\theta)\pi(\theta)\,d\theta} \end{aligned} \tag{5.9}$$

if θ is continuous, and is

$$f(\theta|x_1, \ldots, x_n) = \frac{f(x_1, \ldots, x_n, \theta)}{\sum_{\theta_i\in\Theta} f(x_1, \ldots, x_n, \theta)} = \frac{\ell(x_1, \ldots, x_n|\theta)\pi(\theta)}{\sum_{\theta_i\in\Theta} \ell(x_1, \ldots, x_n|\theta)\pi(\theta)}$$

if θ is discrete. When additional data is acquired, the posterior becomes the prior, and the cycle repeats.

These are familiar notions if one has studied expectations formation in macroeconomics, particularly rational expectations, or has had some exposure to game theory. There, an economic agent has a subjective distribution regarding relevant state variables and uses it to make decisions. As information accumulates, the subjective distribution is updated. It is much the same here, although the formalisms are a bit different.

The Bayesian view that θ is a random variable and the use of subjective distributions is markedly different from the frequentist view that θ is a fixed unknown parameter to be estimated, which is the view taken in the previous sections of this chapter. Controversy has raged over which of the two views is more appropriate to scientific inference for nearly a century. The attitude here is that the debate is largely a waste of time and that one can learn something useful from data using either approach. The main problem with Bayesian inference that has impeded applications is that one must actually do the integration in Equation (5.9).

Recent advances in numerical integration, specifically the development of efficient Markov chain Monte Carlo methods (Tierney 1994), have changed the situation and one may expect to see more Bayesian applied work in the future.

Once the posterior $f(\theta|x_1, \ldots, x_n)$ is in hand, one can use some measure of central tendency such as the posterior mean

$$\hat{\theta} = \int \theta f(\theta|x_1, \ldots, x_n)\, d\theta,$$

the posterior median

$$\hat{\theta} = \theta_{.5},$$

or the posterior mode

$$\hat{\theta} = \underset{\theta \in \Theta}{\operatorname{argmax}}\ f(\theta|x_1, \ldots, x_n)$$

as an estimator of θ. A Bayesian 95% confidence interval is $[\theta_{.275}, \theta_{.975}]$, where $\theta_{.275}$ and $\theta_{.975}$ denote, respectively, the .275 and .975 quantiles of $f(\theta|x_1, \ldots, x_n)$. If θ is a vector, then the marginal posterior density

$$f(\theta_i|x_1, \ldots, x_n) = \int \cdots \int f(\theta_1, \ldots, \theta_p|x_1, \ldots, x_n) \prod_{j \neq i}^{p} d\theta_j$$

may be computed and $f(\theta_i|x_1, \ldots, x_n)$ used as above to obtain an estimator or set a confidence interval. We shall illustrate these ideas with an example.

Example 5.1. Let $X_1, \ldots, X_n$ be a random sample from the Bernoulli distribution with parameter p and let the prior be the beta with parameters α and β,

$$\pi(p) = \frac{\Gamma(\alpha + \beta)}{\Gamma(\alpha)\Gamma(\beta)} p^{\alpha-1}(1-p)^{\beta-1}.$$

The likelihood is

$$\ell(x_1, \ldots, x_n|p) = p^y(1-p)^{n-y},$$

where $y = \sum_{i=1}^{n} x_i$. The joint density of $X_1, \ldots, X_n$ and p is

$$\begin{aligned} f(x_1, \ldots, x_n, p) &= \ell(x_1, \ldots, x_n|p)\pi(p) \\ &= \frac{\Gamma(\alpha + \beta)}{\Gamma(\alpha)\Gamma(\beta)} p^{y+\alpha-1}(1-p)^{n-y+\beta-1}. \end{aligned}$$

Referring to the entry for the beta distribution in the Appendix, we have

$$\int_0^1 \frac{\Gamma(n+\alpha+\beta)}{\Gamma(y+\alpha)\Gamma(n-y+\beta)} p^{y+\alpha-1}(1-p)^{n-y+\beta-1}\,dp = 1,$$

from which we deduce that the marginal density is

$$\begin{aligned} f(x_1, \ldots, x_n) &= \int_0^1 f(x_1, \ldots, x_n, p)\,dp \\ &= \frac{\Gamma(\alpha+\beta)}{\Gamma(\alpha)\Gamma(\beta)} \frac{\Gamma(y+\alpha)\Gamma(n-y+\beta)}{\Gamma(n+\alpha+\beta)} \end{aligned}$$

and the posterior is

$$\begin{aligned} f(p|x_1, \ldots, x_n) &= \frac{f(x_1, \ldots, x_n, p)}{\int f(x_1, \ldots, x_n, \theta)\,dp} \\ &= \frac{\Gamma(n+\alpha+\beta)}{\Gamma(y+\alpha)\Gamma(n-y+\beta)} p^{y+\alpha-1}(1-p)^{n-y+\beta-1}, \end{aligned}$$

which is a beta density with parameters $y+\alpha$ and $n-y+\beta$. A prior density like this that has the property that the posterior density is in the same parametric family as the prior density is called a natural *conjugate prior*.

Again referring to the entry for the beta distribution in the Appendix, we see that the mean of the posterior density is $(y+\alpha)/(\alpha+\beta+n)$. After rearranging terms, the mean of the posterior density becomes

$$\mathscr{E}(p|x_1, \ldots, x_n) = \left(\frac{n}{\alpha+\beta+n}\right)\frac{1}{n}\sum_{i=1}^{n} x_i + \left(\frac{\alpha+b}{\alpha+\beta+n}\right)\frac{\alpha}{\alpha+\beta}.$$

Thus, the Bayes estimate of p is a weighted average of the maximum likelihood estimate, which is the sample mean $\hat{p}_n = (1/n)\sum_{i=1}^{n} x_i$, and the mean of the prior density, which is $\alpha/(\alpha+\beta)$. As sample size increases, the sample mean gets weighted more heavily and essentially becomes the estimate for large n. This is a general characteristic of Bayes estimators: as sample size increases, the likelihood becomes increasingly dominant, with the consequence that Bayes estimates and maximum likelihood estimates will be similar for large n.

5.5 The Wald Test

Consider testing

$$H\colon h(\theta^o) = 0 \quad \text{against} \quad H\colon h(\theta^o) \neq 0,$$

where $h(\theta)$ is a continuously differentiable function of θ. Assume estimators $\hat{\theta}_n$ and $\hat{V}_n$ are available that satisfy

$$\lim_{n\to\infty} \hat{\theta}_n = \theta^o \quad \text{a.s.}$$

$$\sqrt{n}(\hat{\theta}_n - \theta^o) \xrightarrow{\mathscr{L}} N(0, V)$$

$$\lim_{n\to\infty} \hat{V}_n = V \quad \text{a.s.}$$

The function $h(\theta)$ maps $\theta \in \Theta \subset \Re^p$ into $\Re^q$; that is, $h(\theta)$ is a vector of dimension q and θ is a vector of dimension p. We also assume that $(\partial/\partial\theta')h(\theta^o)$ has rank q, which is much the same as assuming that the rows of $h(\theta)$ do not contain the same equation written down twice.

We can derive the asymptotic distribution of $h(\hat{\theta}_n)$ by application of Taylor's theorem and Slutsky's theorem similarly to Section 5.3.3. This is often called the *delta method*. It is as follows.

Expand a typical row of $h(\theta)$ by Taylor's theorem (Bartle 1976, p. 206) to obtain

$$\sqrt{n}[h_i(\hat{\theta}_n) - h_i(\theta^o)] = \frac{\partial}{\partial\theta'} h_i(\bar{\theta}_n)\sqrt{n}(\hat{\theta}_n - \theta^o),$$

where $\bar{\theta}_n$ is on the line segment joining θ^o to $\hat{\theta}_n$. Because $\hat{\theta}_n$ converges almost surely to θ^o and $\bar{\theta}_n$ is between θ^o and $\hat{\theta}_n$, it follows that $\bar{\theta}_n$ converges almost surely to θ^o. Because $(\partial/\partial\theta')h_i(\theta)$ is continuous, $(\partial/\partial\theta')h_i(\bar{\theta}_n)$ converges almost surely to $(\partial/\partial\theta')h_i(\theta^o)$. If we apply this argument to each row of $h(\theta)$ and put $H(\theta) = (\partial/\partial\theta')h(\theta)$, then we can write

$$\sqrt{n}[h(\hat{\theta}_n) - h(\theta^o)] = [H(\theta^o) + o_s(1)]\sqrt{n}(\hat{\theta}_n - \theta^o),$$

recalling that $o_s(1)$ denotes a $q \times p$ matrix whose elements converge almost surely to zero. Applying Slutsky's theorem (Theorem 4.6 with following remarks), we have

$$\sqrt{n}[h(\hat{\theta}_n) - h(\theta^o)] \xrightarrow{\mathscr{L}} N[0, H(\theta^o)VH'(\theta^o)].$$

The Wald test statistic is

$$W_n = nh'(\hat{\theta}_n)[H(\hat{\theta}_n)\hat{V}_n H'(\hat{\theta}_n)]^{-1}h(\hat{\theta}_n).$$

When $H\colon h(\theta^o) = 0$ is true, Corollary 4.1 implies

$$W_n \xrightarrow{\mathcal{L}} \chi^2_q,$$

where χ^2_q denotes the chi-squared distribution on q degrees of freedom. Therefore, an asymptotically level α test is to reject $H\colon h(\theta^o) = 0$ when W_n exceeds the $(1-\alpha)$th quantile of χ^2_q. This is the Wald test.

When $A\colon h(\theta^o) \neq 0$ holds, W_n will become increasingly large as n increases because W_n/n converges almost surely to a positive constant in that case.

5.6 The Lagrange Multiplier Test

Consider testing

$$H\colon h(\theta^o) = 0 \quad \text{against} \quad H\colon h(\theta^o) \neq 0,$$

where $h(\theta)$ is a continuously differentiable function of θ such that $(\partial/\partial\theta')h(\theta^o)$ has rank q. Let $X_1, \ldots, X_n$ be a random sample from the density $f(x|\theta)$ where θ is an unknown parameter in the known parameter space Θ. The normalized log likelihood is

$$s_n(\theta) = \frac{1}{n}\sum_{i=1}^{n} \log f(x_i|\theta).$$

The constrained maximum likelihood estimator is

$$\tilde{\theta}_n = \operatorname*{argmax}_{h(\theta)=0} s_n(\theta).$$

If $H\colon h(\theta^o) = 0$ is true, then $\tilde{\theta}_n$ is strongly consistent for θ^o (Problem 8). Forming the Lagrangian

$$\mathcal{L}(\theta, \lambda) = s_n(\theta) + \lambda' h(\theta),$$

the first-order conditions are

$$0 = \frac{\partial}{\partial\theta}\mathcal{L}(\tilde{\theta}_n, \tilde{\lambda}_n) = \frac{\partial}{\partial\theta}s_n(\tilde{\theta}_n) + H'(\tilde{\theta}_n)\tilde{\lambda}_n$$

$$0 = \frac{\partial}{\partial\lambda}\mathcal{L}(\tilde{\theta}_n, \tilde{\lambda}_n) = h(\tilde{\theta}_n)$$

where $H(\theta) = (\partial/\partial\theta')h(\theta)$ and λ is the vector of Lagrange multipliers. Expanding using Taylor's theorem, and using arguments similar to those used to derive the delta method in Section 5.5, we have

$$0 = \sqrt{n}\frac{\partial}{\partial\theta}s_n(\theta^o) + [\mathcal{J} + o_s(1)]\sqrt{n}(\tilde{\theta}_n - \theta^o) + \tilde{H}_n'\sqrt{n}\tilde{\lambda}_n \quad (5.10)$$

$$0 = [H + o_s(1)]\sqrt{n}(\tilde{\theta}_n - \theta^o), \quad (5.11)$$

where $\mathcal{J} = \int[(\partial^2/\partial\theta\,\partial\theta')\log f(x|\theta^o)]\,f(x|\theta^o)\,dx$, which we assume is nonsingular, $H = H(\theta^o)$, and $\tilde{H}_n = H(\tilde{\theta}_n)$. Multiplying the first equation by $[H + o_s(1)][\mathcal{J} + o_s(1)]^{-1}$, which inverse must exist for large n, and using $[H + o_s(1)]\sqrt{n}(\tilde{\theta}_n - \theta^o) = 0$ from Equation (5.11), we have

$$[H + o_s(1)][\mathcal{J} + o_s(1)]^{-1}\tilde{H}_n'\sqrt{n}\tilde{\lambda}_n$$
$$= -\sqrt{n}[H + o_s(1)][\mathcal{J} + o_s(1)]^{-1}\frac{\partial}{\partial\theta}s_n(\theta^o).$$

As in Section 5.2.2,

$$\sqrt{n}\frac{\partial}{\partial\theta}s_n(\theta^o) = \frac{1}{\sqrt{n}}\sum_{i=1}^{n}\frac{\partial}{\partial\theta}\log f(x_i|\theta^o) \xrightarrow{\mathcal{L}} N(0, \mathscr{I}),$$

where $\mathscr{I} = \int[(\partial/\partial\theta)\log f(x|\theta^o)][(\partial/\partial\theta)\log f(x|\theta^o)]'f(x|\theta^o)\,dx$. Also

$$\tilde{\mathscr{I}}_n = \frac{1}{n}\sum_{i=1}^{n}\left[\frac{\partial}{\partial\theta}\log f(x_i|\tilde{\theta}_n)\right]\left[\frac{\partial}{\partial\theta}\log f(x_i|\tilde{\theta}_n)\right]' \to \mathscr{I} \quad \text{a.s.},$$

$\tilde{H}_n \to H$ a.s., and $\mathscr{I} = -\mathcal{J}$. Applying Slutsky's theorem (Theorem 4.6), we have

$$\sqrt{n}\tilde{\lambda}_n \xrightarrow{\mathcal{L}} N\left[0, (H\mathscr{I}^{-1}H')^{-1}\right].$$

This fact forms the basis for the *Lagrange multiplier test*, which is also known as *Rao's efficient score test*. The test statistic is

$$R_n = n\tilde{\lambda}_n'\tilde{H}_n\tilde{\mathscr{I}}_n^{-1}\tilde{H}_n'\tilde{\lambda}_n$$

or, using the first-order conditions,

$$R_n = n\frac{\partial}{\partial\theta'}s_n(\tilde{\theta}_n)\,\tilde{\mathscr{I}}_n^{-1}\frac{\partial}{\partial\theta}s_n(\tilde{\theta}_n).$$

When $H\colon h(\theta^o) = 0$ is true, Corollary 4.1 implies

$$R_n \xrightarrow{\mathscr{L}} \chi_q^2,$$

where χ_q^2 denotes the chi-squared distribution on q degrees of freedom. Therefore, an asymptotically level α test is to reject $H\colon h(\theta^o) = 0$ when R_n exceeds the $(1-\alpha)$th quantile of χ_q^2. This is the Lagrange multiplier test.

When $A\colon h(\theta^o) \neq 0$ holds, R_n will become increasingly large as n increases because R_n/n converges almost surely to a positive constant in that case.

5.7 The Likelihood Ratio Test

The *likelihood ratio statistic* for testing

$$H\colon h(\theta^o) = 0 \quad \text{against} \quad H\colon h(\theta^o) \neq 0$$

is

$$\Lambda_n = \frac{\max_{h(\theta)=0} \prod_{i=1}^n f(x_i|\theta)}{\max_{\theta\in\Theta} \prod_{i=1}^n f(x_i|\theta)} = \frac{\prod_{i=1}^n f(x_i|\tilde{\theta}_n)}{\prod_{i=1}^n f(x_i|\hat{\theta}_n)},$$

where

$$\hat{\theta}_n = \underset{\theta\in\Theta}{\operatorname{argmax}}\ s_n(\theta)$$

$$\tilde{\theta}_n = \underset{h(\theta)=0}{\operatorname{argmax}}\ s_n(\theta).$$

One rejects $H\colon h(\theta^o) = 0$ for small values of Λ_n. Equivalently, one rejects for large values of

$$L_n = -2\log\Lambda_n = 2n[s_n(\hat{\theta}_n) - s_n(\tilde{\theta}_n)],$$

where

$$s_n(\theta) = \frac{1}{n}\sum_{i=1}^n \log f(x_i|\theta).$$

Using Taylor's theorem to expand $s_n(\tilde{\theta}_n)$ about $\hat{\theta}_n$, we have

$$L_n = -2n\frac{\partial}{\partial\theta}s_n(\hat{\theta}_n)(\tilde{\theta}_n - \hat{\theta}_n) - n(\tilde{\theta}_n - \hat{\theta}_n)'\frac{\partial^2}{\partial\theta\,\partial\theta'}s_n(\bar{\theta}_n)(\tilde{\theta}_n - \hat{\theta}_n).$$

Using $(\partial/\partial\theta)s_n(\hat{\theta}_n) = 0$ and the same arguments that we used in Sections 5.5 and 5.6, we have that $(\partial^2/\partial\theta\,\partial\theta')s_n(\bar{\theta}_n) = \mathcal{I} + o_s(1)$, where $\mathcal{I} = \int[(\partial^2/\partial\theta\,\partial\theta')\log f(x|\theta^o)]f(x|\theta^o)\,dx$. Therefore,

$$L_n = -n(\tilde{\theta}_n - \hat{\theta}_n)'[\mathcal{I} + o_s(1)](\tilde{\theta}_n - \hat{\theta}_n). \tag{5.12}$$

Again using Taylor's theorem and similar arguments,

$$\sqrt{n}\frac{\partial}{\partial\theta}s_n(\tilde{\theta}_n) = [\mathcal{I} + o_s(1)]\sqrt{n}(\tilde{\theta}_n - \hat{\theta}_n). \tag{5.13}$$

Combining Equations (5.12) and (5.13), and using $\mathcal{J} = -\mathcal{I}$, we have

$$L_n = n\frac{\partial}{\partial\theta'}s_n(\tilde{\theta}_n)[\mathcal{J} + o_s(1)]^{-1}\frac{\partial}{\partial\theta}s_n(\tilde{\theta}_n).$$

This is essentially the same expression that we obtained for R_n in Section 5.6. The same argument used there applies and we may summarize as follows.

The likelihood ratio test statistic is

$$L_n = -2\log\Lambda_n = 2n[s_n(\hat{\theta}_n) - s_n(\tilde{\theta}_n)].$$

When $H\colon h(\theta^o) = 0$ is true,

$$L_n \xrightarrow{\mathcal{L}} \chi^2_q,$$

where χ^2_q denotes the chi-squared distribution on q degrees of freedom. An asymptotically level α test is to reject $H\colon h(\theta^o) = 0$ when L_n exceeds the $(1-\alpha)$th quantile of χ^2_q.

When $A\colon h(\theta^o) \neq 0$ holds, L_n will become increasingly large as n increases because L_n/n converges almost surely to a positive constant in that case.

5.8 Bayesian Hypothesis Testing

Recall the hypothesis testing setup from Subsection 5.1.2: We have data $x_1, \ldots, x_n$ presumed to be generated by a random sample $X_1, \ldots, X_n$ from a density $f(x|\theta)$. The parameter space Θ is divided into two sets Θ_H and Θ_A that are mutually exclusive, $\Theta_H \cap \Theta_A = \emptyset$, and exhaustive, $\Theta_H \cup \Theta_A = \Theta$. The task is to choose between the two hypotheses

$$H\colon \theta \in \Theta_H \quad \text{and} \quad A\colon \theta \in \Theta_A.$$

In Bayesian analysis, once the posterior density $f(\theta|x_1, \ldots, x_n)$ is in hand, deciding between H and A is simply a matter of computing the posterior probability of each hypothesis:

$$P(H|x_1, \ldots, x_n) = P(\Theta_H|x_1, \ldots, x_n) = \int_{\Theta_H} f(\theta|x_1, \ldots, x_n)\, d\theta$$

$$P(A|x_1, \ldots, x_n) = P(\Theta_A|x_1, \ldots, x_n) = \int_{\Theta_A} f(\theta|x_1, \ldots, x_n)\, d\theta$$

and choosing the hypothesis with larger posterior probability.

For instance, in Example 5.1 we obtained the following posterior for a binomial likelihood with a beta prior:

$$f(p|x_1, \ldots, x_n) = \frac{\Gamma(n+\alpha+\beta)}{\Gamma(y+\alpha)\Gamma(n-y+\beta)} p^{y+\alpha-1}(1-p)^{n-y+\beta-1},$$

where $y = \sum_{i=1}^{n} x_i$. To decide between

$$H: p \geq \frac{1}{2} \quad \text{and} \quad A: p < \frac{1}{2}$$

one would compute

$$P(H|x_1, \ldots, x_n) = \int_{1/2}^{1} f(p|x_1, \ldots, x_n)\, dp$$

$$P(A|x_1, \ldots, x_n) = \int_{0}^{1/2} f(p|x_1, \ldots, x_n)\, dp$$

and choose H if $P(H|x_1, \ldots, x_n) \geq P(A|x_1, \ldots, x_n)$.

Testing a sharp null such as

$$H: \theta = \theta^* \quad \text{against} \quad H: \theta \neq \theta^*$$

is problematical in the Bayesian system of inference because it usually requires the use of a prior that puts positive probability on a single point in a continuum; that is, the distribution function of the prior will have a jump discontinuity at $\theta = \theta^*$ of height $P(\theta = \theta^*) > 0$ and will be continuous elsewhere. The consequence is that the outcome of the test is too heavily influenced by the value that is assigned to $P(\theta = \theta^*)$ for most people's taste; see Casella and Berger 1987 and the references therein. There are also some technical annoyances. The prior will be a mixture and one will have to employ the general methods of integration discussed in Subsection 3.1.1 in connection with Figure 3.2 to compute the posterior distribution $F(\theta|x_1, \ldots, x_n)$ and to compute the posterior probabilities $P(H|x_1, \ldots, x_n)$ and $P(A|x_1, \ldots, x_n)$.

5.9 Problems

1. Let $g_n(x)$ be a sequence of continuous functions on a closed and bounded interval $[a, b]$, let $g(x)$ be continuous on that interval, and let

$$\lim_{n\to\infty} \sup_{x\in[a,b]} |g_n(x) - g(x)| = 0.$$

Show that if $x^o \in [a, b]$ and $\lim_{n\to\infty} x_n = x^o$, then

$$\lim_{n\to\infty} |g_n(x_n) - g(x^o)| = 0.$$

Hint: Consider that

$$\begin{aligned} |g_n(x_n) - g(x^o)| &\le |g_n(x_n) - g(x_n)| + |g(x_n) - g(x^o)| \\ &\le \sup_{x\in[a,b]} |g_n(x) - g(x)| + |g(x_n) - g(x^o)|. \end{aligned}$$

2. Verify that

$$\begin{aligned} \frac{d}{d\theta} \int \left[\frac{d}{d\theta} \log f(x|\theta)\right] f(x|\theta)\, dx &= \int \left[\frac{d}{d\theta} \log f(x|\theta)\right] \left[\frac{d}{d\theta} f(x|\theta)\right] dx \\ &\quad + \int \left[\frac{d}{d\theta} \log f(x|\theta)\right]^2 f(x|\theta)\, dx. \end{aligned}$$

Why does $(d/d\theta) \int [(d/d\theta) \log f(x|\theta)] f(x|\theta)\, dx = 0$?

3. Referring to Subsection 5.2.2, use the uniform strong law of large numbers and $\lim_{n\to\infty} \hat{\theta}_n = \theta^o$ a.s. to conclude that a strongly consistent estimator of $\mathcal{I}$ is

$$\hat{\mathcal{I}}_n = \lim_{n\to\infty} \frac{1}{n} \sum_{i=1}^{n} \left[\frac{d}{d\theta} \log f(x_i|\hat{\theta}_n)\right]^2.$$

4. Referring to Subsection 5.2.2, use Slutsky's theorem, $\sqrt{n}(\hat{\theta}_n - \theta^o) \xrightarrow{\mathcal{L}} N(0, \mathcal{I}^{-1})$, and $\lim_{n\to\infty} \hat{\mathcal{I}}_n = \mathcal{I}$ a.s. to show that

$$\hat{\theta}_n - \frac{1.96}{\sqrt{n\hat{\mathcal{I}}_n}} \le \theta \le \hat{\theta}_n + \frac{1.96}{\sqrt{n\hat{\mathcal{I}}_n}}$$

is an approximate 95% confidence interval for θ.

5. Let $X_1, \ldots, X_n$ be iid uniform on $(0, \theta)$; that is, the density is $f_X(x) = \theta^{-1} I_{[0,\theta]}(x)$. (i) Show that $P(\max_{1\le i\le n} X_i \le t) = [F_X(t)]^n$. (ii) Compute the mean and variance of $\tilde{\theta}_n = [(n+1)/n] \max_{1\le i\le n} X_i$. (iii) Show that $\tilde{\theta}_n = [(n+1)/n] \max_{1\le i\le n} X_i$ converges in probability to θ. (iv) Compute the mean and variance of $\hat{\theta}_n = (2/n)\sum_{t=1}^{n} X_i$. (v) Show that $\hat{\theta}_n = (2/n)\sum_{t=1}^{n} X_i$ converges in probability to θ. (vi) Which of the two is the better estimator and why?
6. Suppose that $X_1, X_2, \ldots$ is a sequence of independent and identically distributed random variables with mean $\mathscr{E}X = \mu$, variance $\mathscr{E}(X-\mu)^2 = 1$, third central moment $\mathscr{E}(X-\mu)^3 = 0$, third raw moment $\mathscr{E}X^3 = \mu^3 + 3\mu$, fourth central moment $\mathscr{E}(X-\mu)^4 = 3$, and fourth raw moment $\mathscr{E}X^4 = \mu^4 + 6\mu^2 + 3$. Then $\mathscr{E}(1/n)\sum_{i=1}^{n} x_i^2 = 1 + \mu^2$ and one could define a method of moments estimator as

$$\hat{\mu}_n = \left[\frac{1}{n}\sum_{i=1}^{n}(x_i^2 - 1)\right]^{1/2}.$$

This equation can be rewritten as

$$\sqrt{n}(\hat{\mu}_n - \mu) = \frac{1}{2\bar{u}_n}\left[\frac{1}{\sqrt{n}}\sum_{i=1}^{n}(x_i^2 - 1 - \mu^2)\right]$$

by using Taylor's theorem to expand $(v)^{1/2}$ about $v = \mu^2$. Recall that $\bar{u}_n$ is on the line joining $\hat{\mu}_n$ to μ so that if $\hat{\mu}_n$ were to converge to μ, then so would $\bar{u}_n$. (i) Compute the mean of $(X_i^2 - 1 - \mu^2)$. (ii) Compute the variance of $(X_i^2 - 1 - \mu^2)$. (iii) Use Chebishev's inequality to show that $\hat{\mu}_n$ converges in probability to μ. (iv) Determine the asymptotic distribution of $(1/\sqrt{n})\sum_{i=1}^{n}(x_i^2 - 1 - \mu^2)$ by applying the central limit theorem. (v) Determine the asymptotic distribution of $\sqrt{n}(\hat{\mu}_n - \mu)$ by applying Slutsky's theorem to your answer to part (iv). (vi) What happens to this argument if $\mu = 0$?
7. Let (Y_i, X_i), $i = 1, 2, \ldots$, be a sequence of independent and identically distributed random variables whose moments to the fourth order exist. Define

$$\begin{pmatrix}\hat{\alpha}\\ \hat{\beta}\end{pmatrix} = \underset{\alpha,\beta}{\operatorname{argmin}} \frac{1}{n}\sum_{i=1}^{n}\left[Y_i - \alpha - \beta X_i\right]^2.$$

Derive the asymptotic distribution of $(\hat{\alpha}, \hat{\beta})'$.
8. Referring to Section 5.6, show that if $H\colon h(\theta^o) = 0$ is true, then $\tilde{\theta}_n$ is strongly consistent for θ. Hint: The proof is basically the same

as in Subsection 5.2.2 except that to obtain the inequality $s_{n_j}(\tilde{\theta}_{n_j}) \geq s_{n_j}(\theta^o)$ one uses the fact that both $\tilde{\theta}_{n_j}$ and θ^o satisfy the constraint $h(\theta) = 0$.

9. Let $X_1, \ldots, X_n$ be a random sample from the normal $n(x|\theta, \sigma^2)$ density and suppose that the prior density is $\pi(\theta) = n(\theta|\mu, \tau^2)$. Assume that the values of σ^2, μ, and τ^2 are known. Show that the posterior density of θ is the normal density with mean and variance

$$\mathscr{E}(\theta|X_1, \ldots, X_n) = \frac{\tau^2}{(\sigma^2/n) + \tau^2}\bar{x} + \frac{\sigma^2/n}{(\sigma^2/n) + \tau^2}\mu$$

$$\mathrm{Var}(\theta|X_1, \ldots, X_n) = \frac{(\sigma^2/n)\tau^2}{(\sigma^2/n) + \tau^2}.$$

10. (Neyman-Pearson lemma) Let $X = (X_1, \ldots, X_n)$ have density $f(x|\theta)$, where $x = (x_1, \ldots, x_n)$, and consider testing

$$H{:}\,\theta = \theta_H \text{ against } A{:}\,\theta = \theta_A.$$

Let W_1 be a size α test with rejection region

$$R_1 = \{x{:}\, f(x|\theta_A) > kf(x|\theta_H)\}$$

for some k and let W_2 be any other size α test with rejection region R_2. Then the test W_1 is more powerful than the test W_2. Prove this claim by completing the following steps. Show that the fact that both tests are size α implies

$$\int_{R_1 \cap \tilde{R}_2} f(x|\theta_H)\,dx = \int_{\tilde{R}_1 \cap R_2} f(x|\theta_H)\,dx.$$

Justify each equality and inequality below:

$$\begin{aligned}
\int_{R_2} f(x|\theta_A)\,dx &= \int_{R_1 \cap R_2} f(x|\theta_A)\,dx + \int_{\tilde{R}_1 \cap R_2} f(x|\theta_A)\,dx \\
&\leq \int_{R_1 \cap R_2} f(x|\theta_A)\,dx + k\int_{\tilde{R}_1 \cap R_2} f(x|\theta_H)\,dx \\
&= \int_{R_1 \cap R_2} f(x|\theta_A)\,dx + k\int_{R_1 \cap \tilde{R}_2} f(x|\theta_H)\,dx \\
&\leq \int_{R_1 \cap R_2} f(x|\theta_A)\,dx + \int_{R_1 \cap \tilde{R}_2} f(x|\theta_A)\,dx \\
&= \int_{R_1} f(x|\theta_A)\,dx.
\end{aligned}$$

Show that W_1 is the likelihood ratio test.

11. (Interchange of integration and differentiation) Let the random variable $X = (X_1, \ldots, X_n)$ have density $f_X(x)$, where $x = (x_1, \ldots, x_n)$. Let $(d/d\alpha)g(x, \alpha)$ be continuous in α and dominated by an integrable function $b(x)$ over the interval $I = (\alpha_0, \alpha_1)$ in the sense that $\sup_{\alpha \in I} |(d/d\alpha)g(x, \alpha)| \leq b(x)$ and $\int b(x) f_X(x)\, dx < \infty$. Let $\{h_n\}$ be a sequence of positive numbers tending to zero. Given a fixed value of α, why does there exist $\bar{h}_n$ with $0 < \bar{h}_n < h_n$ such that

$$\frac{g(x, \alpha) - g(x, \alpha + h_n)}{h_n} = \frac{d}{d\alpha} g(x, \alpha + \bar{h}_n)?$$

Why does

$$\frac{\int g(x, \alpha) f_X(x)\, dx - \int g(x, \alpha + h_n) f_X(x)\, dx}{h_n} = \int \frac{d}{d\alpha} g(x, \alpha + \bar{h}_n) f_X(x)\, dx?$$

Why does

$$\lim_{n \to \infty} \frac{\int g(x, \alpha) f_X(x)\, dx - \int g(x, \alpha + h_n) f_X(x)\, dx}{h_n} = \frac{d}{d\alpha} \int g(x, \alpha) f_X(x)\, dx?$$

Why does

$$\lim_{n \to \infty} \int \frac{d}{d\alpha} g(x, \alpha + \bar{h}_n) f_X(x)\, dx = \int \lim_{n \to \infty} \frac{d}{d\alpha} g(x, \alpha + \bar{h}_n) f_X(x)\, dx?$$

Hint: Theorem 2.3. Why does

$$\int \lim_{n \to \infty} \frac{d}{d\alpha} g(x, \alpha + \bar{h}_n) f_X(x)\, dx = \int \frac{d}{d\alpha} g(x, \alpha) f_X(x)\, dx?$$

Appendix: Distributions[1]

Bernoulli

Density: $f_X(x|p) = p^x(1-p)^{1-x}$

Support: $\mathscr{X} = \{x: x = 0, 1\}$

Parameters: $\Theta = \{p: 0 \le p \le 1\}$

Mean: $\mathscr{E}X = p$

Variance: $\operatorname{Var} X = p(1-p)$

MGF: $M_X(t) = (1-p) + pe^t$

Beta

Density: $$f_X(x|\alpha, \beta) = \frac{\Gamma(\alpha+\beta)}{\Gamma(\alpha)\Gamma(\beta)} x^{\alpha-1}(1-x)^{\beta-1}$$

Support: $\mathscr{X} = \{x: 0 \le x \le 1\}$

Parameters: $\Theta = \{(\alpha, \beta): \alpha > 0,\ \beta > 0\}$

Mean: $$\mathscr{E}X = \frac{\alpha}{\alpha+\beta}$$

Variance: $$\operatorname{Var} X = \frac{\alpha\beta}{(\alpha+\beta)^2(\alpha+\beta+1)}$$

MGF: $$M_X(t) = 1 + \sum_{k=1}^{\infty} \left(\prod_{r=0}^{k-1} \frac{\alpha+r}{\alpha+\beta+r} \right) \frac{t^k}{k!}$$

Binomial

Density: $$f_X(x|n, p) = \binom{n}{x} p^x(1-p)^{n-x}$$

Support: $\mathscr{X} = \{x: x = 0, 1, \ldots, n\}$

Parameters: $\Theta = \{(n, p): n = 1, 2, \ldots;\ 0 \le p \le 1\}$

Mean: $\mathscr{E}X = np$

[1] *Source:* Casella and Berger 1990, Johnson and Kotz 1969, 1970a, 1970b, 1972.

Variance: $\operatorname{Var} X = np(1-p)$

MGF: $M_X(t) = [pe^t + (1-p)]^n$

Cauchy

Density: $f_X(x|\mu, \sigma) = \frac{1}{\pi\sigma}\left[1 + \left(\frac{x-\mu}{\sigma}\right)^2\right]^{-1}$

Support: $\mathscr{X} = \{x: -\infty < x < \infty\}$

Parameters: $\Theta = \{(\mu, \sigma): -\infty < \mu < \infty, \sigma > 0\}$

Mean: does not exist

Variance: does not exist

MGF: does not exist

Chi-squared

Density: $f_X(x|\nu) = \frac{1}{\Gamma(\nu/2)2^{(\nu/2)}} x^{(\nu/2)-1} e^{-x/2}$

Support: $\mathscr{X} = \{x: 0 < x < \infty\}$

Parameters: $\Theta = \{\nu: \nu = 1, 2, \ldots\}$

Mean: $\mathscr{E}X = \nu$

Variance: $\operatorname{Var} X = 2\nu$

MGF: $M_X(t) = \left(\frac{1}{1-2t}\right)^{\nu/2}, \quad t < \frac{1}{2}$

Double exponential or *Laplace*

Density: $f_X(x|\mu, \sigma) = \frac{1}{2\sigma} e^{-\frac{|x-\mu|}{\sigma}}$

Support: $\mathscr{X} = \{x: -\infty < x < \infty\}$

Parameters: $\Theta = \{(\mu, \sigma): -\infty < \mu < \infty, \sigma > 0\}$

Mean: $\mathscr{E}X = \mu$

Variance: $\operatorname{Var} X = 2\sigma^2$

MGF: $M_X(t) = \frac{e^{\mu t}}{1-(\sigma t)^2}, \quad |t| < \frac{1}{\sigma}$

Exponential

Density: $f_X(x|\beta) = \frac{1}{\beta} e^{-x/\beta}$

Support: $\mathscr{X} = \{x: 0 < x < \infty\}$

Parameters: $\Theta = \{\beta: \beta > 0\}$

Mean: $\mathscr{E}X = \beta$

Variance: $\operatorname{Var} X = \beta^2$

MGF: $M_X(t) = \frac{1}{1 - \beta t}, \quad t < \frac{1}{\beta}$

F

Density:
$$f_X(x|\nu_1, \nu_2) = \frac{\Gamma\left(\frac{\nu_1 + \nu_2}{2}\right)}{\Gamma\left(\frac{\nu_1}{2}\right)\Gamma\left(\frac{\nu_2}{2}\right)} \left(\frac{\nu_1}{\nu_2}\right)^{\nu_1/2} \times \frac{x^{(\nu_1 - 2)/2}}{\left[1 + \left(\frac{\nu_1}{\nu_2}\right)x\right]^{(\nu_1 + \nu_2)/2}}$$

Support: $\mathscr{X} = \{x: -\infty < x < \infty\}$

Parameters: $\Theta = \{(\nu_1, \nu_2): \nu_1, \nu_2 = 1, 2, \ldots\}$

Mean: $\mathscr{E}X = \frac{\nu_2}{\nu_2 - 2}, \quad \nu_2 > 2$

Variance: $\operatorname{Var} X = 2\left(\frac{\nu_2}{\nu_2 - 2}\right)^2 \frac{\nu_1 + \nu_2 - 2}{\nu_1(\nu_2 - 4)}, \quad \nu_2 > 4$

MGF: does not exist

Gamma

Density: $f_X(x|\alpha, \beta) = \frac{1}{\Gamma(\alpha)\beta^\alpha} x^{\alpha - 1} e^{-x/\beta}$

Support: $\mathscr{X} = \{x: 0 < x < \infty\}$

Parameters: $\Theta = \{(\alpha, \beta): \alpha > 0, \ \beta > 0\}$

Mean: $\mathscr{E}X = \alpha\beta$

Variance: $\operatorname{Var} X = \alpha\beta^2$

MGF: $M_X(t) = \left(\frac{1}{1 - \beta t}\right)^\alpha, \quad t < \frac{1}{\beta}$

Geometric

Density: $f_X(x|p) = p(1-p)^{x-1}$

Support: $\mathscr{X} = \{x: x = 1, 2, \ldots\}$

Parameters: $\Theta = \{p: 0 \le p \le 1\}$

Mean: $\mathscr{E}X = \dfrac{1}{p}$

Variance: $\operatorname{Var} X = \dfrac{1-p}{p^2}$

MGF: $M_X(t) = \dfrac{pe^t}{1-(1-p)e^t}, \quad t < -\log(1-p)$

Hypergeometric

Density: $f_X(x|n, D, N) = \dfrac{\binom{D}{x}\binom{N-D}{n-x}}{\binom{N}{n}}$

Support: $\mathscr{X} = \{x: \max(0, D+n-N) \le x \le \min(n, D),$
$x = 0, 1, \ldots, n\}$

Parameters: $\Theta = \{(n, D, N): n, D \le N;\ n, D, N = 1, 2, \ldots\}$

Mean: $\mathscr{E}X = \dfrac{nD}{N}$

Variance: $\operatorname{Var} X = \dfrac{nD}{N}\dfrac{(N-n)(N-D)}{N(N-1)}$

MGF:
$$M_X(t) = \frac{(N-n)!(N-D)!}{N!} \times F(-n, -D, N-D-n+1, e^t)$$

$$F(\alpha, \beta, \gamma, x) = 1 + \frac{\alpha\beta}{\gamma}\frac{x}{1!} + \frac{\alpha(\alpha+1)\beta(\beta+1)}{\gamma(\gamma+1)}\frac{x^2}{2!} + \frac{\alpha(\alpha+1)(\alpha+2)\beta(\beta+1)(\beta+2)}{\gamma(\gamma+1)(\gamma+2)}\frac{x^3}{3!} + \cdots$$

Logistic

Density: $f_X(x|\mu, \sigma) = \dfrac{1}{\beta}\dfrac{e^{-\frac{x-\mu}{\sigma}}}{(1+e^{-\frac{x-\mu}{\sigma}})^2}$

Support: $\mathscr{X} = \{x: -\infty < x < \infty\}$

Parameters: $\Theta = \{(\mu, \sigma): -\infty < \mu < \infty, \sigma > 0\}$

Mean: $\mathscr{E}X = \mu$

Variance: $\operatorname{Var} X = \dfrac{\pi^2\sigma^2}{3}$

MGF: $M_X(t) = e^{\mu t}\Gamma(1-\sigma t)\Gamma(1+\sigma t), \quad |t| < \dfrac{1}{\sigma}$

Lognormal

Density: $f_X(x|\mu, \sigma^2) = \dfrac{1}{\sqrt{2\pi}}\dfrac{1}{x\sigma}e^{-\frac{1}{2}\left(\frac{\log x-\mu}{\sigma}\right)^2}$

Support: $\mathscr{X} = \{x: 0 < x < \infty\}$

Parameters: $\Theta = \{(\mu, \sigma^2): -\infty < \mu < \infty, \sigma^2 > 0\}$

Mean: $\mathscr{E}X = e^{\mu+\sigma^2/2}$

Variance: $\operatorname{Var} X = e^{2(\mu+\sigma^2)} - e^{2\mu+\sigma^2}$

MGF: does not exist

Negative binomial

Density: $f_X(x|r, p) = \dbinom{r+x-1}{x}p^r(1-p)^x$

Support: $\mathscr{X} = \{x: x = 0, 1, \ldots\}$

Parameters: $\Theta = \{(r, p): r = 1, 2, \ldots; 0 \le p \le 1\}$

Mean: $\mathscr{E}X = \dfrac{r(1-p)}{p}$

Variance: $\operatorname{Var} X = \dfrac{r(1-p)}{p^2}$

MGF: $M_X(t) = \left[\dfrac{p}{1-(1-p)e^t}\right]^r, \quad t < -\log(1-p)$

***Normal** or **Gaussian** (multivariate)*

Density: $f_X(x_1, \ldots, x_m|\mu, \Sigma)$
$= (\det\Sigma)^{-1/2}(2\pi)^{-m/2}e^{-\frac{1}{2}(x-\mu)'\Sigma^{-1}(x-\mu)}$

Support: $\mathscr{X} = \{(x_1, \ldots, x_m)': -\infty < x_i < \infty, i = 1, \ldots, m\}$

Parameters: $\Theta = \{(\mu, \Sigma): \mu \in \mathscr{R}^m, \Sigma\ m \times m \text{ positive definite}\}$

Mean: $\mathscr{E}X = \mu$

Variance:	$\text{Cov}(X, X') = \Sigma$
MGF:	$M_X(t) = e^{t'\mu + t'\Sigma t/2}$

***Normal** or **Gaussian** (univariate)*

Density:	$f_X(x\|\mu, \sigma^2) = \frac{1}{\sigma\sqrt{2\pi}} e^{-\frac{1}{2}\left(\frac{x-\mu}{\sigma}\right)^2}$
Support:	$\mathscr{X} = \{x: -\infty < x < \infty\}$
Parameters:	$\Theta = \{(\mu, \sigma^2): -\infty < \mu < \infty, \sigma^2 > 0\}$
Mean:	$\mathscr{E}X = \mu$
Variance:	$\text{Var}\, X = \sigma^2$
MGF:	$M_X(t) = e^{\mu t + t^2\sigma^2/2}$

Pareto

Density:	$f_X(x\|\alpha, \beta) = \frac{\beta\alpha^\beta}{x^{\beta+1}}$
Support:	$\mathscr{X} = \{x: \alpha < x < \infty\}$
Parameters:	$\Theta = \{(\alpha, \beta): \alpha, \beta > 0\}$
Mean:	$\mathscr{E}X = \frac{\beta\alpha}{\beta - 1}, \quad \beta > 1$
Variance:	$\text{Var}\, X = \frac{\beta\alpha^2}{(\beta-1)^2(\beta-2)}, \quad \beta > 2$
MGF:	does not exist

Poisson

Density:	$f_X(x\|\lambda) = \frac{e^{-\lambda}\lambda^x}{x!}$
Support:	$\mathscr{X} = \{x: x = 0, 1, \ldots\}$
Parameters:	$\Theta = \{\lambda: 0 \le \lambda < \infty\}$
Mean:	$\mathscr{E}X = \lambda$
Variance:	$\text{Var}\, X = \lambda$
MGF:	$M_X(t) = e^{\lambda(e^t - 1)}$

t

Density:	$f_X(x\|\nu) = \dfrac{\Gamma\left(\frac{\nu+1}{2}\right)}{\Gamma\left(\frac{\nu}{2}\right)} \dfrac{1}{\sqrt{\nu\pi}} \left(1+\dfrac{x^2}{\nu}\right)^{-(\nu+1)/2}$
Support:	$\mathscr{X} = \{x: -\infty < x < \infty\}$
Parameters:	$\Theta = \{\nu: \nu = 1, 2, \ldots\}$
Mean:	$\mathscr{E}X = 0, \quad \nu > 1$
Variance:	$\operatorname{Var} X = \dfrac{\nu}{\nu-2}, \quad \nu > 2$
MGF:	does not exist

Uniform *(continuous)*

Density:	$f_X(x\|a, b) = \dfrac{1}{b-a}$
Support:	$\mathscr{X} = \{x: a \le x \le b\}$
Parameters:	$\Theta = \{(a, b): -\infty < a < b < \infty\}$
Mean:	$\mathscr{E}X = \dfrac{b-a}{2}$
Variance:	$\operatorname{Var} X = \dfrac{(b-a)^2}{12}$
MGF:	$M_X(t) = \dfrac{e^{bt} - e^{at}}{(b-a)t}$

Uniform *(discrete)*

Density:	$f_X(x\|N) = \dfrac{1}{N}$
Support:	$\mathscr{X} = \{x: x = 1, 2, \ldots, N\}$
Parameters:	$\Theta = \{N: N = 1, 2, \ldots\}$
Mean:	$\mathscr{E}X = \dfrac{N+1}{2}$
Variance:	$\operatorname{Var} X = \dfrac{(N+1)(N-1)}{12}$
MGF:	$M_X(t) = \dfrac{1}{N} \sum_{j=1}^{N} e^{jt}$

Weibull

Density:	$f_X(x\|\gamma, \beta) = \frac{\gamma}{\beta} x^{\gamma-1} e^{-x^\gamma/\beta}$
Support:	$\mathscr{X} = \{x: 0 < x < \infty\}$
Parameters:	$\Theta = \{(\gamma, \beta): \gamma, \beta > 0\}$
Mean:	$\mathscr{E}X = \beta^{1/\gamma}\Gamma\left(1 + \frac{1}{\gamma}\right)$
Variance:	$\operatorname{Var} X = \beta^{2/\gamma}\left[\Gamma\left(1 + \frac{2}{\gamma}\right) - \Gamma^2\left(1 + \frac{1}{\gamma}\right)\right]$
MGF:	does not exist for all γ

References

Abramowitz, M., and Stegun, I. A. (1964). *Handbook of Mathematical Functions With Formulas, Graphs, and Mathematical Tables*. Washington, DC: U.S. Government Printing Office.

Bansal, R., Gallant, A. R., Hussey, R., and Tauchen, G. (1993). Computational aspects of nonparametric simulation estimation. In D. A. Belsley (ed.), *Computational Techniques for Econometrics and Economic Analysis* (pp. 3–22). Boston: Kluwer Academic Publishers.

Bartle, R. G. (1976). *The Elements of Real Analysis, Second Edition*. New York: Wiley.

Billingsley, P. (1995). *Probability and Measure, Third Edition*. New York: Wiley.

Casella, G., and Berger, R. L. (1987). Reconciling Bayesian and frequentist evidence in the one-sided testing problem. *Journal of the American Statistical Association*, *82*, 106–111.

Casella, G., and Berger, R. L. (1990). *Statistical Inference*. Pacific Grove, CA: Wadsworth & Brooks-Cole.

Chung, K. L. (1974). *A Course in Probability Theory, Second Edition*. New York: Academic Press.

Cox, D. R., and Hinkley, D. V. (1974). *Theoretical Statistics*. London: Chapman and Hall.

Dunes Hotel. (1984). *Gaming Guide* (Brochure). Las Vegas, NV: Dunes Hotel and Country Club.

Gallant, A. R. (1980). Explicit estimators of parametric functions in nonlinear regression. *Journal of the American Statistical Association*, *75*, 182–193.

Gallant, A. R. (1987). *Nonlinear Statistical Models*. New York: Wiley.

Gallant, A. R., and Long, J. R. (1997). Estimating stochastic differential equations efficiently by minimum chi square. *Biometrika*, *84*, 125–141.

Gallant, A. R., and Nychka, D. W. (1987). Seminonparametric maximum likelihood estimation. *Econometrica*, *55*, 363–390.

Gallant, A. R., and Tauchen, G. (1996). Which moments to match? *Econometric Theory*, *12*, 657–681.

Gourieroux, C., Monfort, A., and Renault, E. (1993). Indirect inference. *Journal of Applied Econometrics*, *8*, S85–S118.

Hansen, L. P. (1982). Large sample properties of generalized methods of moments estimators. *Econometrica*, *50*, 1029–1054.

Hansen, L. P., and Singleton, K. J. (1982). Generalized instrumental variables estimators of nonlinear rational expectations models. *Econometrica*, *50*, 1269–1286.

Johnson, N. L., and Kotz, S. (1969). *Distributions in Statistics: Discrete Distributions*. New York: Wiley.

Johnson, N. L., and Kotz, S. (1970a). *Distributions in Statistics: Continuous Univariate Distributions-1*. New York: Wiley.

Johnson, N. L., and Kotz, S. (1970b). *Distributions in Statistics: Continuous Univariate Distributions-2*. New York: Wiley.

Johnson, N. L., and Kotz, S. (1972). *Distributions in Statistics: Continuous Multivariate Distributions*. New York: Wiley.

Lehmann, E. L. (1983). *Theory of Point Estimation*. New York: Wiley.

Lehmann, E. L. (1986). *Testing Statistical Hypotheses, Second Edition*. New York: Wiley.

MGM Grand Hotel. (1984). *Keno* (Brochure). Las Vegas, NV: MGM Grand Hotel.

Newey, W. K. (1990). Efficient instrumental variables estimation of nonlinear models. *Econometrica*, *58*, 809–837.

Patterson, J. L., and Jaye, W. (1982). *Casino Gambling*. New York: Putnam Publishing Group.

Pollard, D. (1984). *Convergence of Stochastic Processes*. New York: Springer-Verlag.

Pratt, J. W. (1961). Length of confidence intervals. *Journal of the American Statistical Association*, *56*, 549–567.

Royden, H. L. (1988). *Real Analysis, Third Edition*. New York: Macmillan.

Schuster, H. G. (1988). *Deterministic Chaos*. New York: VCH Publishers.

Theil, H. (1961). *Economic Forecasts and Policy, Second Edition*. Amsterdam: North-Holland.

Tierney, L. (1994). Markov chains for exploring posterior distributions. *The Annals of Statistics*, *22*, 1701–1727.

Wald, A. (1949). Note on the consistency of the maximum likelihood estimate. *Annals of Mathematical Statistics*, *20*, 595–601.

Zellner, A., and Theil, H. (1962). Three-stage least squares: Simultaneous estimation of simultaneous equations. *Econometrica*, *30*, 54–78.

Index